God's Church for

# God's Church for God's World

*The Lambeth Conference Report, 2022*

Edited by

Stephen Spencer

scm press

© The Anglican Consultative Council 2023

Published in 2023 by SCM Press
Editorial office
3rd Floor, Invicta House,
108–114 Golden Lane,
London EC1Y 0TG, UK
www.scmpress.co.uk

SCM Press is an imprint of Hymns Ancient & Modern Ltd
(a registered charity)

Hymns Ancient & Modern® is a registered trademark of
Hymns Ancient & Modern Ltd
13A Hellesdon Park Road, Norwich,
Norfolk NR6 5DR, UK

British Library Cataloguing in Publication data
A catalogue record for this book is available
from the British Library

978-0-334-06551-7

Typeset by Regent Typesetting
Printed and bound in Great Britain by
CPI Group (UK) Ltd

# Contents

## Part 3  Witnessing Together – *The Lambeth Calls*

# Foreword

*The Archbishop of Canterbury*

The Lambeth Conference has been and continues to be a wonderful opportunity to understand what it means to be God's Church for God's World. The delay in the conference, from 2020 to 2022, allowed bishops and spouses to begin to grapple with this question in Phase 1, which the conference (Phase 2) itself built on in all kinds of ways. This period following the conference, Phase 3, allows all of this to continue across the Churches of the Anglican Communion.

Looking back at global and national events over the last two years it is clear there was a window of opportunity, in July and August last year, for bishops and spouses to travel in large numbers to Canterbury, enjoy the hospitality of Canterbury Cathedral and the University of Kent, and then return home safely afterwards. The Covid-19 pandemic, which had dominated our lives for the last two years, was in retreat and global travel had become possible once again.

Meanwhile, the Lambeth Conference Company, working from its base at the Anglican Communion Office in London and guided by the Design Group chaired by Archbishop Thabo Makgoba of Southern Africa and supported by a Working Group chaired by Bishop Emma Ineson of the Church of England, had put in place meticulous and comprehensive plans for the smooth running of the conference, from recruiting those who gave bishops and spouses a friendly welcome at the airport to those who arranged connections, accommodation, meals and all manner of events in and around the conference. Through great skill and commitment these careful preparations came together, and 635 bishops, 464 spouses, 45 ecumenical guests, 177 volunteers, 356 staff and event crew, and 42 interpreters assembled for the once-in-a-decade event. I thank God profoundly for all of this.

Lambeth 2022 was a high-risk conference. The cost was significant and many individuals and bodies had contributed generously towards this. There was the risk that not enough bishops and spouses would come to make it credible. The whole event could so easily have been disrupted or cancelled by the Covid pandemic. But the conference took place as planned from start to finish. Many of those who attended have communicated their appreciation for all that happened, not least for the forging and renewing of friendships across provinces and regions. It has energised the Anglican Communion in an extraordinary way.

There were many who came to Canterbury with foreboding about divisions within the Anglican Communion, especially over same-sex marriage. These divisions found expression at certain points in the conference with some, for example, choosing to forgo communion in the opening and closing services in the Cathedral. This was sad but also simply reflected divided opinion across the Communion. However, the listening and speaking that took place within the conference hall allowed bishops to come to acknowledge one another's views. A particular point of tension was on the Tuesday afternoon over the Human Dignity Call but, by the grace of the Holy Spirit, I was able to find the words to show that no one could or would be excluded from the room. I was gratified by the warm reception of my statement and deeply grateful that we were able to move on to the rest of the business of the conference with open ears, hearts and minds. I thank God for this.

I also thank God for the spouses' programme within the conference. In my view this was the most effective and maybe the most transformative part of the conference in terms of building relationships and spiritual confidence. It went superbly and I am delighted that there is now follow-up including the setting up of an Anglican Communion Spouses' Network.

The 2022 Conference broke new ground with the Calls process, replacing the passing of resolutions at earlier conferences. I must confess that I had questions about it beforehand, and there were some teething problems with gathering feedback at the conference, but having seen the way the discussions took place over the week as a whole I am now completely committed to it as a structure that needs to be continued. I look forward to the revised Calls being disseminated across the Anglican Communion and their specific requests being received and implemented by provinces, dioceses, parishes, the Anglican Consultative Council and by its commissions and networks and other agencies across the world. Some have commented that with the launch of this process we may have taken a major step forward in our ecclesiology, which will offer material for much reflection as we move towards visible, organic unity, based on subsidiarity and solidarity.

I am very grateful to Stephen Spencer of the Anglican Communion Office and the other contributors for producing this report. It offers an opportunity to read and reflect on the insights of bishops in the pre-conference conversations; it provides access to the immense wisdom that was shared by the invited speakers at the conference; and it allows us to relive and rejoice again in the movement of God's Spirit among bishops and spouses over those 12 days in Canterbury. Also, it allows me once more to express my huge appreciation and gratitude to all those who helped to turn the dream of having another Lambeth Conference into the rich reality of the actual event last summer.

I now look forward to the next phase of the Lambeth journey, Phase 3, in which bishops and the wider church are invited to be caught up, once more, in the adventure of being God's Church for God's World.

+ *Justin Cantuar*

# Preface

*Stephen Spencer*

The first anniversary of the 2022 Lambeth Conference is a good moment to look back on the whole journey, from the pre-conference phase through to the conference itself, and forward to what lies ahead. The publication of this report offers an opportunity to do this, providing windows on to the journey, allowing reflection on what it all means and, especially, on what it reveals of the way God is leading the Churches of the Anglican Communion forward in the mission of Christ.

This report is to be read in conjunction with two other publications. The first is *Celebrating our Journey*, the magazine-type overview of what happened each day of the conference, with many evocative photographs and links to online recordings of the services and plenary sessions. This was produced by Janet Miles of the Lambeth Conference Company and published online in February 2023.[1] The second is *Now You Are God's People*, a collection of the Bible studies and expositions of 1 Peter drawn from the conference and including the retreat addresses. Edited by Justin Welby with Jennifer Strawbridge, the book is due for publication in 2023.[2]

This report concentrates on providing the key addresses and sermons from the conference itself, along with a number of short reports on what took place before and during the event to set the context, and the revised version of the Lambeth Calls, recently released online. In these ways it describes the core content of a complex, multi-faceted and remarkable gathering. Many of those who attended would describe the conversations and forging of friendships as the most important element of the conference, while others would highlight the worship led by Pete Gunstone's remarkable music group, others the prayerfulness of the retreat, and others the uplifting liturgies in Canterbury Cathedral. All of this, of course, cannot be captured in an official report. This book is a presentation of the insights and wisdom shared from the pulpit and platform around which all of that took place. It also includes the key outputs of the conference, the ten Lambeth Calls, and finally a short description of what is coming next in the follow-up Phase 3. Much of what was presented at the conference has ongoing significance for the Anglican Communion and its publication here allows further study and reflection upon it.

The conference that took place in 2022, however, was a part of something much bigger, an ongoing series of gatherings that have occurred every ten years or so since 1867, which together constitute the Lambeth Conference. This can best be understood not as a synod with legislative powers over the Anglican Communion nor, on the other hand, as a kind of retreat with no business taking place. It is something between the two: an ongoing, reflective and purposeful conversation of colleagues around the key challenges and opportunities of their work, in particular the conversation of bishops and their spouses about mission and unity and the encouragement of one another in this. It is a conversation that takes place in an intentional way once a decade.

This time around the coming together was understood to be in three phases. Phase 1 is described in Part 1 'Listening Together: The Journey to Lambeth 2022'. This phase began in earnest in 2021 with a centrally facilitated season of prayer, online study groups ('Bishops' Conversations' and 'Spouses' Global Conversations') and a course on reconciliation ministry ('Ministry in a Conflicted World'). There is a summary of what bishops shared with one another in Chapter 3 'Bishops' Conversations 2021', the opening round of conversation within the three phases. In many ways this first phase was all about bishops and spouses speaking and listening to one another, sharing what they were facing in their ministries, and their questions and hopes. In the official terminology of the conference, this phase was all about *listening together*.

Phase 2 of the conversation, the one in Canterbury, is described as *walking together*, not least because it involved plenty of actual walking from venue to venue at the University of Kent. This phase widened the conversation to include the contributions of a wide range of invited speakers, some of whom travelled to Canterbury to address the bishops and spouses and others who came from among those at the conference. This happened for the spouses in their 'Strengthening Sessions' and for the bishops in their plenaries. Many of the addresses they heard are printed in Part 2, which constitutes the heart of this report (but, sadly, there is not enough space to include all of them). They include the keynote addresses of Archbishop Justin and a diverse range of presentations by other speakers, which contain perspectives from across the world. All of this, furthermore, was interpreted into nine languages, a remarkable feat of organisation. This phase was also about bishops engaging with the themes, in their small Bible study groups, in the extensive range of seminars and in discussion of the Lambeth Calls.

The Calls are a set of ten statements drafted by advisory groups, which present current Anglican thinking on key conference topics. The bishops in their discussion sessions had the opportunity to provide feedback on what needed correcting or adding or deleting. The revised and updated version of these Calls has recently been released and they are included here, at the start of Phase 3, called *witnessing together* (Part 3). In this phase member churches are invited to study, discuss and, when they so choose, receive the Calls for implementation and development in their provinces. This phase is also about relationships among bishops and spouses being renewed and widened, especially through renewal and extension of the Bible study groups. This phase is planned to continue for three years.

I am very grateful to all who have contributed chapters and especially grateful to Kari Loureiro who has helped to transcribe many of the addresses, and to SCM Press for taking on publication of this report. The varied yet integrated chapters that follow reflect the nature of the Lambeth Conference itself, an ongoing, reflective and purposeful conversation of colleagues who are together serving a purpose greater than them all, the mission of Christ.

### Notes

1 www.lambethconference.org/resources/resources-guide/.
2 Justin Welby with Jennifer Strawbridge, *Now You Are God's People: Reflections on 1 Peter for God's Church in God's World* (London: SCM Press, forthcoming in 2023).

# Contributors

PART I

# Listening Together

## *The Journey to Lambeth 2022*

# I

# Introducing the Lambeth Conference

## The Lambeth Conference and the Anglican Communion[1]

The first Lambeth Conference took place in 1867 when the Archbishop of Canterbury, Charles Thomas Longley, invited the bishops of what would become the Anglican Communion to gather for a conference at Lambeth Palace.

There were two main issues that led to this invitation: First, a growing desire, expressed by many bishops around the world, to gather in order to pray, to study scripture and to confer together and, second, to address difficult pastoral and theological issues that were causing divisions between bishops around the world. These issues related to how the Christian gospel was and should be expressed in different cultures. It was therefore missiological and pastoral.

The conference was not attended by all the bishops who were invited, and it did not solve all the issues presented to it. The Archbishop of York and several other bishops who were invited did not attend. There was concern that the conference might claim the power of a synod but, while the conference passed 13 resolutions, Archbishop Longley made it clear, despite the hopes of some, that it was not a general synod for Anglican churches around the world. This principle remains: the Lambeth Conference does not have the power to legislate for or compel action in the churches of the Anglican Communion.

A Lambeth Conference continues to be a place in which bishops from around the Communion gather to confer and to express their collegiality and their common sense of witness to the world. As the important Inter Anglican Standing Commission of Unity, Faith and Order (IASCUFO) paper, *Towards a Symphony of Instruments*, notes, 'The Lambeth Conference can be seen as a conciliar event in a non-juridical mode. Here the bishops come precisely to confer and not to take decisions that are binding on the member churches.' The Lambeth Conference is one of the four Instruments of Communion of the Anglican Communion and, as another of the Instruments, it is the Archbishop of Canterbury who calls them together.

The four Instruments of Communion are the Archbishop of Canterbury, the Lambeth Conference, the Anglican Consultative Council and the Primates' Meeting.

It is important to note what the Anglican Communion is, and what it is not. It is a communion, a fellowship or a family of churches. Each church, comprised of provinces, dioceses and churches, is interdependent, autonomous and self-governing. As a Christian world communion, the Anglican Communion does have an identity and structure. The Instruments of Communion can and do make decisions and can and do speak out in our world as a witness to the Gospel of Christ. The Instruments can encourage the member churches and can provide help and guidance based on prayer, wisdom and experience, but they cannot bind or compel. The decisions of the Instruments and the traditions and common practices of the churches of the Communion are put into effect and made real by the decisions of the decision-making bodies of the churches themselves. Each church will also consider how it receives any matters that it believes are important and it is notable that Anglican churches have different understandings of what is meant by reception. The Anglican Communion has an influence and an authority though, as mentioned, without juridical authority over or within the churches that make it up.

The Lambeth Conference brings together bishops from around the world. Each has influence and authority in their own diocese and according to the laws and practices of their own church. Bishops have, though, never exercised that ministry of oversight in isolation. In the Anglican tradition, they do so in consultation with their fellow bishops and in collaboration with the clergy and all the faithful. The Anglican Communion is not itself a 'church' but a body made up of member churches, each of which is part of the one, holy, catholic and apostolic church of Jesus Christ.

## The Place of the Lambeth Conference within the Anglican Communion

Lambeth Conferences have played a significant part in helping shape the life of the churches of the Anglican Communion down the years and across cultures. Each Lambeth Conference has given priority to ensuring the bishops have time to pray together, to worship together, to study the scriptures together and to confer together. And, as the church always exists in and seeks to serve God's world, there have always been serious issues that the bishops of the communion have needed to face when they come together.

Over successive Lambeth Conferences the mind of the bishops was expressed through published resolutions. These resolutions have touched on every area of the life and mission of the church. The resolutions have called on churches (both Anglican churches and ecumenical sister churches) and governments, on individuals and on society at large. But the authority of any resolution is limited. Member churches have distinct processes for receiving decisions from Lambeth Conferences and discerning and deciding to what extent they will have authority in their context.

The Lambeth Conference has always played an important role within the Anglican Communion and for the churches that make up the Communion. It has encouraged and enabled significant decisions to be made by the member churches. It has resourced discernment on the call to God's mission in myriad cultures across the Communion and world.

## Preparing for Lambeth 2022

Preparations for this conference were set in motion by the Secretary General of the Anglican Communion, Archbishop Josiah Idowu Fearon, who convened a Design Group to oversee planning of the event. Archbishop Justin proposed the membership of the group, beginning with the chair, Archbishop Thabo Makgoba of Southern Africa, who had been part of the design group of the previous Lambeth Conference in 2008. The other members were Bishop Emma Ineson of the Church of England, Bishop George Sumner of The Episcopal Church, Bishop Joel Waweru of the Anglican Church of Kenya, Mrs Mathilde Ntahoturi of the Anglican Church of Burundi, Archbishop Melter Tais of the Church of the Province of South East Asia, the Revd Cathrine Ngangira of the Church of England (youth representative), Bishop Pradeep Samantaroy of the Church of North India, Lord Stephen Green from the United Kingdom, the Revd Professor Robert Heaney of Virginia Theological Seminary and Bishop Nigel Stock of the Church of England.

With the postponement of the 2020 conference because of the Covid-19 pandemic and the need for fresh facilitation of a 2022 conference, a Working Group was appointed to take forward the work of the Design Group. This was chaired by Bishop Emma Ineson and included Bishop Anthony Poggo of Lambeth Palace, Bishop Joseph Galgalo of the Anglican Church of Kenya, Bishop Pradeep Samantaroy, and Matthew Frost and Lord Stephen Green – both from the United Kingdom.

The work of these two groups was supported and implemented by the Lambeth Conference Team, based at the Anglican Communion Office in London. This was led by Phil George and included Janet Miles, Rachel

Westall, Caroline Thompson, Kari Loureiro and Brad Frey (seconded from Christian Aid). This team, in turn, recruited a wide range of volunteers and contractors to put in place all the elements of a large and complex event. They were also supported in various ways by the staff teams at the Anglican Communion Office and Lambeth Palace. Behind all this the Lambeth Conference Trustees managed the fundraising and disbursement of funds to pay for it all, an empowering ministry.

## Archbishop Justin's Letter to Primates, January 2022

Your Graces, my Lords, my dear sisters and brothers in Christ, in the name of the Lord Jesus Christ I send warm greetings to every one of you. The psalmist declares in Psalm 33 'may your unfailing love rest upon us, O Lord, even as we put our hope in you'. So may you know that you are in our prayers as you prepare for the year ahead in the ministry to which you are called by the Holy Spirit in the service of Jesus Christ under the authority of God.

As we start the year my heart is full of hopeful anticipation of meeting together for the fifteenth Lambeth Conference July–August 2022. It will be a time of community as we meet our sisters and brothers from around the globe. It will be a time of breaking bread and celebration as we offer hospitality to one another. It will be a time for prayer, for Bible study and worship as we listen to God. And it will be a time to have important conversations about issues facing the church and the world.

That is why I am convinced more than ever that our conference theme – exploring what it means to be God's Church for God's World – is vitally important. Around the globe many people are experiencing great suffering. We have only to look at our news screens for a second to see situations of injustice and inequality. Our conversations at the Lambeth Conference will happen in a world grappling with huge challenges, above all the climate crisis, but also the pandemic, racial inequality, conflict and mass migration, persecution, and rapid scientific and technological change. And within the life of the Anglican Communion among us there are a wide range of issues and questions we must address.

When we meet we must ask God 'What will our mission and our work for social justice and for the church look like for the 21st-century world?' How can the Anglican Communion share the task of transformation in the name of Jesus Christ? One of the beautiful things about the Anglican Communion is that it is a hugely diverse international community spanning 165 countries. Bishops invited to the Lambeth Conference represent the hopes and challenges impacting Christians, churches and communities all around the world, as do their spouses. As we prepare for our conference conversations, may we hold our communities that we serve uppermost in our hearts and prayers. May we come with a readiness to share our ministry experiences and a willingness to listen and to learn from one another. May we seek God's will for the Anglican Communion that we may walk, listen and witness together.

During 2022, in preparation for the Lambeth Conference, we will continue with our listening phase of the conference journey. Last year many of you took part in our online Bishops' Conversations, which met for prayer, for Bible study and for early discussions. This year we are inviting bishops to take part in a new online discussion series about ministry in a conflicted world. Bishops, and in many places spouses too, are ministering in situations facing great challenge. They may be based near a war zone or in one, or dealing with the reality of rising tides due to climate change, or living in a hugely divided and polarised society, or persecuted. The new discussion series will look to the model of Christ and explore habits of leadership that equip us for ministry in such situations. By taking part, you'll meet with other bishops from around the world and learn from their context. You will also hear contributions from theologians and practitioners whose ministry has been informed in particularly complex and divided situations. I invite you to join in these discussions which will be so important in building our understanding of one another's context before the conference.

In the months ahead the pandemic will, sadly, continue to impact all of us. But it remains our hope and prayer that we will be able to welcome as many bishops as possible from the Anglican Communion for an in-person event in Canterbury. During the year the conference planning team will advise you on how to make your travel plans. They are also making provisions for some of the events to be made available online for those who may find getting to the event impossible due to travel or health challenges. We are now recommending that all delegates travel direct to Canterbury for a programme of welcome and warm hospitality at the University of Kent instead of the original hospitality initiative we called the Big Hello. I pray that everyone will take the opportunity to join us at Canterbury for this important time of pre-event prayer, preparation and growing to know one another.

I so thank all those involved for everything they have done to support the planning to this point. We remain hopeful, hope-filled, about the wonderful opportunity the conference presents for gathering and exploring what it means to be God's Church for God's World in 2022.

Thank you for all that you do and for your fellowship that we share in service in the Lord Jesus Christ. May God bless you and those whom you love and those whom you serve. And may God bless and strengthen all in the Anglican Communion. Amen.

## Notes

1 This chapter draws on https://www.lambethconference.org/wp-content/up loads/2022/06/History-and-Purpose-of-the-Lambeth-Conference-and-the-2022-Lambeth-Calls-process-FINAL-1.pdf. For a detailed and comprehensive overview of the history and theology of the Lambeth Conference, see Paul Avis and Benjamin M. Guyer (eds), *The Lambeth Conference: Theology, History, Polity and Purpose* (London: Bloomsbury T&T Clark, 2017).

# 2

# The Listening Phase

## Listening to Voices from Around the World

Before the Listening Phase officially began a number of initiatives were taken to help prepare Anglicans for the Lambeth Conference. One of these was a project launched at Lambeth Palace, under the direction of Graham Kings, which brought together a wide range of contributors from the global South as well as the global North to present papers at three conferences and then in three books. These were on the three key themes of Archbishop Justin's ministry at Lambeth, namely reconciliation, evangelism and prayer, combined with the three dispositions of the Lambeth Conference – namely, walking together, listening together and witnessing together. The papers were published by the Anglican Communion Office and Forward Movement, the first in 2019 on reconciliation, as *Walking Together: Global Anglican Perspectives on Reconciliation*, the second also in 2019 on evangelism, as *Witnessing Together: Global Anglican Perspectives on Evangelism and Witness*, and the third was in 2020 on prayer and the religious life, with the title *Listening Together: Global Anglican Perspectives on Renewal of Prayer and the Religious Life*. The three volumes, edited by Muthuraj Swamy (the convenor of the conferences) and Stephen Spencer, presented the views of 46 scholars and church leaders and helped to counteract the preponderance of voices from the global North in the literature surrounding the Lambeth Conference.

Another important publication, again promoting the theme of the conference, was the production of a practical approach to mission by a group of scholars mostly from the global South. *God's Church for God's World: A Practical Approach to Partnership in Mission*, edited by Robert S. Heaney, John Kafwanka and Hilda Kabia, was published in 2019 by Church Publishing. Drawing on mission experience in different parts of the world, the book offered best practices for listening and partnership as the foundation for mission, both for the bishops coming to the Lambeth Conference and for the wider church.

## Prayers of Hope for the World, January to February 2021

The official journey to the Lambeth Conference started with a season of prayer called 'Prayers of Hope for the World', which was launched online on Sunday 10 January 2021. It linked the theme of 'God's Church for God's World' with a daily rhythm of prayer focusing on themes such as hope, peace, proclaiming the Good News, responding to the pandemic, the planet, poverty, politics and justice, and people. Prayers were written by bishops, spouses of bishops, clergy, mission partners and youth from around the world. Many voices contributed including that of the Archbishop of York, Stephen Cottrell (the Church of England), Bishop Michael Curry (The Episcopal Church), Archbishop Thabo Makgoba (Anglican Church of Southern Africa), Archbishop Daniel Sarfo (Kumasi, Ghana), Bishop Pradeep Samantaroy (Amritsar, North India), Archbishop Samy Shehata (Egypt) and Archbishop Linda Nicholls (Anglican Church of Canada).

## A Focus on 1 Peter

The book of 1 Peter was the biblical focus for the Lambeth Conference. An official commentary on 1 Peter was developed with contributions from an international group of 35 New Testament scholars from Anglican and other churches, who gathered in Lambeth Palace in November 2018 for the St Augustine's Seminar. Funded by St Augustine's Foundation, Canterbury, the group created a commentary and a series of supporting films which were made available in the run-up to the conference. The seminar was convened by Canon Professor Jennifer Strawbridge, who also edited the commentary. The English version of the commentary was published by SCM Press in 2020, and also translated into Spanish, Portuguese and French, with copies sent all around the world. The commentary and videos on 1 Peter were written and prepared before the conference was rescheduled as a result of the Covid-19 pandemic. Further work was done for the conference, with updated materials and additional videos made available for the event in 2022.

The commentary, offered not just to bishops but to the church at large, and which is still available from SCM Press, offers a close reading of the text from beginning to end, drawing on a multiplicity of voices and engaging in a number of foundational themes for the Christian community according to the apostolic author: hope, holiness, suffering, joy, witness, hospitality, exile, resurrection, leadership. Tackling the themes raised by the epistle including slavery, exile and refugees, patriarchy, hierarchy, oppression, gender justice, and the risk of hospitality, the book engages with these topics not only through commentary but also through short excursuses which draw the reader more deeply into some of the difficult questions.

## Science and Faith

It was Archbishop Justin's wish that issues around science and faith should be part of the discussion at the Lambeth Conference. He was aware that being informed by science, collaborating with the scientific community and bringing the ethical voice of faith to scientific debate needed to be a major part of the church's mission in a world increasingly shaped by science and technology. For this reason, before the conference in a series of filmed discussions, he and other contributors from both the scientific and faith communities explored why it was vital that the church engages with science in the 21st century. Contributors included Professor Andrew Briggs, Professor of Nanomaterials, Oxford University, Bishop Steven Croft of the Church of England, Archbishop Thabo Makgoba, Primate of Southern Africa, Dr Heather Payne, Senior Professional Adviser to the Welsh Government, Professor Eunice Kamaara, Professor of African Christian Ethics at Moi University, Kenya, Archbishop Josiah Idowa-Fearon, Secretary General of the Anglican Communion, Dr Anna Pearson, Research Scientist in Quantum Natural Language Processing, Cambridge Quantum Computing, Oxford, Bishop Paul Korir of the Church of Kenya, Bishop David Njovu of Lusaka, Central Africa, Bishop Pradeep Samantaroy of Amritsar, North India, and Bishop Cleophas Lunga of Matabeleland, Zimbabwe.

These discussions were continued at the conference itself and a Lambeth Call was shared on the topic. Members of the newly formed Anglican Communion Science Commission also met for the first time during the event.

## The Bishops' Conversations

See Chapter 3.

# Ministry in a Conflicted World, February to April 2022

'Ministry in a Conflicted World' was a formational leadership course for bishops. It was responding to the challenge of ministering as a bishop in contexts of division and conflict. The series aimed to look at the person of Jesus and how his approach to leadership brought hope, restoration and reconciliation.

Over 310 bishops registered for the course. Groups met at different times to accommodate different time zones. Language diversity was accommodated through translation of resources as well as interpretation in six languages. The series offered theological and practical input on three habits that can shape ministry and leadership. The series was delivered by Lambeth Conference Company in partnership with Difference, part of the Archbishop of Canterbury's Reconciliation Ministry based at Lambeth Palace.

The first session, 'Be Present', explored a theology of incarnation and lament, allowing discussion of what it means to be 'present' in ministry with those who are suffering, marginalised or disagree with one another. Contributions on film were offered by Canon Joseph Zebedayo Bilal Kenyi of South Sudan and the Revd Dr Manfred Deselaers of the Catholic Church in Germany.

The second session, 'Be Curious', explored a theology of encounter, discussing what it means to minister across divides, with a curiosity that seeks to listen, grow understanding and enable fractures to be healed. Filmed contributions were offered by Pastor Ray Minniecon of the Forgiveness Project in Australia and the Revd René August, a reconciliation trainer based at The Warehouse, South Africa.

The third session, 'Reimagine', explored a theology of hope and reconciliation, allowing discussion of how churches can reimagine approaches to mission and community work to bring transformation. Filmed contributions were offered by Bishop Dinis Sengulane of Mozambique, Bishop Eleanor Sanderson of Aotearoa New Zealand (now of York in the Church of England), Bishop Joseph Galgalo of the Church of Kenya, the Revd Dr Julie Gittoes of the Church of England, and Dr Paulo Ueti, a theological educator from Brazil.

# 3

# Bishops' Conversations 2021

All active bishops were invited to take part in what were called 'Bishops' Conversations' run on zoom, with six sessions from July to December 2021, once a month for two hours, with up to 25 bishops in each group. The sessions enabled them to begin to engage with 1 Peter, then to look at some of the realities around the Communion and the world at large and to share these with one another, and to pray together. There were 511 participants over the course of the sixth months. The following is a compilation of what they shared with one another, drawn from the feedback sheets written by the group facilitators. It provides a description of what bishops shared with one another before they and their spouses arrived in Canterbury in July 2022, offering a varied and rich portrait of their outlooks and views; the compilation is drawn to a large extent from their own words, one key component of the conversation that became the Lambeth Conference of 2022. As the months went by bishops shared more and more deeply of their experience and views. They were supported by a diverse team of bishop convenors and facilitators from around the Anglican Communion. Also, each month a new film was released in support of each theme, featuring bishops from different provinces sharing relevant thoughts and ministry experiences. The following provides a summary of the most prominent themes that emerged through the six months of conversation, as shown by the reports sent in each month by the facilitators. As far as possible, the themes are presented in the bishops' own words.

## Churches have changed

The Covid-19 pandemic has been a severe test for churches across the Communion, especially when they have had to close their buildings and move online: 'Some of the membership has been lost, and some income as well, but in many places church congregations have become creative in their use of technology, a learning curve that has often resulted in their reaching hitherto unreached people.' Church buildings have been converted into vaccination centres; clinics have distributed dry rations, feeding the poor and vulnerable. Anglicans 'have joined hands to end hunger and to offer trauma counselling'. 'Leaders have advocated dignified burials for Covid victims and for treating people with honour and love, because they are created in God's image.' As the bishops of South Sudan put it, 'Within the church there is great faithfulness, perseverance, hope, humility and resilience. There is much prayer and a belief in the power of prayer and of freely and sacrificially offering ourselves to God's service.'

## Bishops need to listen

'We need to listen, especially when people who we meet often think we are there to talk rather than listen' – to young people who are passionate about the climate emergency, to indigenous voices who offer insights into how to care for creation; to the victims of racism, violence and abuse; to communities threatened by the move away from fossil fuel economies; and especially to one another when we disagree on key issues. Also, there is a need to listen to science, on the pandemic (to overcome vaccine hesitancy and ignorance), on the climate crisis and how to address that, and on the effects of social media: 'Scientists have lots to share with us – can they speak to us at Lambeth?'

## Give and receive hospitality

'We need to learn how we receive hospitality from God in creation and how we are called to give and receive it from our neighbours and wider society, especially those on the margins.' 'We need to develop a sense of spirituality around creation care: strengthen indigenous approaches to nature protection in which nature is seen as the extension of our bodies – an alternative to the colonial, imperialistic approach, and take ethical positions on issues like plastic, non-fossilised fuels, use of petroleum products, etc.' Above and beyond this, 'hospitality is first received from God, then offered to one another and then returned to God for his glory'.

## Repentance for past failings

'We must be willing to say sorry for our complicity in the suffering around us and our inaction in areas we could have made a difference. What do we change? We change our attitudes of insensitivity about the pain of the others.' 'No one should feel that they are aliens or foreigners but should be included as the same people of God equal and dignified. For this to happen structures that perpetuate inequality and injustice must change.' Also, 'we must be sure that any part of our Communion which is suffering is supported by other parts of our fellowship'. And 'we need to desire God's light to be cast into the darkness in our lives, families and churches'.

## The importance of discipleship

More and more of the bishops are recognising how discipleship and learning are central to the life of the church. Up to now, there has sometimes been 'shallow teaching of the Christian faith combined with a lack of follow-up of converts'. But now 'the church cannot wait for people to come to it so that they can become disciples, rather, we as the church need to go out to the people wherever they are, by going out to those communities we usually do not visit and being with them, learning from them and making them disciples'. 'Discipleship is not something we do alone but in the community.' Furthermore, 'as we reach out to people in discipleship we too are being discipled'.

## The need to speak out

'Jesus called us to be salt and light, not milk and honey. We are not called to bring sweetness, but to challenge and persevere.' A bishop from an indigenous community shared that 'being an indigenous person, I feel the pain and continue to feel the injustices to the indigenous people and the struggle of the indigenous people in my country'. So, across the world, 'The church needs to be a voice against racism, colonialism, poverty, extremism and ongoing unjust issues related to the pandemic', not least inequity in vaccine distribution.

## The need for servant leadership

Among bishops there is recognition and admission of the presence of over-domineering and autocratic leadership in some of our churches, and unfortunately in some places church members expect this. Rather, the leadership of a bishop should emulate that of Jesus, as a servant leader who is strong in the faith, serving with humility. As the bishops of South

Sudan put it, 'We need to take off pride and clothe ourselves with humility and be accessible to the people we serve. We need to think about how we stay in the midst of our flock, and not at a distance.' For others, 'diakonia' (service) is an essential aspect of episcopal leadership – literally feeding the flock as well as metaphorically feeding the flock. Such leadership 'comes from the heart, wholeheartedly – it becomes your life'.

## For unity

Above all, bishops are vessels of unity: 'the diversity in the communion moves us to become instruments of unity and reconciliation'. We can 'agree to disagree agreeably but only if everyone shares this approach. Much grace is required in all circumstances, to demonstrate generosity under God.' And in response to disagreement, 'focus on common goals rather than on internal squabbles'. So 'now is the time for discernment of our unity and time for listening in our unity. We need to try to embrace humility with authority. It is important to listen to one another. Humility and experiencing where other people are coming from is also important.'

## For the whole of life

'The good news must also bring physical care. The gospel is holistic. We must preach and also develop people's lives and ensure they have enough food and drink and clothing. Health must not be forgotten. Spirits and bodies matter in parallel.' So courageous leadership is needed on the big issues of mission, such as creation care and finding a prophetic voice concerning inequality across the world. 'God is asking us to be agents of transformation in society, ensuring that inequalities are not perpetuated.'

## Looking ahead to Lambeth 2022

'These six months of conversations have created excitement. We want Lambeth to connect and expand our hearts and spirits.' 'Can Lambeth create an environment of eager expectation about what God is doing?' Yes, if we 'celebrate our diversity as opposed to amplify our differences', and 'when we understand ourselves as part of a global fellowship this brings a lot of encouragement and strength'.

Also, there is a 'desperate need for LC22 to make a substantive statement about the climate'. Some want resolutions to come out of Lambeth next year that they can sign up to and stick to, with big targets and small achievable steps to get there. The bishops at Lambeth should develop a common vision on climate change as a shared challenge: 'the Lambeth Conference is a platform to "trumpet" this message across the world, making it a universal priority'.

## Concluding comments on the conversations as a whole

'We have had a wonderful time! Can't wait for more of this at the Lambeth Conference!'

'I am very grateful for these meetings that we have had, it was a pleasure to get to know you and to meet you … We are the same in our suffering, frailness and human vulnerability … we have more in common than we often think we do or imagine or accept. A huge thank you for sharing your personal heartfelt stories in your families and parishes – in these ways we are able to create a Communion. I thank the Lord for all of this. I will be praying for you and ask that you pray for us.'

'One expects differences because of nationality but the uniqueness of each personality will stick out for me. Thank you for sharing your vulnerability and reminding us of our humanity as bishops.'

'I am so blessed to be part of this group – God has been in the midst of this – God has been taking our cares and anxiety so that we don't need to carry it ourselves.'

## A prayer from the bishops of South Sudan

Guide us always to communicate biblical truth to your people so that they follow your ways and do your will.
We pray for the unity of your church in general and the Anglican Communion in particular.
We pray that you help us imitate you, Jesus, in suffering, in selfless leadership, in unity and love for one another.
Protect us from Covid-19.
And guide us in how to advocate for a reduction of global warming.
In Jesus' name, Amen.

# 4

# Spouses' Global Conversations

The postponement of the Lambeth Conference in March 2020 became an opportunity for the group planning the spouses' programme to draw spouses together for support and encouragement before the conference. The 'Global Conversations' were developed with a particular focus on sharing together the ways that spouses in their different contexts were responding to the challenges of the Covid-19 pandemic. A series of four sessions were designed to engage spouses either in person or by meeting online. The aims of the programme were to strengthen relationships, to encourage them in their situations now and in their shared learning at the conference, and for the group to develop into an ongoing support network. It was hoped that spouses would understand and share the skills and resources they already have and use them to bring hope and help in the current crisis. A team of facilitators from across the different regions were identified and brought together across the different regions to partner with spouses and deliver the programme.

Caroline Welby wrote to Primates and their spouses (where applicable) and invited them to consider gathering a group of bishops' spouses in their province. Groups of spouses met by province in Brazil, Burundi, Canada, England, the Indian Ocean, South East Asia and South America. For some spouses, the Global Conversations were the catalyst for them to meet for the first time and this was a supportive and empowering experience.

Subsequently, there were conversations that included spouses from across a number of different provinces. These included a grouping in Oceania involving spouses from Australia, Aotearoa New Zealand, Polynesia and Melanesia (who were coping with civil unrest as the group met), and Portuguese-speaking spouses from Brazil, Portugal and Mozambique and Angola, who met together online. What was originally planned as a conversation between spouses from Kenya and England extended to include spouses from Jerusalem and the Middle East, Alexandria, South Sudanese living in Kenya, and a representative from The Episcopal Church.

The experience of the groups was that the suffering of the Covid pandemic was common to all although it impacted in different ways in different places. Spouses saw that they were not alone but could learn from one another and be encouraged by what God was doing among them. Zoom proved itself to be a good medium for retreat, prayer and reflection, with the use of break-out rooms as well as whole-group gatherings. Many found that these conversations offered an opportunity to express themselves more freely than they could in their home contexts. They found it encouraging to hear members describe their faith journeys, which they had to do more fully and clearly than usual because of communicating with those who were not so familiar with their story.

As well as serving to connect spouses, the Global Conversations helped the Spouses' Planning Group to identify a group of global facilitators, many of whom went on to be involved in the planning and delivery of the sessions for the spouses at conference.

As attention now turns to Phase 3 of the Lambeth Conference and the establishing of a Network of Bishops' Spouses in the Anglican Communion, there is much to draw on from all of this, including the lessons learned from the Global Conversations, the relationships formed both online and in person at the conference, the equipping of the facilitators who have developed their skills, and the resources and activities that were developed which provide a wealth of material to draw on.

Since the conference the Portuguese and Spanish spouses have continued their online conversations, and included spouses from other provinces. Other groups have resumed their conversations, or will be resuming them. The new Network of Bishops' Spouses will seek to support and extend this.

# PART 2

# Walking Together

## *The Conference in Canterbury 2022*

# 5

# The Welcome

## Welcome to Canterbury by Archbishop Justin[1]

My dear sisters and brothers in Christ: It is a source of great joy that you
have journeyed from around the Anglican Communion to be part of this
historic occasion in Canterbury. Many of you have also taken part in
online meetings during 2021–22, as part of our prayers and preparations
for the event. Thank you for your fellowship and time.

Two years ago, we could hardly have believed the course of world
events that was about to unfold with the outbreak of the Covid-19
pandemic. This, along with the ongoing challenges like the climate emergency, war and conflict in many countries and the huge inequalities of
our world, continue to have a deep impact on us all. As we gather for the
fifteenth Lambeth Conference, the privilege and responsibility of meeting
feels even more significant.

The business of this conference is to discern the Holy Spirit's directing
in what it means to be 'God's Church for God's World', as we seek to
'walk, listen and witness together'. We are living at a time where there is
much to fragment and divide the world – but Christ calls his church to
be one in witness and in worship so that Jesus is presented to the world.
That is why the conference's biblical focus on the book of 1 Peter is so
important. Peter's First Epistle addressed a church at a period of history
facing many challenges. It is a book that explores themes of suffering,
despair, joy, exile and alienation – the hope of Christ and the call to the
church in the midst of these. Then and now – 1 Peter calls the church
beyond the power dynamics of the world, to live holy lives rooted in the
servanthood of Christ.

As we embark upon our journey together in 2022, we pray for God's
Holy Spirit to guide us, as we seek God's will for the global witness of the
Anglican Communion in the decade ahead.

## Note

1 From *Official Programme: God's Church for God's World*.

# 6

# Some Facts and Figures
# About the Conference

635 bishops attended the conference in Canterbury

464 spouses attended

45 ecumenical guests represented other churches

82 countries were represented at the conference

39 of the 42 provinces of the Anglican Communion were represented, as well as 4 Extra Provincial Territories

Bursaries were awarded to 289 bishops and 263 spouses

There were a minimal number of Covid infections – 19 recorded

88 Bible study groups for bishops

63 Bible study groups for spouses

31 seminars

48 specially invited speakers

178 participants signed up to renew or start diocesan companionship links

136 accredited media representatives at the conference

177 volunteers, stewards and airport hospitality team – 46 stewards aged between 19 and 38, 356 staff and event crew

42 interpreters

9 languages interpreted in the main venues

27 services of Morning, Evening and Night Prayer

9 Strengthening Sessions for spouses involving 30 people and six languages in the delivery

9.4 million people reached through social media

368,000 people streamed the opening service from Canterbury Cathedral

# 7

# Retreat

The conference started in prayer, Bible study and contemplation. The bishops met at Canterbury Cathedral and started to reflect on the theme of 'God's Church for God's World' and the book of 1 Peter. Spouses also met for a retreat, based at the University of Kent.

Contributors at the Bishops' Retreat (over two days) included

The Revd Prebendary Dr Isabelle Hamley, Secretary for Theology and Ecumenical Relations and Theological Adviser to the House of Bishops, England

The Revd Dr Paul Swarup, now Bishop of Delhi in the Church of North India

Dr Esther Mombo, Professor of African Church History, Gender and Theology at St Paul's University in Limuru, Kenya

Dr Paulo Ueti, Theological Education Adviser for the Anglican Alliance and Anglican Communion Office, based in Brazil

The Revd Canon Jennifer Strawbridge, Associate Professor in New Testament Studies at Oxford University

Their addresses are published separately.

The spouses met to look at what it means to be 'Called by Name' and 'Known and Loved'. Contributors included:

Mrs Caroline Welby

Canon Paula Gooder from St Paul's Cathedral, England

Sister Veronica, Community of the Sisters of the Church, Soloman Islands

Spouses were able to choose from a range of activities including imaginative contemplation of scripture and the power of storytelling.

# 8

# Opening Sermon in Canterbury Cathedral

*Bishop Vincentia Kgabe, Diocese of Lesotho,*
*Southern Africa*

As we gather for this fifteenth Lambeth Conference we carry in our hearts, and impressed on our minds, matters and situations that challenge and trouble our respective countries, regions, dioceses and provinces. We also gather to celebrate the diversity and gifts that have been generously given to us for mission and ministry in God's Church for God's World. As Peter puts it, 'like good stewards of the manifold grace of God, serve one another with whatever gift each of you has received' (1 Peter 4:10).

The readings set for today's Eucharist have recurring keywords that can be summed up in two themes – namely, *servant leadership* and *hospitality*. To be a servant-leader is to show hospitality.

At consecrations the following words are often read:

The Church is the Body of Christ, the people of God and the dwelling-place of the Holy Spirit. In baptism, the whole Church is summoned to witness to God's redeeming love who reveals Godself to God's people through the *normal*, the *physical*, the *temporal*, and the *mundane* things of this life and thus to work for the coming of God's Kingdom.

To serve this royal priesthood, God has given particular ministries. Bishops are ordained to be Shepherds of Christ's flock and guardians of the faith, to proclaim God's word and to lead God's people in mission. Obedient to the call of Jesus Christ and in the power of the Holy Spirit, Bishops are called to gather God's people and celebrate with them the sacraments of the new covenant. Thus, formed into a single communion of faith and love, the Church in each place and time is united with the Church in every place and time.

In this part of the Charge within the Consecration service there is a reminder, and also an invitation, to serve God's people and to practise hospitality wherever we have been planted, and to do this in season and out of season. There is no limit to how we can do it. As the church, we are called to practise hospitality and we are called to serve.

## Hospitality

Hospitality in the Oxford Dictionary is defined as 'the friendly and generous reception and entertainment of guests, visitors, or strangers'. In the African context, hospitality is defined as 'that extension of generosity, giving freely without strings attached. It can also be seen as unconditional readiness to share.' It can be seen as the willingness to *give*, *help*, *assist*, love, and *carry* one another's burdens without necessarily putting profit or rewards as the driving force. This is what in Southern Africa we call *ubuntu* – that a person is a person through other persons – *Umntu ngumtu nga bantu*.

This hospitality is demonstrated in our Old Testament reading by the widow who welcomed and fed a stranger with her diminutive food supplies. This act of hers could have resulted in death by starvation, as the text states: 'she told Elijah that she is gathering sticks so that she may go home and prepare a meal for herself and her son, that they may eat it and die' (1 Kings 17:12).

In our second reading Peter urges us to be hospitable as he writes 'be hospitable to one another without complaining. Like good stewards of the manifold grace of God; serve one another with whatever gift each of you has received' (1 Peter 4:9, 10). And in John's Gospel Jesus is quoted as saying: '"So if I, your Lord and Teacher, have washed your feet, you also ought to wash one another's feet"' (John 13:14).

Hospitality can be a powerful and also a vulnerable thing to do: *powerful* because you allow people into your space and share what you have with them. In most cases, the host is in control. It is a *vulnerable* thing to do because in most cases you allow a stranger or strangers into your space, into your domain. And all you have is trust that all goes well until the last guest departs. To welcome a guest into your home also involves being open to that person's presence by showing interest in what that person has to offer.

Our readings today remind us that serving/service or servant-leadership and hospitality go together: for the widow hosted Elijah and served him food. And through Elijah God promised her that 'the jar of meal will not be emptied and the jug of oil will not fail until the day that God sends rain on the earth' (1 Kings 17:14).

Jesus Christ demonstrates this also in our Gospel reading, during the meal with friends and disciples, when he moves away from the table, takes a basin filled with water and demonstrates a new way of serving – by washing their feet – and directs that they should do that for one another. This is both an act of hospitality and service, and love is central to this act.

How do we do this as a church? How do Anglican churches demonstrate hospitality in a world that is experiencing some serious pain and strife? We do this by following the model that has been set for us by our Saviour, and this model is not self-centred or inward-looking. It calls us not to be navel gazing but seek first God's Kingdom and his righteousness, and all the things we wish, yearn and call for will be given as well.

We have it within us to serve the world and bring healing by sharing what we have been freely given and without the fear that we will end up empty. God is a God who provides and assures us that 'those who trust in the Lord for help will find their strength renewed. They will rise on wings like eagles; they will run and not get weary; they will walk and not grow weak' (Isaiah 40:31). Our jar will not be emptied, neither our jug fail. We serve a God who provides.

How do we as the church demonstrate hospitality to one another? For many, the church has been a place of pain and hurt. We have it within us to serve God's people, not only those who look like us, or speak the same language as us or who are of the same socio-economic or political class as us.

This gathering has the power and is capable of bringing healing to the world and church. Peter reminds us 'to maintain constant love for one another, for love covers a multitude of sins'. My prayer is that during our time together, may

God's name be hallowed and not ours!
God's will be done and not ours!
God's Kingdom come and not ours!
Amen.

# 9

# Daily Worship

## Robert Jones, Archdeacon of Worcester, Church of England

The pattern of worship at the conference was modelled on that of the 2008 conference. There were two main acts of sung worship in the main venue, the Holy Eucharist at the start of the day and Evening Prayer at the end of the day. Some bishops attended an alternative morning Eucharist in another venue. There were also more reflective services of Morning and Night Prayer in the chaplaincy centre. The Cathedral liturgies included the opening and closing Eucharists and the retreat (with a parallel spouses' retreat at the university campus). The Eucharists and Evening Prayer in the main venue were supported by Pete Gunstone's very talented music group.

The day began at 6.30am with Morning Prayer in the chaplaincy, followed by the Eucharist at 7.15am in the main venue. Evening Prayer took place at 6pm in the main venue. Night Prayer took place at 9.30pm in the chaplaincy. For many, the distances between accommodation and these venues, alongside the need to queue for meals, made attending these services difficult. Some commented that a Eucharist in the middle of the day, before lunch, would have attracted a greater number of participants.

As before, there was a common conference liturgy with each service having a specific provincial flavour. The liturgy was presided over by bishops from the particular province being highlighted, for which they also provided a video in place of a sermon, reflecting on intentional discipleship in their province and, of course, the response to the Covid-19 pandemic. Prayers of Intercession were led by the chaplaincy team to give a sense of the bishops being prayed for. Holy Communion was distributed in both kinds by intinction (at Archbishop Justin's request) by members of the province assisted by the Community of St Anselm. Music was chosen by the director of music in consultation with the provinces. Spouses were included in the daily worship together with bishops.

This was supported by a conference lectionary prepared by Professor Jennifer Strawbridge to fit in with the daily Bible study and to avoid an overload of scripture and words. At the Eucharist there was a reading from 1 Peter and a related Gospel passage; at Evening Prayer a psalm and a New Testament reading.

The reflective services held in the chaplaincy centre consisted of Morning Prayer and Night Prayer, and were led by the Community of St Anselm, who together with the liturgical team and the pastoral team were embedded in the chaplaincy team. Prayer ministry was offered here too.

The following provinces helped to lead the Eucharists: the Anglican Church in Aotearoa New Zealand and Polynesia; Iglesia Anglicana de la Region central de America; the Episcopal Church in the Philippines; the Episcopal Church in Jerusalem and the Middle East; the Church of Pakistan (United); the Church of the Province of West Africa.

The following provinces led Evening Prayer: the Anglican Church in Tanzania; the Church in Wales; the Anglican Church in Melanesia; the Church of the Province of South East Asia; the Province of the Episcopal Church of South Sudan; Hong Kong Sheng Kung Hui; Iglesia Anglicana de Chile.

There was a common Order of Service produced in the eight official languages of the conference (French, Spanish, Portuguese, Japanese, Korean, Swahili, Juba Arabic and Burmese) for use each day. People were asked to bring their headsets to worship and, if necessary, follow the readings in their own Bibles as other local languages were used as well, such as Farsi and Welsh. There was also use of a video link and recorded content to involve provinces and bishops not able to attend in person.

# 10

# Spouses' Programme

## Vision for the Conference

Archbishop Justin chose to invite spouses to the Lambeth Conference alongside the bishops, based on his experience of visiting the provinces of the Anglican Communion. Having met bishops and spouses in their context and seen the burdens of responsibility many spouses are expected to carry he wanted to recognise the significant contribution they bring to the life of the church. His invitation to spouses was also an acknowledgement of the cost that episcopal ministry has on the family, something that is so often borne principally by the spouse.

For some, including some spouses, there was the question of whether a conference of bishops could be opened to others. Spouses came to the previous Lambeth Conference in 2008 but followed a largely separate programme of events and activities in parallel to the bishops' conference. For the 2022 conference, however, it was decided to hold a joint conference with separate sessions arranged for spouses when the bishops were engaged in business sessions.

The decision was taken that same-sex spouses could not be invited to the 2020 conference. However, several spouses were in Canterbury during the 2022 conference and it was possible for Caroline Welby to meet with them while the conference was taking place. This was a powerful encounter for all which enabled deep listening to one another and led to the opportunity for a further meeting with other spouses on another occasion.

## Planning

A Spouses' Planning Group was appointed that operated under the oversight of the main Lambeth Conference Design Group. The Spouses' Planning Group was convened by Caroline Welby and chaired by Linda Baines, wife of the Bishop of Leeds, England. Linda had been present at the 2008 conference and led on the art project that spouses had contributed to. Members of the planning group included Comfort Fearon, Jane Namurye, Linda Baines, Rebecca Cottrell, Eamonn Mullally, Lizzie Jeanes, Ashella Ndhlovu and Bev Jullien. Additional members joined during the lockdown, including Carmen Regina Duarte, Tabitha Waweru and Caroline Bauerschmidt.

It was agreed that spouses would participate alongside bishops in the acts of worship, the Bible expositions and main plenary sessions. Bishops and spouses would follow the same series of Bible studies but in separate small groups of bishops or spouses. The main seminar programme would be open to both bishops and spouses.

At the heart of the programme were to be the spouses' 'Strengthening Sessions', designed in response to a clear indication that some spouses would come to the conference expecting an element of training. As planning progressed, three clear themes emerged which would provide something for everyone: leadership, community action and personal wholeness.

## Welcome Day

On the Welcome Day when bishops spent time in their own groups, spouses had the opportunity to meet in provincial or regional groupings. The Spanish- and Portuguese-speaking spouses met in cross-provincial groups. This was helpful at the outset as not all spouses have regular opportunities to meet together in provinces. The planning group were keen for spouses to meet with people from their own province or region first in order to have a familiar group to move out from to engage with the much larger conference community. For the second part of the afternoon, spouses moved to their own venue where they met with their Bible study group in which they would remain for the rest of the conference.

It was important to the Spouses' Planning Group that the venue used for many of the spouses' sessions conveyed a strong sense of welcome, as the aspiration was to create a sense of 'safe space' where spouses felt 'at home' and were 'held' and would be able to share together. Caroline Welby wrote to the Primates and their spouses before the Primates' Meeting in March 2022 asking if they would bring fabric that was recognisably from their province. These fabrics were incorporated into the design for the stage setting and wall hangings which included words of praise and welcome in the different conference languages, and used as runners for the Bible study group tables. The visual impact was striking and effective.

## Spouses' Retreat

A separate retreat was planned for spouses and this took place on site at the university while the bishops were at Canterbury Cathedral. Spouses were seated at tables in their Bible study groups in their own venue. In the introductory session, Caroline Welby encouraged spouses to share their hopes for the time together at the conference as they began to get to know one another. Paula Gooder, from St Paul's Cathedral, London, spoke on the themes of 'Born into a Living Hope, 1 Peter 1:3' and 'Called by Name and Known and Loved'. In response to these inputs, spouses from Guatemala, Cameroon, Australia and the USA were invited to share something of their own story and testimony and this sharing was then taken up in the small groups, called table groups. These table groups were composed of the same people throughout the conference.

On the Thursday afternoon, spouses were able to choose from a range of activities including a walk in Blean Woods nature reserve, a walking tour of the sites of Canterbury, Ignatian contemplation of scripture, a workshop looking at lament and 'the gift of tears', or taking part in 'The Big Sing'. A range of creative workshops were also available including 'Testimony in Paint', banner making, storytelling and creative writing. A number of spouses took the time to enjoy 'Tranquillity in the Trees' in one of 20 hammocks suspended in the woods on the University campus.

The spouses' retreat continued on Friday morning with the second input from Paula Gooder and concluded with a Eucharist at which Sister Veronica from the Sisters of the Church in Melanesia presided. Leah Vasey Saunders from the Liturgy Team shaped and held the liturgical aspects of the spouses' retreat and other key moments in the spouses' programme. Geraldine Latty, Carey Luce and other musicians from the team led the spouses in sung worship. These planned elements were supplemented by groups of spouses from different provinces who offered to sing to conclude the Bible study sessions in the spouses' venue each day.

Led sung worship was a key element of the spouses' programme – from the retreat, through to a plenary event mid-conference, to the final session. Having a spouses-dedicated venue enabled this and it meant that everything in the spouses' programme was placed within the context of prayer and worship.

## Spouses' 'Strengthening Sessions'

On five occasions, when the bishops were engaged in the Lambeth Calls, spouses were offered the choice of nine 'Strengthening Sessions'. These were offered in three strands: Personal Wholeness, Leadership and Community Action. These sessions were intended to respond more specifically to issues or felt needs, identified by the spouses themselves through a consultation process that the Spouses' Planning Group conducted early on in the planning stages.

Rob Dawes, the Development Manager with the Mothers' Union, and Cathy James, an independent community development facilitator, were engaged to lead on the development of these sessions. They brought together a talented team of 30 facilitators from around the Communion made up of spouses and other facilitators from Mothers' Union, Anglican Alliance, Anglican Communion Office and the Lambeth Palace Reconciliation Team (many of whom had been engaged in the Global Conversations). This group was involved in the original design of the sessions, meeting over zoom, as well as in the delivery at conference, working in pairs which always included a spouse. In recognition of the language needs among the spouses, on each occasion one of the sessions was either led in, or had translation into, French, Spanish, Portuguese, Kiswahili and Juba Arabic. Spouses who needed Japanese or Burmese had translators who were available to attend their chosen sessions with them.

In each time slot, nine choices were offered, as the intention was to limit attendance to around 45 spouses to ensure that the sessions could be highly interactive. The sessions were designed to draw on the wisdom and experience in the room rather than to teach from the front. The content was intended to increase spouses' confidence in who we are in God, to strengthen existing gifts and uncover new ones, and to identify practical resources and tools that release others to bring hope and help in families, churches and communities. As well as being helpful to spouses attending the conference, the sessions were also designed for spouses to take away and use in their own contexts following the event. While involving so many people in the design and delivery of the sessions added to the planning complexity, the breadth and inclusiveness of the team communicated an important principle.

## Building Resilience Seminar

Midway through the conference all of the spouses were invited to attend a double session looking at 'Building Resilience'. These sessions sought to address the challenges that spouses face in their family, church and community life. These include living as a persecuted minority in places of physical conflict, criticism from others, or challenges in their marriages or as parents, with accompanying feelings of loneliness or isolation. The seminar was led by Canon Sarah Snyder, Director of the Rose Castle Foundation and previously Reconciliation Director at Lambeth Palace. Other contributors included spouses from Pakistan, South Sudan and New Zealand who shared from their own experience of challenge and sources of support and strength.

In response to the plenary inputs, spouses spent time in their table groups sharing their own experience of challenge and also the strategies that they have developed in response. Spouses were invited to shape a piece of clay into a pinch pot that held a tea light, symbolising both the pressures we experience but also the hope that we carry. The afternoon ended with a largely impromptu time of singing and dancing, with spouses from different places offering songs that were taken up by the rest of the room. Spouses took away a pinch pot from the seminar, but not the one they had made. This was symbolic of the solidarity experienced from listening to and sharing one another's stories.

It is important to record that the seminar took place on the Tuesday afternoon, when Archbishop Justin was addressing the bishops on the need for listening to one another on the issue of human sexuality. This was an unintended juxtaposition but it meant that spouses as well as bishops experienced a significant deepening of relationships at the same time, an unexpected moment of grace.

## Spouses' Marquee and Project Focus

It was important to the Spouses' Planning Group that spouses had an informal space of their own where they could relax and meet during what was a very busy conference schedule. A marquee was sited in an open area central to the campus with views over Canterbury Cathedral. The Mothers' Union provided a team of local volunteers who ensured that refreshments were always available and contributed to the welcome alongside Kay Hunter Johnson from Women on the Frontline and other members of the spouses' team. The marquee offered an important space either simply to sit and be with other spouses or to work alongside one another in shared craft activities.

The Spouses' Planning Group had been advised that some spouses preferred to have something to do, and a project focus was identified by profiling the work of Days for Girls in the marquee. Days for Girls seeks to advance menstrual equity, health, dignity and opportunity through the provision of reusable sanitary pads and health education. The Days for Girls team at the conference were able to engage in conversation with spouses in order to discuss the potential of the project and how it might be taken up in different communities within the Communion. Spouses were able to take away sample kits in order to progress conversations. The Days for Girls team also contributed to a seminar in the main programme open to bishops and spouses under the title 'Menstruation Matters'.

## Hospitality

The Lambeth Conference 2022 was pervaded with the hospitality and welcome extended by Archbishop Justin and Caroline Welby. During the conference all of the bishops and spouses were invited to supper at the Old Palace in Canterbury, held across a series of evenings. On the Wednesday the whole conference community travelled to London for a day hosted at Lambeth Palace and focused on the environment and sustainable development.

The Spouses' Planning Group wanted to create a space for spouses that was welcoming and enabled everyone to feel at home as quickly as was possible. This was largely achieved through a large team of individuals, each working in their gifts and strengths towards a shared purpose. It was felt that, by grace, more was accomplished than might have been expected. Spouses felt connected to one another and reported having a greater understanding of, and love for, such a diverse Anglican family.

## Concluding Sessions for Spouses

On the final Saturday morning spouses were invited to attend a plenary session to consider together 'What am I taking away?' Spouses were encouraged to reflect on the conference and to consider what they had received from the time together in Canterbury and what they might seek to apply back in their home context.

On the Sunday morning, spouses met in their provincial or regional groupings to reflect together on the conference and to consider how they might seek to continue to connect and support one another on their return home.

## Looking Ahead

Many spouses and bishops hope to build on what happened at Canterbury, although as there is a high turnover of bishops as they retire, and others take over, this will need support. The forming of a Spouses' Network, to enable relationships to continue to grow across provinces and within provinces and to offer ways that those who have not met since the conference can re-engage, has been agreed by the ACC Standing Committee. The hope is that it will draw in existing spouses as well as new spouses for training, equipping and sharing experience and practice. The Spouses' Network will initially be able to draw on the resources developed for the Strengthening Sessions and seek to develop other resources to enable the work of connecting and supporting to continue during Phase 3 and beyond.

# 11

# Ecumenical Guests

The following representatives from other churches attended and contributed to the Lambeth Conference:

Bishop Antonio ABLON of the Iglesia Filipina Independiente

Bishop Ivan ABRAHAMS of the World Methodist Council

Archbishop ANGAELOS of the Coptic Orthodox Church

Bishop Maga ASHKARIAN of the Armenian Orthodox – Cilicia

Metropolitan Mor Polycarpus AUGIN AYDIN of the Syrian Orthodox Church

Archbishop Donald BOLEN of the Roman Catholic Church

Fr Martin BROWNE OSB of the Roman Catholic Church

The Revd Anne BURGHARDT of the Lutheran World Federation

Archbishop Anil COUTO of the Roman Catholic Church

Fr Anthony CURRER of the Roman Catholic Church

Bishop Johan DALMAN of the Church of Sweden

The Revd Dr Casely ESSAMUAH of the Global Christian Forum

Bishop Brian FARRELL LC of the Roman Catholic Church

Fr Markos HENDERSON of the Patriarchate of Jerusalem

Bishop Tor JORGENSEN of the Lutheran Church of Great Britain

Metropolitan Seraphim KYKKOTIS of the Patriarchate of Alexandria

The Revd Professor Dirk LANGE of the Lutheran World Federation

The Revd Dr Hanns LESSING of the World Communion of Reformed Churches

Archbishop Bernard LONGLEY of the Roman Catholic Church

Bishop Jan Otto MYRSETH of the Church of Norway

Archbishop NIKITAS of the Ecumenical Patriarchate

Metropolitan Silouan ONER of the Patriarchate of Antioch

Commissioner Jane PAONE of the Salvation Army

Archimandrite Stefan PONJARAC of the Serbian Orthodox Church

Bishop Harald REIN of the Old Catholic Churches of Utrecht

Bishop Matt REPO of the Church of Finland

The Revd Dr Thomas SCHIRRMACHER of the World Evangelical Alliance

Obispo Maximo Rhee TIMBANG of the Iglesia Filipina Independiente

The Most Revd Bernd WALLET of the Old Catholic Churches of Utrecht

The Revd Dr David WELLS of the Pentecostal World Fellowship

Mrs Susan Wells of the Pentecostal World Fellowship

The Revd Dr William WILSON of the Pentecostal World Fellowship

Mar Awraham YOUKHANIS of the Assyrian Church of the East

# 12

# Bible Studies on 1 Peter

## Retreat Reflections

Five retreat reflections, one for each book of 1 Peter, were offered by five members of the St Augustine Seminar at the opening retreat of the conference. These reflections, given by Isabelle Hamley (in French), Paul Swarup, Esther Mombo, Paulo Ueti (in Portuguese) and Jennifer Strawbridge, were submitted in advance and printed in the retreat booklets. They offered a carefully designed balance of exegesis, reflection and challenge and set a positive tone for engagement with 1 Peter at the conference. They are published separately.

## Bible Studies

Bishops undertook Bible studies in small groups, called table groups. These table groups were composed of the same people throughout the conference. If given only three words to sum up the Lambeth Conference Bible Studies, they would be 'in my context'. These words dominated the bishops' time together in Bible study and their subsequent reflections. These words, highlighted in the booklet, allowed them quickly to go deep with their group members and to speak from their context and learn about the context of others. The way the Bible studies were set up, then, enabled encounter. Asking questions that engaged 1 Peter through 'your context' was a conscious decision of the St Augustine Seminar members who drew together the Bible studies. The intention was to encourage listening and personal reflection and to discourage 'right' answers and preaching at one another. This seems to have worked well, evidenced by how close some of the Bible study groups became, and is something worth considering when planning Bible studies at future conferences. It is interesting to learn from answers to the 'in my context' questions that at least three Bible study groups discovered that a member of their group had killed a lion!

Other features of the Bible studies included the handy booklets which were beautifully produced, and many bishops carried them throughout the conference. The booklets provided space for writing and reflection, reproduced the pictures well, and had clearly demarcated sections. The booklets worked well in conjunction with the I Peter Commentary (some mentioned how well they complemented each other) and with the Archbishop of Canterbury's expositions immediately before the Bible study time.

The preparation sessions for facilitators were well attended and engendered some helpful questions. They were led by Jennifer Strawbridge, Paul Swarup and Paulo Ueti. Interestingly, the only significant criticism picked up by facilitators was that bishops wanted more time in Bible study together.

## Expositions

Like the Bible studies, the biblical expositions also enabled encounter between text and context. Focusing on I Peter, they were theologically deep yet accessible. The use of videos in all but one exposition allowed for voices from around the Communion to contribute and to add more depth to the expositions. Reflections on suffering, hospitality, holiness, hope, and the roaring lion, for example, enabled everyone to listen to and learn from contexts across the globe as well as connect them with I Peter. Interviews with seven bishops/spouses on holiness, hospitality and lions also enabled stories to be shared and for those present to listen and learn from brothers and sisters in regions very different from their own. The combination of videos and spoken text was carefully balanced. The scripts of the expositions themselves needed continual re-working each day as a result of concerns about timing (every exposition went over the allocated time). They are published separately.

## Taking the Studies Forward

Access to the video material from the expositions is being provided separately so that it can be used in other Bible studies across the Communion, as are the Bible study materials. The words of the expositions are also being published as a text, creating a trilogy of materials, with this text standing alongside the studies and commentary. There are hopes that the St Augustine Seminar may continue in some form as a resource for theological and biblical reflection for the wider Communion.

# 13

# Seminars

The conference was enriched by a wide range of seminars. These were delivered by conference participants and others specially invited to offer papers. Using the educational facilities of the University of Kent, seminars were an essential part of the programme, one that allowed participants to hear about issues and from voices that were not present on the main conference platform.

The following seminars were offered and all were attended by conference participants (between around 30 and 150 at each):

- A Call to Courageous and Confident Engagement with Science: Introducing the Lambeth Call on Science and Faith and the work of the Anglican Communion Science Commission
- A Symphony of Instruments: How the Anglican Communion expresses its unity
- Anglican Communion Safe Church Commission: Providing support where there is abuse
- Anglicans in Health: Building trust and countering fake news
- Building a Confident, Science-engaged Church across the Anglican Communion
- Church Planting
- Elevating Indigenous Wisdom and Experience in the Anglican Communion
- God's Justice: Just relationships between women and men, girls and boys
- Intentional Discipleship for a Jesus-shaped Life
- International Anglican Liturgical Consultation (IALC)
- Justice, Democracy and Corruption: Nurturing prophetic voices in public life
- Leading with Integrity with those of Other Faiths
- Menstruation Matters
- Mission through Anglican Schools
- Missional Formation with Young People
- Models of Partnership

- Re-imagining Our World: The Anglican Communion and the Sustainable Development Goals
- Rethinking Mission: Exploring power, privileges and partnerships
- The Church and Religious Freedom: Lament, learning and hope
- The Communion Forest: An act of hope in the face of climate crisis
- The Environment and Living with the Fifth Mark of Mission
- The Other Pandemic: Responding to the mental health concerns sweeping across our world
- Theological Education in Africa: Challenges and opportunities
- Theological Education in Asia, Latin America and the Caribbean: Challenges and opportunities
- Thy Kingdom Come: Life-changing prayer for evangelism
- Transforming Conflict and Division: The role of the church
- Unity, Faith and Order: Dialogue and action
- Welcoming the Stranger: The church response to migration and modern-day slavery/human trafficking
- Youth and Livelihoods: The impact of the pandemic

## Reports on Some of the Seminars

### Environment: Living the Fifth Mark of Mission

About 140 participants took part in this seminar organised by the Anglican Alliance and the Environment Network. It was offered in nine languages, and through a series of small-group discussions in the table groups participants shared different ways in which they are striving 'to safeguard the integrity of creation and sustain and renew the life of the earth' in the face of the triple environmental crisis of climate change, biodiversity loss and pollution. How can creation-care be part of daily discipleship? Archbishop Julio Murray of Central America and chair of the Environment Network introduced the Lambeth Call on the Environment and Canon Rachel Mash and Mandisa Gumada, a youth worker from South Africa, reflected on the contribution of young people to the crisis. Archbishop Julio spoke on how Anglicans are engaging with the COP process and Canon Rachel Carnegie talked about the next steps of engaging with the Lambeth Call on the Environment and the Communion Forest initiative.

This seminar, early in the conference, set the agenda for the environmental theme that ran through the whole event and was especially highlighted on the London Day. It was also significant in raising the voices of the many bishops active in environmental responses around the Communion. One outcome was the strong support for the Communion

43

Forest initiative and also for the Lambeth Call on the Environment later in the week. All this work is being followed up by the Anglican Alliance and the Environment Network, and by the Anglican UN Office on the COP process.

### Youth and Livelihoods: The impact of the pandemic

Young people everywhere are particularly impacted by unemployment and loss of livelihoods, especially from the Covid-19 pandemic and deepening economic crisis. This seminar heard from young people about the way that livelihood challenges can lead to risks such as unsafe migration, addiction and conflict. There was also discussion on positive models of where churches can ally themselves with youth in developing skills and opportunities to build lives of hope.

Clifton Nedd, co-convenor of Anglican Communion Youth Network and Anglican Alliance regional Caribbean facilitator, chaired the session and set the context. With a video made by the Anglican Youth Network giving examples and insights, Clifton gave a global overview that set out the statistics to show how and why youth are particularly affected. Bible verses framed the seminar and the participants were asked how they work to support youth to live flourishing lives. This was followed by a panel discussion where Rachel Lindley, CEO of Five Talents UK, interviewed Archbishop Joseph Atem of South Sudan, and Bishop Dushanta Rodrigo of Colombo, Church of Ceylon. They discussed the challenges young people face in their region and what the churches can do to support the livelihoods of the young. These questions were then discussed in group work and participants were invited to share their experiences of the challenges young people face in their context. They explored what bishops and spouses can do to empower young people in livelihoods and identified the specific assets within the church to help. Finally, participants were asked what they were now inspired to do. After brief feedback from the groups, the chair shared information on available resources/organisations. To conclude, the participants were invited to engage in conversations with their young people on return to their dioceses using the seminar resources. The seminar was planned by a working group comprising the Anglican Youth Network, the Anglican Alliance, Five Talents and CAPA (Council of Anglican Provinces of Africa). This working group is continuing to meet, developing further webinars and resources to take this initiative to connect bishops and youth in their own contexts.

## A Call to Courageous and Confident Engagement with Science: Introducing the Lambeth Call on Science and Faith and the work of the Anglican Communion Science Commission

Professor Andrew Briggs of Oxford University, Bishop Emily Onyango of the Church of Kenya, Dr Heather Payne, a health adviser to the Welsh government, and Bishop Steven Croft of the Church of England led a seminar for around 35 delegates on the first Saturday of the conference focused on the Lambeth Call on Science and Faith and the new Anglican Communion Science Commission. The seminar looked at the key areas of cosmology, learning from the church response to Covid-19, agriculture, and gender-based violence. Participants were asked what their priorities would be for the work of the Commission, recognising that the contexts in which they find themselves is key. The seminar leaders then mapped these on to each of the Five Marks of Mission. It was revealing that the highest number of priorities were in the area of the second Mark – that is, teaching, baptising and nurturing new believers. The Science Commission will pick up and take forward work on many of these priorities over the next five years.

## Building a Confident, Science-engaged Church across the Anglican Communion

This seminar was led by members of the ECLAS team. ECLAS stands for Equipping Christian Leaders in an Age of Science. The team presented the ways in which ECLAS has worked in conferences for senior church leaders, funded scientists in congregations and new work in seminaries, and undertaken primary research on church attitudes to the sciences. Again there was some careful listening to the priorities of participants which ranged from teaching conservation agriculture to ethical questions around technology to exploring the ways that we know things.

## Theological Education in Asia, Latin America and the Caribbean: Challenges and opportunities

This seminar, chaired by Archbishop Howard Gregory of the West Indies, considered the recent Guatemala Appeal on Theological Education, an appeal written in the wake of the migration crisis in the Americas.[1] This was introduced by Paulo Ueti, and responses and other reflections were offered by Bishop Sally Hernández of Mexico City, Bishop Anantha Raj

Chelliah of the Church of South India, the Revd Thomas Sharp on behalf of the Young Anglican Theologians Project, and Professor Katherine Grieb, Director of the Centre for Anglican Communion Studies at Virginia Theological Seminary. Contributions from the floor ranged far and wide as traditional approaches to theological education were compared and contrasted with the Appeal's call to move theological education 'off the balcony and onto the road' (using John Mackay's phrase) – that is, out of the seminaries (perceived as 'ivory towers') and into the struggle for basic rights for migrants. It was noted that one strength of the document was its biblical exegesis, showing how central the idea of migration is to the biblical narratives. Many in the seminar agreed that there is a migration crisis and that it should shape part of the curriculum of theological education. Some disagreed with the idea that theological education was some kind of escape into an alternative reality separated from the missionary life of churches and that seminary education did not take place in the 'real world'. There was a lively discussion.

### Theological Education in Africa: Challenges and opportunities

The seminar on theological education in Africa was chaired by Bishop Victor Atta-Baffoe of Ghana and considered the Statement from an All Africa Council of Churches' consultation in Nairobi in November 2021, which called for a pan-African approach to theological education 'for sustainable growth in churches and society in relation to the Africa Union's Agenda 2063', not least by digging deep into church traditions, especially those 'cooked in an African pot in an African kitchen'. Responses and reflections came from the Venerable Kofi deGraft-Johnson, General Secretary of CAPA, Professor Esther Mombo of St Paul's University, Kenya, Bishop Vincentia Kgabe of Lesotho (previously Rector of the College of the Transfiguration, South Africa), and with an external perspective offered by Professor Katherine Grieb. Once again, contributions from the floor enriched and broadened the discussion. This seminar did almost the exact opposite of the first one, affirming the importance of theological seminaries, recognising both the challenges they face and the opportunities they have, especially if they work together and draw on African initiative and leadership. This conversation was taken further at a consultation in Botswana organised by USPG with the support of the Anglican Communion Office in November 2022.

## Mission through Anglican Schools

Anglican churches provide primary and secondary school education as part of their mission throughout the Communion. The seminar discussed whether churches have a shared vision for education and explored the church's purpose and role in promoting mutual understanding and respect, serving the common good and ensuring an Anglican identity in church schools. The seminar attempted to respond to these questions through case studies and sharing perspectives. The seminar was organised by the Anglican Alliance.

After welcoming participants, the chair, Archbishop Paul Kwong from Hong Kong, opened the seminar by exploring why the provision of school education is central to Anglican mission. This was followed by a panel discussion in which the Revd Nigel Genders, Chief Education Officer for the Church of England, spoke about how to grow faith through connecting church, school and home for mission among children and young people. Bishop Emmanuel Lomoro of Rokon, South Sudan, spoke about education during times of conflict, including promoting girls' education. Archbishop Kay Goldsworthy of Perth, Australia, talked about Anglican identity in schools and the potential for an Anglican Communion Schools' Network. After the panel discussion participants were invited to go into groups to explore how an Anglican school programme can serve mission and the common good, including mental well-being, and also how an Anglican Communion Schools' Network could help the work they were doing locally in education. The concept of such a network was supported after wider discussion with participants.

## Anglicans in Health: Building trust and countering fake news

The seminar aimed to examine how people cope with conflicting information. With misinformation and fake news undermining confidence in health messages, faith leaders can play a key role as trusted sources of accurate information. The church has four powers: local presence; time for the long haul; understanding of context; and their credibility and trust. This seminar explored how the church can build confidence and trust and enable communities to promote health and become more media savvy. This seminar was organised by the Anglican Alliance in collaboration with the Anglican Health and Community Network.

The chair, Bishop Michael Beasley of the Church of England, set the scene before interviewing the panel: Archbishop Ande Titre of the Anglican Church of Congo and Dr Marion Watson of the Jenner Institute at

Oxford University. Each talked about their experience of the issues in terms of health information, where they get accurate information based on scientific evidence and how they use media well to convey accurate facts. After this, Dr Sally Smith, Health Network coordinator, asked the participants to form small groups to explore how they best speak about health in the public domain in their various contexts and how the church can do this well. What media channels do they need to speak into and how can they work effectively with media? After the group discussion and feedback, the chair and Dr Sally Smith provided information on the Anglican Health and Community Network and described how it is looking to convene further webinars on this topic.

## The Communion Forest: An act of hope in the face of climate crisis

The climate emergency requires multiple, urgent responses, including protecting and restoring the earth's forests and other ecosystems. The Communion Forest is both a practical and symbolic response and a global initiative consisting of local activities. This seminar explored the theology and practicalities of the initiative, sharing existing examples of ecosystem protection and restoration, woven into the life and mission of the church. The seminar was offered in English and Spanish and was organised by the Anglican Alliance and the Anglican Environment Network.

Archbishop Julio Murray of Central America and chair of Environment Network led the seminar. The Revd Canon Rachel Mash, Convenor of the Anglican Communion Environment Network and who is based in South Africa, introduced the topic and had an in-depth discussion with Elizabeth Wathuthi, the Kenya climate justice advocate. They discussed issues connected to environmental justice, including the legacy of the late Bishop Wamukoya of Swaziland, the seriousness of the climate emergency and how it affects people across the Communion, the need to make connections across the Communion and world, and the need to link climate with issues like migration, impacts on women and young people and food security.

All this means that a range of responses is needed. These were taken up in small discussion groups. Dr Elizabeth Perry, Advocacy and Communication Manager of the Anglican Alliance, introduced the Communion Forest concept. She shared examples from across the Communion. Canon Rachel Mash then interviewed panel members: Bishop Marc Andrus of the Episcopal Church, who talked about how he is weaving creation care into the spiritual and liturgical life of his diocese; Brother Christopher John SSF, who shared how he is engaged in advocacy over illegal logging in the Solomon Islands; and Bishop Francisco Duque of Colombia, who spoke of the inter faith aspect of his work on ecosystem restoration. Participants then shared their stories in groups. Bishop Graham Usher of the Church of England shared a spiritual and theological reflection on ecology. Participants were invited to sign up for future webinars. This seminar contributed to the launch of the Communion Forest initiative, a key legacy of the Lambeth Conference. Several of the bishops attending the seminar have subsequently engaged with the Communion Forest team, joined webinars and started an initiative or shared existing work.

## Welcoming the Stranger: The church response to migration and modern-day slavery/human trafficking

More people than ever are on the move, leaving their homes for other areas or crossing borders, often forcibly displaced by conflict, economic crisis, climate change or trafficking. Churches are often front-line responders, committed to welcoming the stranger and raising awareness about the risks and signs of human trafficking. This seminar, organised by the Anglican Alliance and the Anglican Working Group on Migration, shared experiences of displacement in different contexts and how churches are responding to migration and trafficking.

Speakers included Archbishop Maimbo Mndolwa of Tanzania, in the chair, Bishop Silvestre Romero of Guatemala, and Bishop David Rice of San Joaquin who spoke about migration in Central America and the USA and how bishops and churches are responding. Bishop Alastair Redfern, former Bishop of Derby and chair of the Clewer Initiative, made a presentation on human trafficking drawing on a video from the Initiative, reflecting on theological and practical responses. Bishops and spouses discussed how to offer leadership in their own contexts in response to migration and human trafficking. The Revd Rachel Carnegie, director of the Anglican Alliance, shared ways of connecting and networking across the Communion and ecumenically, including through the Anglican Alliance, Clewer Initiative and Anglican Migration Working Group. The seminar served to highlight how migration and human trafficking are issues of profound concern across the Communion.

## The Other Pandemic: Responding to mental health concerns sweeping across our world

Clergy across the Communion, medical practitioners and survey data all report increasing levels of mental ill-health in our communities and among our caring professions. Drawing on Jesus' ministry of restoring health and wholeness, this seminar, organised by the Anglican Alliance and the Anglican Health and Community Network, explored how churches can respond. How can they support mental and spiritual well-being, help with grief and trauma care, promote resilience and care for the carers?

Bishop Murray Harvey of Australia, in the chair, welcomed everyone and outlined a global overview. Ruth Rice, Director of Renew Well-being in the UK, described how local churches support mental well-being through their community life as well as through the care of clergy and lay leaders. Bishop Juan David Alvarado of El Salvador spoke about trauma healing with youth caught up in gang violence. Participants discussed what the religious and cultural issues at play were. Then the Revd Zanele Ndwandwe, a senior nurse, priest and bishop's spouse from South Africa, spoke on the impact of the Covid-19 pandemic on mental health, including gender issues. Abagail Nelson from Episcopal Relief and Development in the Episcopal Church spoke about building resilience and care for carers with a global perspective. Participants discussed how the church can support mental health, including the mental well-being of clergy and other carers. They also explored ways to partner with other agencies working in this area, and learned from one another's responses from different contexts. The Anglican Health and Community Network will follow up with a webinar.

## Re-imagining Our World: The Anglican Communion and the Sustainable Development Goals

With only eight years to go, the efforts to achieve the UN Sustainable Development Goals (SDGs) need extraordinary commitment. This seminar offered space to consider how, as God's Church for God's World, we can emerge from the pandemic and re-imagine our world. Through panel discussion and group work, the seminar offered practical ways to link the Five Marks of Mission and the SDGs around the pillars of prayer, action, advocacy and communication. This seminar was offered in the nine conference languages and was planned by the Anglican Alliance and the Anglican UN Office.

Chairing the seminar, Archbishop Albert Chama of the Church of the Province of Central Africa reflected on the SDGs in light of the Anglican Communion's Five Marks of Mission. A video on the SDGs was followed by a panel discussion on church and community responses. Bishop Brent Alawas, of the Episcopal Church of the Philippines, introduced Asset-Based Church and Community Transformation. Catherine Le Tissier, the spouse of Archbishop Nick Drayson, Province of South America, described how indigenous Anglican women bring their skills and vision to transform communities in her part of Argentina. Bishop Julius Wanyoike, from the Diocese of Thika, Kenya, spoke about the value of the Church and Community Mobilisation Process (CCMP), also known as Umoja, as part of the church's holistic mission. This led into a group-work session where participants discussed how the holistic mission of their church related to the SDGs. The chair invited feedback from these discussions to the whole meeting. Jack Palmer-White, the Anglican Communion Permanent Representative to the United Nations, and the Revd Rachel Carnegie, the Executive Director of the Anglican Alliance, made a presentation on the SDG campaign 'Re-imagining our World', especially on its advocacy and action. An Anglican Alliance Contextual Bible Study Resource was also launched. With a similar title of 'Re-imagining our World Together', it offers Bible studies on the Five Marks of Mission and the SDGs. To conclude the seminar, participants were invited to write individual reflections on postcards. The Anglican Alliance and the Anglican UN Office will take its insights into future strategy.

### Note

1 https://www.anglicancommunion.org/media/490557/TEAC_Guatemala-Appeal-on-Theological-Education_2206212_en.pdf.

# 14

# The London Day and Queen's Message

On Wednesday 3 August the conference visited Lambeth Palace in London for a day of prayer, reflection and action on the environment and sustainable development. Archbishop Justin and Caroline Welby welcomed everyone to the garden of their London home:

This garden is one of the oldest in England. We know that when the Archbishop of Canterbury purchased this land in 1197 there was already a garden here. And when we look at the Domesday Book of 1086 there was a garden here, so we think this garden is probably over 1,000 years old. It would have been some swampy land with a few crops which has not been built on except for the marquee today. We are thrilled that you can see it. The garden today is an illustration of climate change. There are very few of us who can remember in this country a time when even the trees were turning brown from lack of water and from heat. Today with its theme of sustainable development and the climate emergency, I hope this brings home to us how serious this is, as we gather together. For many of you it is already a terrible disaster. But let us remember that the climate emergency causes people to move. And when people move, there are wars and we enter into a downward spiral.

The garden is one of my favourite places. Underneath this end of the marquee is a labyrinth, the grass labyrinth, which is one of my favourite places for prayer. The prayer stations this morning, particularly the one near the beehives, struck me very forcefully as a reminder that all things are created by our Lord and Saviour. So I hope that you use this time as a time of renewal and refreshment from God's creation of good company.

We are honoured to have our guests from other faith communities here as well as our ecumenical guests. Also, in particular, His Excellency the Papal Nuncio, and his eminence, the Cardinal Archbishop of Westminster. We also welcome the leaders of the Hindu community, the Sikh community, the Jewish community and the Chief Rabbi of the Commonwealth, and Imam Qasim from Manchester. All of you are profoundly welcome and I hope that we will make you feel even more welcome.

## A Message from Her Majesty the Queen

The Bishop of London, Sarah Mullaly, read out the following message:

It is with great pleasure that I send my warm greetings as you continue your meeting in the fifteenth Lambeth Conference. As we all emerge from the pandemic, I know that the conference is taking place at a time of great need for the love of God – both in word and deed.

I am reminded that this gathering was necessarily postponed two years ago, when you had hoped to mark the centenary of the Lambeth Conference that took place in 1920, in the aftermath of the First World War. Then, the bishops of the Anglican Communion set out a path for an ongoing commitment towards Christian unity in a changing world; a task that is, perhaps, even more important today, as together you look to the future and explore the role of the church in responding to the needs of the present age.

Now, as so often in the past, you have convened during a period of immense challenge for bishops, clergy and lay people around the world, with many of you serving in places of suffering, conflict and trauma. It is of comfort to me that you do so in the strength of God.

We also live in a time when the effects of climate change are threatening the lives and livelihoods of many people and communities, not least the poorest and those less able to adapt and adjust. I was interested to learn that the focus of your programme at Lambeth Palace today is reflection and dialogue on the theme of the environment, a cause close to the heart of my late husband, and carried on by The Prince of Wales and The Duke of Cambridge.

Throughout my life, the message and teachings of Christ have been my guide and in them I find hope. It is my heartfelt prayer that you will continue to be sustained by your faith in times of trial and encouraged by hope at times of despair.

I send my warmest good wishes to you all for a successful conference and may God bless you in your ministry and service in his world.
ELIZABETH R.
3rd August, 2022

## The Communion Forest

The conference community was invited to take part in the launch of the Anglican Communion Forest, a worldwide environmental initiative set up to encourage Anglicans in tree planting, the creation of wetlands, and coastal restoration projects. The Lambeth Call on the Environment and Sustainable Development was also shared on this day. Bishops from across the globe pledged their support for the Communion Forest. Each area of the Anglican Communion will decide locally how they wish to create and enhance landscape protection. The 'Forest' could include woodland, grasslands, meadows, wetlands, coastal habitats and more. The pledge was marked by a symbolic planting of a tree. The first tree of the Communion Forest was planted in the Lambeth Palace garden by Archbishop Justin and Archbishop Julio Murray of Panama, together with the Archbishop of Cape Town, Thabo Makgoba, and Elizabeth Wathuti, a Kenyan environmental activist.

The conference community walked around the gardens of Lambeth Palace to different prayer stations, to read and reflect on prayers about the environment shared by bishops from around the world.

Archbishop Justin commented on the theme and activity of the day:

> Scripture is full of rich descriptions of our natural world and God's love for His creation. It is the call of the church to treasure this gift, to stand alongside our brothers and sisters around the Anglican Communion who are already affected by climate change, and to safeguard the environment upon which all of us depend. I pray the tree planted today in Lambeth Palace will be the beginning of one of the world's most widespread and diverse environmental projects. We hope to see landscape protection and care for creation exhibited by churches and parishes in every corner of the world as a historic legacy of the 2022 Lambeth Conference.

Archbishop Julio Murray, of Iglesia Anglicana de la Region Central de America (IARCA), who led the Anglican Communion delegation to the COP meetings on climate change, reminded everyone that

> the focus today is prayer, fellowship and reflection on the themes of the environment and sustainable development. It is a fact that the present times are challenging and also decisive times. Our countries face many crises, but none with the scope as shocking as climate change. Its impacts vary among regions, generations, age, classes, income groups and gender. Based on the information provided by the Intergovernmental Panel on Climate Change (IPCC), it is evident that people who are already most vulnerable and marginalised will also experience the greatest impacts. As we face the triple environmental crisis: climate change, biodiversity loss and pollution, we also recognise the threat to millions of people and their livelihood. The poor, especially in de-

veloping countries, are expected to be disproportionately affected and consequently in need of adaptation and mitigation strategies in the face of climate change.

The response to the climate crisis has been inadequate, in the level of resources and in the level of urgency. With this as part of the facts, here we are: Bishops of the Anglican Communion at the Lambeth Conference, we will have an opportunity to prepare a call to government leaders and other actors, to re-imagine actions and strategies to slow down the devastating effects on the life of human beings, locally and globally. Faith actors should leverage both their capacity and influence to advocate for urgent, bold climate action by leaders and key stakeholders. We also need your capacity to transform hearts and minds away from destructive attitudes and behaviours towards responsible creation care. Young people are asking for the faith leaders to do more, leaders such as Elizabeth Watuti, a young climate activist, who addresses us now.

Elizabeth Watuti of the Green Generation Initiative, Kenya:

We have a shared moral responsibility to ensure that this amazing planet, our common home, remains safe and habitable for present and future generations. I have come here today because I believe that the world needs your united voice and powerful leadership to help make that happen.

Almost a year ago I was invited to speak at the opening ceremony of the Cop26 climate conference in Glasgow. At that time the summit was being described as humanity's last best chance to avoid catastrophic climate change and I was allocated four minutes to address world leaders directly. The responsibility of that moment weighed very heavily upon me and I had to do a lot of soul searching about what I might say, because I did not know what there was left to say to move world leaders to act at the speed and scale we know is needed. In the end I chose to use my four minutes with world leaders to shine a spotlight on the impact that the climate crisis is already bringing to bear across the African continent. Right now, a historic drought worsened by climate change is bringing immense suffering to millions of my fellow Kenyans and to other communities living in neighbouring countries across the whole of Africa. Earlier this year I travelled to Wajir county in the north-eastern part of my country and there I witnessed a shocking example of the impacts of the interconnected climate, nature and food crisis. I drove for hours down dusty roads lined with shrivelled carcases of decimated local wildlife populations. I held in my dusty arms livestock that were dying. I heard stories of hungry and desperate people who were losing all hope for their future.

Climate-driven disasters are of course not only happening in Kenya. Over the last few years deadly heatwaves and fires have swept through Algeria; devastating floods have taken many lives in Uganda, Nigeria and South Africa, and we know that there is more to come. I used my speech at Cop26 to share real human stories from people who are rarely given a voice in decision-making processes, and I have chosen to do the same here today, not to shock or blame anyone but rather in the hope and with the prayer that we may truly allow ourselves to feel the immense suffering that our way of doing things is causing. This is because I believe an open heart is where the seed of true action lies within each of us.

The global community has been coming together to negotiate outcomes at environmental and climate conferences for many more decades than I have been alive, and yet we still find ourselves at the precipice of an interconnected and worsening climate-nature-pollution crisis. Why are we not doing what we know we must? In my view, what is holding us back from dealing with the interconnected climate-nature-pollution crisis is not a lack of scientific knowledge or technology. These are human problems and the solutions to them lie in the human head, heart and mind. I believe in our human capacity to care deeply and to act collectively. I believe in our ability to do what is right if we let ourselves feel it in our hearts. And I believe that we can absolutely find our way out of the planetary crisis that we face, but to do so we will need to change our way of thinking and start telling new stories about what is important and what is possible. And this is where I think the faith community has a vital role to play. Right now, the life-sustaining and sacred relationship between nature and humanity is not being recognised or valued or protected. We are perpetuating an ecocidal economic system that is destroying nature faster than it can regenerate. We are not being good stewards, we are not being good planetary stewards. But it does not have to be this way. A future with a stable climate, clean air, clean water and food security for all is possible. An international and cooperative solidarity is how we will achieve it. What is needed now is courageous and urgent action from each and every one of us to change course while we still can, born of compassion and respect for ourselves and all life on earth.

The global community will be convening in Egypt in November for the Cop27 climate conference and again in Montreal in December for the Cop15 biodiversity conference. My urgent appeal to all of you ahead of these critical moments is please do more to help. Help us by using your power, resources and influence to call on world leaders, the business community and citizens everywhere to take the climate and nature crisis seriously and act with urgency to follow through on promises that have been made before and not met. This is not just a moment for compassion but also a moment for action and reform. We must break our deadly reliance on fossil fuels and invest massively in a clean energy future and access for all. We must also transform our global food systems and protect and restore the earth's ecosystems. Countries must also raise their ambition to limit global warming to 1.5 degrees Celsius and assist others to meet this challenge by mobilising finance and resources, including a dedicated finance facility to help poor countries cope with climate-related loss and damage. What we will gain by solving the nature, food and climate crisis together will be improved human health, security and well-being everywhere. This is the only pathway to a healthy and dignified life that allows people to provide for themselves and their families, and it is my sincere hope that we can walk together towards the kind of future that I think we all want.

## A Message from António Guterres, the Secretary General of the United Nations

The following message came through a video link:

To my dear friend the Archbishop of Canterbury and other friends, the Lambeth Conference is an opportunity to discuss and deliberate core and indeed universal lessons of faith and values. This year's gathering takes place amid a series of challenges that cloud our work. From conflicts like the war in Ukraine and climate catastrophe, to mistrust and division, to poverty, inequality and discrimination to the ongoing effects of the global pandemic. These challenges resist easy solutions. But your inspiring teams, summoning us to walk, listen and witness together, offer a blueprint for progress. It calls upon all people to bring value to life not through words but through action and service to others and to deliver economic and environmental justice that the world needs more than ever: economic justice through an equal economic recovery with all countries accessing the financing and debt relief they need to invest in their people at this critical time; social justice, by reducing inequalities, investing in the health, education and well-being of all people and supporting the most vulnerable including refugees, migrants and women and girls; and environmental justice, by addressing the planetary emergency of climate change and supporting all countries as they decarbonise their economies and build green futures. Above all, there can be no justice of any kind without peace. But embracing peace, forgiveness and tolerance and, more importantly, by living these values every day we can move one step closer to the sustainable, equal and just world that every person deserves. Thank you for being part of this essential endeavour.

# 15

# God's World

My prayer for this conference is very simple. It is that everyone here, whoever you are, wherever you have come from, whether as an observer, steward, ecumenical guest, bishop, spouse, with whatever hopes and fears you may bring with you, may leave with your heart full of desire for friendship with Jesus Christ. For to desire Jesus is to desire God. To desire Jesus is to desire to be filled with love for God and, by God, love for his people and love for his word. Whatever else we do over the next two weeks, the one thing that is essential is that we learn again to hunger and thirst for God. And the reason I say this is because we know there is so much to do and often it is God who is pushed aside, by circumstances, by pressures.

As Peter says: 'Although you have not seen him, you love him; and even though you do not see him now, you believe in him and rejoice with indescribable and glorious joy, for you are receiving the outcome of your faith, the salvation of your souls' (1 Peter 1:8–9). It is because of the love of Jesus and for no other reason we are being saved.

Peter writes to churches that hunger and thirst for God, that do rejoice with indescribable joy. And yet they experience suffering. Many – perhaps most of us – come to this conference from places of suffering. Many, certainly a majority, come from places of suffering. I know because I have had the privilege of visiting many of them with Caroline. Some may be sitting here this evening feeling that they are failing in their calling. Or they may come doubting God and his love. Some may come with hidden sins of which they are deeply ashamed. Peter, around whose letter we are gathering, knew fear and failure, sin and questioning.

Yet Jesus Christ stands among us now, looks into my heart and your heart, and offers to bear our burdens, to renew our hopes and faith, forgive our sins and feed us with heavenly food of word and sacrament. He looks deeply into each of us, and there is nothing he does not know. He looks deeply into each of us and loves us. So if you come with inner doubts, inner fears, inner shames, talk to the chaplains, confess, be prayed for, be anointed, receive renewal of your hearts and your love for Jesus Christ.

Many of us come aware of what Peter calls the roaring lions: the sense – and often reality – of attack, hostility, danger and uncertainty. That is the main subject of this address. Although we can know joy and love from Jesus Christ, the distractions and realities of our fallen world – the fears, apprehensions, pressures and burdens – can make the lions seem bigger and bigger and bigger, and more important and more powerful than the great and freely given love of God that we seek, desire, long for, and can find in these days together, and be changed by finding.

Archbishop Jackson Ole Sapit, the Archbishop of Kenya, is a Maasai and so knows much about lions. He told me once that lions roar when they search for prey or when they seek to drive prey into a trap. But when they are really close and they are stalking you, they are silent. As shepherds, as overseers of God's flock, we bishops are commanded to be aware of the roaring lions in order to keep our flocks safe. Sometimes that is easy. At other times, the lions are roaring so loudly that we see and hear nothing but danger all around us. And then they can be silent and even more dangerous.

In these three Presidential addresses I shall look first at God's World, then at God's Church, and then at the vocation we have, as bishops and bishops' spouses, of leading God's Church especially as we remember that God's Church does not exist for our sakes but for the salvation of the world.

Let me say first something about the detailed agenda for this Lambeth Conference. For many years, churches, provinces and dioceses have continued to work marvellously in their own areas. But too often the Anglican Communion has been known – where it is known at all as a Communion – for looking inwards and struggling with its own disagreements, especially on the Christian and Anglican approach to human identity and sexuality. Those disagreements will not be solved at this conference. However, my prayer is that, while we are aware of them because they really matter, we turn as a Communion outwards to the entirety of the world that God loves so much that God gave his only Son to die for its salvation.

We must look outwards because we meet at a time of world crisis. But crises are moments when our cries rise to God and God hears them. God heard the cry of the enslaved Hebrews. God rescued Israel under the Judges. God brought them back from exile. God supremely has given us a new birth – we are born again into a living hope through the resurrection of Jesus Christ from the dead and, as Peter says, into an inheritance, a future possession, that is imperishable, undefiled and unfading, kept in heaven for you who are being protected by the power of God through faith for a salvation ready to be revealed in the last time (1 Peter 1:3–4).

In times of crisis, as we all know – personal crisis and world crisis – we depend on God's power, not our own power. And then we find that we can act. Whatever the crisis may be for you – whether it may be in your diocese or your province, whether it is internal to the church or external to the world – this conference is aimed at calling us to a fresh start, to be the church that God calls us to be, of being involved in the mission, the *missio Dei*, the mission that God prepares and sends us into.

## Crises of our time

The world crisis is complicated. It is a crisis of economics, of war and savagery, of climate change, of international relations, and of culture and belief. It is no surprise, therefore, that for so many of us, in so many places and in so many ways, this is a moment of decision. Because crises do not offer you the opportunity of not making a choice. Not to choose is to choose.

As Christians, we believe in a fallen world, where sin and self-seeking, our rebellion against God, opens the way to all the many evils that surround us and always have surrounded us. Crises in both world and church will be normal, because wherever there are human beings there is sin, and crises are always fuelled by sin.

Since the last Lambeth Conference in 2008, 14 years ago, we have seen the impact of the collapse of the western banking system, the end of globalisation of trade, the Covid-19 pandemic, the catastrophe that we are facing over world food prices and availability (the biggest crisis in food availability in over half a century), a major war involving a nuclear-armed power, as well as hundreds of other conflicts impacting so many of us here and, with growing force, climate change.

On top of those global changes, there has been the great roaring of lions in so many of our own countries. Wars, persecution, civil disorder, poverty have struck hardest at the weakest and the poorest in the flock, killing thousands who have put their trust in Jesus Christ as Saviour and Lord. In many parts of the world, especially those of the global North, culture is also changing immensely rapidly. What are so often called culture wars – the rejection of many of the old ways of settling belief, faith or ethics – find their roots in philosophical changes in the understanding of identity and of what it is to be human. The shock waves of these changes are felt around the world and across the Communion.

Some of the change is good. With most young people in this country, in the global North, there is a passionate commitment that did not exist among those born after the war, to justice, to equality, to freedom and to rejecting self-seeking. There is a deep hatred of hypocrisy – and they see it too much in the church – and there is a prizing of integrity. There is a real commitment to the most vulnerable. There is genuine energy around the world, especially by people under 30, in seeking to ensure that the planet on which we live avoids climate disaster in the next 20, 50, 100 years.

These crises, if we look at them as Christians, are in many ways God giving us choices. This is always how judgement is found – God gives us what we want – and holds a plumbline against us, as we have been and against our societies. There is nothing unusual about crises. For those who are faithful they call us to deeper discipleship, to new directions of obedience and holiness. They transform us and we transform the world around us. That is the aim. But the church that turns inwards, that fails to hear the roaring of the lions, is going to fail.

Look back in church history. In the 5th century, North Africa was the heart of world Christianity; 200 years later the church there was almost wiped out. One of the most recent provinces in the Anglican Communion covers North Africa, but there are missionary dioceses there and very, very few indigenous churches. This wipe-out could happen anywhere in the world today if we ignore the lions, where the shepherds pay no attention to the lions, because they've turned their backs on the flocks, looked at one another, and are involved in mutual dispute.

But should we not be focused on our inner differences, especially on those of sexuality? Well, they do matter greatly, they are at the heart of people's understanding of who they are, as Christians, as human beings. We shall look at them in the context of the Call on Human Dignity. We will look at them again in the second Presidential address, and in the context of our studies of 1 Peter. But they are not everything.

We cannot wait until everything is fixed before being God's Church *for* God's World, because that wait will go on longer than the wait for Jesus to return. And I have to say from the deepest point of my heart, I believe we will not quickly be forgiven if this is another gathering that focuses mainly on ourselves. To someone without food, or caught up in war, or persecuted, or suffering from intense poverty, their daily struggle is uppermost in their minds. They want a church that stands with them.

As shepherds we must, as Pope Francis said, 'smell of the sheep' because we are among them. We must tend to their wounds, guide them to water, protect them from the lions. Unless we understand what is happening in the world, we cannot prepare for the opportunities or the threats it brings, we cannot teach the people of God properly how to face the crises they experience.

## Science and technology

So in the rest of this address I will look into the near future and speak of some of the roars that reverberate around the world. There is a new roar – the roar of science and technology. Scientific commentators have said that the next 40 years are expected to see the greatest changes in science and technology that have ever been seen in human history in that period of time.

In the biological and medical sciences we are already seeing extraordinary advances in the treatment of diseases, from cancer to malaria. The Covid-19 vaccine was developed in less than 18 months. Twenty years ago it would have taken a decade. We already have more power in our phones than NASA had to send astronauts to the moon. Self-driving cars are already a reality. With Artificial Intelligence, machines are already producing conversations that sound convincingly 'human'. At what point do we say they are thinking for themselves and have a soul? Wars are now won and lost because of drones and autonomous weapons. Robotics is advancing rapidly. The list is endless. And these changes give humanity, the whole global population, two possible ways to go.

In the first way, led by churches that are engaged with science and technology, we learn to give thanks to the Lord who gives us brains to think with, and scientific advances to help change lives. In this pathway, this wonderful way, the benefits of knowledge are shared: the ethical questions are thought through; skills in crop change are spread throughout the world so that countries affected by global warming can still feed their population; clean water is made available to countries suffering from drought; diseases that cause so much suffering and death are eradicated; drones and good surveillance are used to stop wars, stop bandits, stop poaching, and to warn of natural disasters.

The second way is all about acquiring power and wealth. The rich gain the benefits of the new technologies and science and they do as they choose. The poor are shut out of the gains and live as best they can. The wealthy have choice; the poor suffer the consequences.

There are many bishops here from Sudan. In the 1890s, at the Battle of Omdurman just outside Khartoum, a small British force won, not because they were braver, although they were outnumbered six to one, but because they had machine guns and their enemies had spears and muskets. That difference will be as nothing to the clash of forces in which one army fights with automatic weapons controlled from their homeland by people sitting in offices, and the others with rifles and artillery face fearless and merciless machines. The militias that gain access to such weapons will sweep to power. Competing power groups will use the supply of weapons to wage proxy wars.

Medicine will be no better in this path. We know that rich countries, to our eternal shame, failed to share the advantages of the Covid vaccine. That will be repeated, along this bad path, with so many diseases, leaving the poor to live short lives serving the powerful. Empires of territory will not re-emerge, I hope, but empires of finance and economy, with scientific and technological power, will. The gifts of God that are offered to the world in these areas will, along this path, be seized for personal and powerful advantage.

That is why we are having a Call to support the creation of a fully funded Anglican Communion Commission on Science and Technology, so that our schools and universities – one of the greatest things we as Anglicans do is education – will become centres for the new knowledge and we will be those in society who are scientifically thoughtful, deeply Christian and contributing well to ethical debate. Above all, that we will be those who see the wonders of the world of technology and science as the gift of God and will use them for God's glory and for the good of all the earth.

A church that refuses to – or is unable to – engage in these areas, my dear sisters and brothers, will have nothing to say to a world whose future is being decided by changes in science and technology.

This lion can be transformed. He can be domesticated and made to serve. But there's another even bigger roar.

## Climate change

In 1945, at the end of one of the most terrible world wars in human history, there were 25 million refugees. Today, there are around 90 million. The impact of climate change on migration will be much greater. According to the International Panel on Climate Change, whose president gave a speech to religious leaders gathered by the Pope with myself and the Patriarch in Constantinople (a gathering of religious leaders representing over 80 per cent of the world's population), by 2050, just 30 years away, there will not be 25 million, or 90 million, but somewhere between 800 million and 1.2 billion people displaced, refugees of climate change. Most of them will come from countries represented here.

Migration means people movements to other regions, and huge people movement causes huge conflict. Climate change is too often seen as a matter of future concern for people in this country, though the heatwave we've just had, of 40 degrees in London, is changing minds, but those in tropical areas and low-lying countries do not need telling that climate change is already a matter of life and death. It will become much more threatening. John Kerry, the US Secretary of State responsible for climate change negotiations, said on the BBC earlier this week that it is not only an existential question, but a question of life or death. He said on the basis of what is happening at the moment, we are not looking at 1.5 degrees, but a 2.5 to 3.2 degree rise in average global temperatures, which takes us well past the worst assumptions. That kind of climate change is not peripheral, it is not on the edges – it is fuel and food for the four Horses of the Apocalypse.

But it is also resolvable by scientific research and campaigning. For example, on New Year's Day every year I burden the people of this country with a five-minute speech on the BBC on some subject or other. You can tell when it's happening because viewers turn the telly off and put the kettle on to avoid listening to me. We film them somewhere interesting every year – it's great fun to do, less fun to listen to. This year I went to Kew Gardens, where they have found a coffee plant that can flourish at higher temperatures than any other coffee plant currently being grown. That will enable farmers to produce climate-resilient crops, protecting their livelihoods and the global supply chain and the economies of their countries.

As the Anglican Communion are we capable of campaigning in this area? Are we able to lead and influence? We did last year at Cop26, but are we going to keep going? Our flocks depend on it, otherwise they will not eat. As those who lead the flocks, will we ensure that the nations of the world face their responsibilities squarely and act decisively? I point you to the very good Call on the Environment and Sustainable Development to be discussed later.

This lion cannot be domesticated and tamed to serve. It can only be killed.

## Persecution

There are other roars at the moment, from religious extremism, war and conflict. Attacks on the church from religious extremists continue all over the world. Since we last met in 2008, thousands of Anglicans have lost their lives as martyrs. Religious extremism is a disease found in every world faith. It is not basically theological, it is sociopathic. It comes from people who are frightened by the changes of the world and who turn inwards. In every major global faith it has the same characteristics: a small group who are violent and who seek to find a place of false security inside the walls of their faith, hiding from the challenges of the modern world.

This is not biblical Christianity. In this we venture out, clad in the armour of God, to 'proclaim the wonderful works of him who brought us out of darkness into his marvellous light'. These roars might cause us to hide, fear-filled from the realities of the world, but the Anglican theological method, based above all in scripture, guided by tradition and reason, opens us to the Holy Spirit's promptings to be engaged, to go out.

We only have to look around this room – look at your neighbours and you will see those who live amid war and government oppression. One of the themes of this conference is reconciliation. Christians have received reconciliation lavishly, by the pouring out of the blood of God's only Son, and we are called to be reconciled reconcilers, and many here are.

## Inequality

And then there's economic injustice and poverty. It is not only greater than it has ever been but also more obvious. A person in a slum in Nairobi can go to an internet café and look at the shops of Shanghai or Mumbai or London, but they cannot go there. The apparent but deceitful temporal treasures of wealth are visible to all, but unreachable for most.

The world economies are joined up financially, so it has never been easier for the rich and the corrupt to hide their money in tax havens or to launder money in the great markets of the world. Wealth has come from the very methods that caused climate change, the despoliation of natural resources. The poorest countries are used for their resources and are then discarded. The only ones who prosper are the people in those countries who get a share from corruption.

There are many exceptions, of course: there are wealthy people who are incredibly generous, often moved by the Spirit of God in Christ. But they are exceptions. A world of privileged fortresses of comfort cannot exist in stability with a world of want and suffering. It is not the way of the Kingdom of God.

Inequalities lead people into sin. Banditry, theft, corruption, become normalised. I remember in Nigeria being held overnight by one of the militia leaders in the Delta. I had gone to see him as part of a reconciliation project and I had a 'safe conduct'; I was with a local leader. But when we got there we found the militia leader drunk and drugged, and we were several hours in a boat from anywhere safe. He said, 'Take these people out and kill them.' But my local colleague persuaded him this was a bad idea. So he said, 'Okay, take him to the hotel', where we were locked in and guarded. And then he said, 'I'll decide whether or not to kill you in the morning.'

By the morning he was sober. He was a polite and hospitable man with a gun, showing us around the town. And as we turned the corner, on one horizon I could see an oil company platform in the marshes pumping oil for a major company. I could see helicopters flying in and out, lights from the generators. I am sure they had excellent air conditioning, excellent medicine, and excellent food and water. Around me, as I stood next to this man, children played in the sewage-filled streets. The militia leader was a very bad man, a killer. But as I went home I wondered if *I* had grown up in his town, seeing that contrast, would I have been any different?

Inequalities lead us to terrible questions. As Christians we are those who have received grace from God and we are called to be those who overflow with grace in the world that God made. 1 Peter says 'be aware' of the lions. But we are not to fear, for all the lions are defeated by the crucified Christ.


## Godless culture

My last lion is a silent one. It comes stealthily. Its bite is so gentle that we are not even aware we are inside its jaws. But it is as much a killer of the sheep, a destroyer of the flock, as any other. It is the culture around us that seeks to construct itself without God.

Whether, in this country, it is the loss of even the memory of Christianity among so many of the youth of the West, or the acceptance of the violence of war and child soldiers, or violence against women in conflict, or the access to pornography around the world, the culture opposed to the Kingdom of God that spreads more and more in the world.

Culture consumes us so cleverly that we do wrong without even being aware of it. One of the most powerful experiences I've had in many years was this April when I was in Canada at the invitation of the Anglican Church of Canada, to visit residential school survivors and to bring an apology for the terrible deeds of the Church of England (before the Anglican Church of Canada existed). The residential schools were set up to take the children of First Nations, indigenous people, to take them, steal them, kidnap them from their homes and ensure that they lost the culture of their people. By eliminating their language, it was hoped that they would forget their culture. Terrible acts were done at the request of the Canadian government by the churches. The Pope has been there this week apologising for the work of the Roman Catholic churches. In those schools there was abuse, cruelty and loss. Children died and were buried in unmarked graves and their parents never told. Brothers and sisters were separated, from the age of three or five.

What is worse, and shakes me to this day, is that through that period no leading Christians, no archbishops, stood up and said, 'This is not

Christ.' They accepted the cultural presupposition that some human beings were more civilised, were better, and had a right to do these things. That has been the history of the church in many times and places as so many of us know. It is always a cause for shame and an urgent call on all Christians, and on our Communion, to repentance and to a fresh commitment to justice and reparation.

As pastors we are called, all of us, to be those who understand the lions. But we have different views of what a lion is. There is a story about a group of blind people who went out walking one day along paths they knew well. What they did not know was that a large lion had eaten, and had then fallen asleep in the middle of their path. As they got close they could hear breathing. 'What is it?' they asked. One found its coat and said, 'It is very warm and cuddly. It will keep me warm on cold nights.' Another found its tail: 'I can use this to keep the flies away.' A third found its mouth: 'I think it is very dangerous and is carrying sharp knives.' They were all right, and they were all wrong. None knew the whole story. But then the lion woke up and devoured them all.

We are shepherds and pastors, co-workers with Peter and the apostles. In our vastly different circumstances we all hear lions roaring. Some are common to us all. Some are prowling only in one province. Some are in parts of the world but not others. But they are all lions. We may not see them clearly, but we can, together, grow in our capacity to deal with them. We must, as God's shepherds, hear the lions, understand them, and be a Communion that will face and defeat them in the power of Christ – not by power, not by might, but by God's powerful Spirit. For every one of us here and everyone in the flock, and everyone in the world, Christ is the conqueror, redeemer and Saviour of all.

# 16

# God's Church

God has created a new nation – a holy nation – and we have been looking at it all week. The believers in Antioch, as I said a week ago, saw it for the first time. So here in this room we are not defined by colour or nationality or language or class or education or background or contacts. We are only defined by Christ. And therefore we are called 'Christian' because there is no other way in this world of defining us. We are not, as Christians around the world, defined by the conquering of territory, we are marked out differently.

Before they were called Christians, the followers of Christ had been a Jewish movement but they now included Gentiles – a new identification therefore emerged. They came from all over the known world and not a lot has changed. We are indigenous and immigrant. We are rich and poor. For some, to own the name of Christ is routine. For others, it is life and death. All of us, in our conversations, have found that growing in our recognition during this last week in our Bible study groups.

Those who are baptised change identity, nationality, their first nationality and their final loyalty. They dance, we dance, to a different tune from the society in which we live. We accept the promise of Christ that in the world there is persecution (John 16:33). So we must hate our lives for Christ's sake (John 12:25). Christians individually and collectively are therefore called to be different to the world around. Let us go back to 1 Peter 2:9:

> But you are a chosen race, a royal priesthood, a holy nation, God's own people, in order that you may proclaim the mighty acts of him who called you out of darkness into his wonderful light. Once you were not a people, you were stateless, you were real aliens and exiles. but now you are God's people; you have a state and a passport. Once you had not received mercy, but now you have received mercy.

Christians are the largest nation on earth. In the first 315 years, Peter's 'holy nation' conquered the world's greatest empire without the sword.

Today there are 2 billion of us. All over the world we run schools, clinics, hospitals. We serve refugees, we wash the feet of those on the street, we feed the hungry, we care for the orphan and the alien. We challenge governments over justice, we set up charities for those caught up in war. Who created the Red Cross? A Christian. Who created the great hospitals in London? The monasteries. We are harried and persecuted, we are hunted as Christians from one killing ground to the next, but we do not hate as our enemies want us to hate. And may I say that this week it is by God's grace, by God's grace, that we have disagreed without hatred. We worship in ancient cathedrals, in modern buildings, in huts, under trees, in the open, in secret when the danger is too great. Some of the greatest art and music in each style of culture springs from Christian scripture and theology. Worldwide notions of justice are taken from the mouth of Jesus, or from the biblical texts we share with Jewish people: the likes of Jeremiah, Ezekiel, Daniel, Isaiah, from the Torah and the minor prophets. The Psalms, after 2,500 to 3,000 years, still speak to us of every emotion, from ecstatic worship to anger and despair. They are still the living prayer book of the Bible, as Bonhoeffer described them. And when nations receive the Bible into their own language, they change for the good and they find fresh identity.

The church is the creation of God and the hope of humanity. The church proclaims that there is hope in death, hope in war, hope in mourning, hope in birth, even birth in a refugee camp. The church proclaims that even if the world hates us, God offers his love, unconditionally; that at this very moment Christ intercedes for us at the right hand of God. The list of things that we celebrate and proclaim could go on for ever, because in each story, as we heard from Archbishop Jackson this morning, there is the story of God's work of transformation. For these stories will go on for ever because they come from the Eternal God.

## The need for repentance

But there is a problem. It is a problem that is found in the Gospels and is plain in the epistles. It is the problem set out in the Old Testament and New. It is the problem of human beings being sinners. For Christ came to save a world that was at enmity with him, that did not recognise him.

He came to save his enemies – you and me. We are enemies, not because God started off hating us – far from it – but because we want to have our own way, to be independent of God, to be free of the constraints of perfect love and unlimited grace. What fools we are!

The reality is that God's Church is – by God's choice – full of human beings and human beings have a lot of sin, so God's Church is full of sinners. The history of the church reveals a body not only full of saints expressing the love of God but of sinners hungry for power. God's Church preached violent crusades, organised the Inquisition, burned people at the stake. God's Church covered up the sins of imperialism, took vast sums of money from slave traders, sought to eliminate the First Nations and indigenous peoples from colonised territories (those peoples whose cross I'm wearing today, as is Caroline). God's Church fanned the flames of antisemitism and provided a seedbed and a theology for the persecution of the Jews and ultimately for the Holocaust. God's Church protected earthly power while surrendering heavenly hope. God's Church split and divided and treated those with whom there was disagreement as enemies, to be tortured, killed, or today to be vilified on social media and insulted in many ways. In May we found in the Lambeth Palace Library, where it ought not to have been, a letter from about 1723 from a slave in Virginia, to the 'Archbishop of London', pleading for teachers of the gospel to be sent to teach the children of slaves. As far as we know, it was never answered.

But all this is not just about the past, however recent, It is also about the present. During my nine and a half years as Archbishop of Canterbury, and before this time, I have heard many stories of abuse that was covered up. I have heard stories of the literal torture of children, young people and vulnerable adults. No part of our church has been exempt – such abuse has taken place in evangelical, in high church and in liberal churches. Abusers have been single or married – of every sort of churchmanship, old and young, ordained or lay, and abuse has been about power.

Worse than that, as you know, until the recent past abuse very often was covered up by the authorities in the church (and there may be some churches where that is still a temptation). And I say these words about abuse knowing there will be some of you here who have been victims of many kinds of abuse: in the church, in your own homes, or elsewhere.

Wherever abuse takes place it is the gravest misuse of power. It is the darkest of dark sins. It is an affront to the gospel of Jesus Christ. And in the church in this country I want to pay tribute to the bravery and resilience of survivors who told us their stories year after year, again and again, until someone listened to them – sometimes for 30 years. And I will continue to apologise with tears in my eyes for the church that let them down so terribly.

Our repentance, here in England and in each church where these sins are found, must involve doing everything we can to make the church a safe place for all people, where everyone can flourish – for power is at the heart of so much that goes wrong. When the shepherds beat the sheep they disobey what 1 Peter says: 'Tend the flock of God that is in your charge, exercising the oversight, not under compulsion but willingly, not for sordid gain but eagerly. Do not lord it over those in your charge, but be examples to the flock.'

The temptations of power are as old as Adam and Eve, Cain and Abel. Power lies behind the greatest paradox, the greatest puzzle of the church: how can it be that institutions based on the gospel, bound up inextricably in the life and death of Jesus, reading the Gospels, can themselves do or tolerate or cover up such evil things as the church has so often done? How can this happen?

The book of Leviticus deals with these issues (they are not new). As Ellen Davis has written, 'Specifically, it focuses on how ordinary Israel (or humanity), being prone to inadvertent error and deliberate sin, might nonetheless host the radical holiness of God' (*Opening Israel's Scriptures*, 2019, p. 63). Another example comes from Isabelle Hamley, who led one of the reflections in the bishops' retreat, in her commentary on Judges, looking at the point where people had gone most terribly wrong.

When as bishops we do not recognise our power we too easily misuse it: 'Instead, as he who called you is holy, be holy yourselves in all your conduct; for it is written, "You shall be holy, for I am holy"' (1 Peter, quoting Leviticus). And as 1 Peter goes on: 'If you invoke as Father the one who judges all people impartially according to their deeds, live in reverent fear during the time of our exile' (1 Peter 1:15–17).

So what must the Anglican Communion do as it faces this paradox, this puzzle of the love of God alongside the sin that we so often commit. How can it change? How do we move forward while recognising we will always be full of sinners?

We must, above all, be a body of those who are reconciled to God and who become reconcilers of others: 'Just as I have loved you, so you must love one another' (John 13:34). How has he loved and how will he love? By washing the feet even of his betrayer, Judas, and of his denier, Peter. Reconciliation in human affairs, as I said earlier this week, is not agreement, it is disagreement in the context of overwhelming and self-giving love: it is disagreeing well. This is the standard for the shepherds, 'for love covers a multitude of sins' (1 Peter 4:8). If it was not in the Bible we would not like that sentence – we would say it is woolly and fishy ... but it is in the Bible!

Look at Mozambique again – I keep talking about Mozambique – one of the two countries in one of our youngest provinces, working effectively across provincial boundaries with Tanzania, with the help of a United Nations group who are constantly surprised by the skill and knowledge in reconciliation that the church has. I am not surprised but the UN group is, because they think we can only do religion. We don't only do religion – we do Christ!

## The need for prayer and witnessing

'Blessed are the peacemakers, for they will be called children of God' (Matthew 5:9). The Communion must become a body of disciples who are serious and purposeful about following Christ. That means prayer, alone and together, aloud and silently, in dialogue with scripture. It means communities of prayer like the Benedictines, the Franciscans, the Melanesian Brothers or the more recent Community of St Anselm, or the about-to-be launched community at the cathedral of St John the Divine in New York, and many others where the heart of life is to desire for God, a hunger to be close to God. We transform our churches when at their heart they have deliberate communities of prayer.

The Communion also must be a body of witnesses, which knows and can – in simple terms – testify to the Good News of Jesus. Very often in the Diocese of Canterbury, in a small rural church, or an urban one, but we're mostly rural, with 20 or 25 people there – at the end of a sermon I challenge people to explain in one minute to the person sitting next to them their answer to a question they might be asked on Monday, when someone says, 'Did you have a good weekend ... what did you do?' And they say, 'Well, I did this on Saturday and on Sunday morning we went to church.' And the person says, 'You went to church, why on earth would you do that?' And the challenge, I say to them, in one minute, with no religious jargon, is to answer that question clearly and simply. As 1 Peter says, 'Always be ready to give an explanation for the hope that is within you, yet with gentleness and grace' (1 Peter 3:15). I can tell you that when I say this in a rural church, and say 'right, one minute, to the person nearest to you, start now', you can see that for a brief moment, quite often for a much longer moment, they hate me. And a minute later I say 'right, turn around, do it the other way round', and the other half hate me. But when I go back they often say, 'You made us think – I don't know why I go to church', and I say, 'Well, do an Alpha Course, a Discoverer's Course, a Pilgrim course, whichever course you like, find out why you go to church and that you are a beloved child of God.'

The Communion therefore must pray, must witness, it must have those who are wise in the world. We will have the Call on Science and Faith tomorrow: How can science serve the Kingdom, rather than the kingdoms of this world, unless we have those who can argue the claims of

God based on the gifts God has given us in science and technology? How can we challenge the selfishness of the richest countries and richest people if we are unable to argue about economics in the power of the Spirit, or against corruption, or decisions on war and peace with an understanding of ethics involved of what it is really like? Look at the failure to share the Covid-19 vaccine. Now multiply this several thousand times into the future, when climate change wreaks havoc around the world, when sea levels rise and the rich are behind their armour-protected walls. Or will we seek together to do what is right? It is the churches, acting together, ecumenically, united, that have the global networks to do right. It is the faiths that can lead changes of attitudes, inspired perhaps by the light of Christ – even unknowingly sometimes.

## The need for unity

The Communion must be united in a way that reveals Jesus Christ. The miracle that God has brought about in the church is not that like-minded people like each other, but people who would cross the street, cross the city, cross the ocean to get away from each other, learn to love one another. We are seeing that this week. But to keep it going is difficult. People will say that by being friends with those with whom we disagree we are changing sides – we are betraying the cause. They said the same to Jesus.

John 17:21 says that when we are one the world will know that Jesus came from the Father. David Ford (former Professor of Divinity at Cambridge University) in his 2021 commentary on John describes that verse as 'the climax of the climax' of the gospel. Dare we contribute to the obstruction of Jesus' prayer? Dare we contribute to the obstruction of God's purpose? We are called by God's grace, not by our choices. 'You have not chosen me, I have chosen you', says Jesus in John 15:16. Each one of us is chosen not by our will but by God's will. That is extraordinary. God knew us, whether we were people of colour, or white, or whether we were gay or straight, whether we were tall or short, or whether we were gifted or suffering from some kind of disability. God knew all of that. And he chose to call us.

We are not at liberty to choose our brothers and sisters, our siblings. Of course, we have groups with different views. Of course, they are God's gift to us because the different view will often challenge us and change our minds. We should seek with passion the visible unity of the church. But that is very difficult, as we heard yesterday when we did the Call on Christian unity. We are not even quite sure what that means (thank you very much to Anne for her extraordinarily powerful presentation on this).

Anglicanism has always seen itself as contingent, temporary, until the visible unity of God's Church is re-established. Anglicanism itself is not sacred, for all church institutions are provisional. Only the purpose of God is sacred, eternal and unfailing. As Christians, our deepest desire (as Archbishop Stephen Cottrell of York said earlier) needs to be to worship, and out of that we witness, and see a world converted. In those intentions we find our call and our eternal future. As 1 Peter says: 'after you have suffered for a little while, the God of all grace, who has called you to his eternal glory in Christ, will himself restore, support, strengthen, and establish you. To him be power for ever and ever. Amen' (5:10–11).

## The need for conversion and revolution

Which brings me to the main point of this address. The greatest challenge for me or for you as a Christian is to be converted every day, 'Conversion of life', as Benedict calls it in his Rule. And that takes us to Intentional Discipleship. It means we must become churches that live by what they say and are constantly revolutionary. That is what Bishop Eleanor Sanderson put before us in her magnificent address this morning. She was challenging us when she spoke of the danger of nominalism (of being just nominal Christians) and asked, 'Are we living among some impressive structures but seriously lacking in life?' That sums up many churches, and explains institutional sin and failure. Revolution means first that our church institutions do justice and love mercy and walk humbly with our God (Micah 6:8), and that we do not tolerate what is wrong because it fits the culture or we have always done it that way, or because our lawyers say so. We are to remain revolutionaries internally in the church, radical in our living, faithful in our theology.

Our institutions must conform to the justice and righteousness of God in how we work as organisations. The church visible is, I am afraid to say, the church institutional, but there is a profound gap between what it does in theory and what the institution does in day-to-day life.

For example, in England it means we needed to reorganise safeguarding. It also meant we needed to look at how our historical resources were invested, not least examining and publishing the gains from money given in 1704 which had been acquired through slavery. Other provinces will find internal injustice, lack of mercy, absence of righteousness, tribalism, racism and nominalism that all corrode our passion and desire for Christ.

We are disciples, followers and learners. The song we sing is the Magnificat in which Mary, inspired by the Holy Spirit, prophesies how

God has shown strength with his arm;
he has scattered the proud in the imagination of their hearts.
He has brought down the powerful from their thrones,
and lifted up the lowly;
he has filled the hungry with good things,
and sent the rich away empty.

That, my dear sisters and brothers, is a statement of revolution not of comfort. The East India Company, which ruled most of India until 1856 and controlled the regions it didn't directly rule, banned the singing of the Magnificat at Evensong, for fear that the indigenous people of India might come to know that God might be on their side, against tyranny. It is a dangerous text.

Let us be clear about revolution. The church is a place of evolution and of revolution without violence. It has too often mixed up change with violence. But we are called to set the world the right way up, for the song to which we dance is to become the song to which all the world dances. We are those who both call out and demonstrate in our actions the fulfilment of Amos' prayer in Amos 5:24: 'Let justice roll down like waters and righteousness like an ever-flowing stream.'

Revolution flows from the Five Marks of Mission. The church is not silenced because we *tell* of Jesus Christ. We are not diverted because we *teach* discipleship. We are not hidden because we *tend* the poor and neediest. We cannot be ignored because we *transform* unjust structures. We cannot be comfortable for our societies because we *treasure* all of creation. We are revolutionaries.

Communism began with a revolution, but as an atheist creed it ignored the sinfulness of people and was consumed by the abuse of power without repentance. The Christian revolution must be one of mercy and forgiveness, generosity and engagement. Revolution should be part of the institutional life of those who proclaim Christ. A church that leaves the world unchanged around it has been changed by the world. A church that leaves people unconverted has been converted to the world. A church that neglects its internal justice, righteousness and mercy will live unjustly, ruthlessly and sinfully. A church that is not a place of peaceful revolution will be a church only of history. But a church that acts righteously, loves mercy, seeks justice, will find the peace of God, the presence of the Spirit and the call of Christ. A church that gives light to the lost will find light in all its relationships and will live in love. A church of God's revolution will be a church that from generation to generation will see a world transformed. It has happened before and it is God's grace that will make it happen again. Come, Holy Spirit! Amen.

# 17

# How to be God's Church
# for God's World?

*Archbishop Justin's Third Keynote Address*

Being sent by God is at the heart of being a Christian.

A key indicator of declining institutions or companies or countries – and churches – is that they may have a vision of what they should do, they may even have a clear strategy, but they cannot turn their strategy into action. There is no implementing of the strategy. So the question is not always 'what should we do?' We do need to ask that question and Archbishop Stephen answered it on Friday morning: we worship and we make disciples. The key question now is 'how?'

As the church we are always travelling on the way, and therefore we have to renew the life of the church on the march, as we go. We cannot stop, take time out, and get everything right before moving on. We have to renew it on the go. And the very obedience of keeping going is one of the main ways in which the church finds renewal and revival. Because when we travel, we travel with God. Look at the Israelites in the wilderness in the Exodus. Travelling is how we build relationship and the heart of the church is deeply relational (see 1 Corinthians 13). It does not matter what we do, what gifts we have, what wonders we carry out, if we do not have love for one another; we are, as Paul writes, a sounding gong or a clanging cymbal. Therefore whatever else comes out of this Lambeth Conference and as we go forward in this next period, at the heart of it must be the deepening and the building of relationship as our first objective – that we grow in love for God and for one another.

When I am asked what kind of bishops we need, my answer is bishops who love God and love people. If you can tick those two boxes none of the other boxes matter nearly so much. But if you cannot tick those, then it does not matter what other boxes you can tick and what you are good at: it is not enough. That is why I so miss the Nigerians, and the Ugandans and the Rwandans. Discussion might have been more complicated. But if we love one another, we will all find renewal. And that really matters. I was asked at the press conference yesterday evening what I felt was my greatest failure in this Lambeth Conference, and I said not to have been able to encourage them enough to be here.

We have agreed the Calls – subject to amendment and your comments. They are not an end in themselves. They are an appeal to each church, province, bishop and diocese, to every Anglican, to be more visibly the people of God.

From St Thomas in South India in the 1st century, to the Jesuits and other missionaries across the world, to the great pioneers of the 19th century and Hudson Taylor and heroes like Ajayi Crowther, the Holy Spirit sends out those whom God is calling.

As geographical knowledge of the Earth opened up through history, so the church responded in fresh ways – the vision came for going into all the earth as Christians learned what all the earth was. As they learned about different societies they responded in sociologically fresh ways, and as we continue to learn about human beings we respond in fresh physiological and psychological ways. As we understand more about DNA and about the chemistry of the brain, we find fresh ways to communicate the gospel better.

Some of you will have heard that the Church of England has spent the last four years on a project called 'Living in Love and Faith'. It has produced a big book of about 400 pages – I had nothing to do with it, by the way, I did not write anything except the Foreword, so I can say that it is an extraordinary work of scholarship based on, and drawing on, a bank of articles by scholars of all opinions around the nature of human identity within the Christian tradition. There are 500,000 words within these articles from scholars in biblical studies, church history, human and biological sciences, ethics, philosophy and systematic theology. The aim in all this was not to give the decisive answer to a particular question but to enable the Church of England to think through the issues of identity and being human, in all their aspects, including human sexuality. The project hid from nothing, and included people of very different views, trusting in the Holy Spirit who leads us into all truth, as John's Gospel promises.

This is just one example of a church in the Anglican Communion journeying together as a body of disciples, engaging, learning, praying, walking, speaking, acting, being visible. And when we look back over the history of the church the moments of greatest growth have been when the global church has seen, recognised and confronted the darkness of the world. There is St Benedict who, as the Roman Empire collapsed, set up schools for disciples, as he called them in his Rule. And he more or less accidentally saved Christian civilisation, which had not been his intention. There is St Francis of Assisi, half a millennium later, who came at a time when the leadership of the church was morally depraved. There are priests in 19th-century London who worked in the slums preaching the gospel and, working together with local doctors, invented epidemiology – the science of understanding how disease spreads. They discovered that cholera was not transmitted through the air but through water. There are more recent martyrs and heroes of the church, such as Archbishop Janani Luwum, the Melanesian martyrs, and so many known only to God. The church in mission is not merely a help to the world: it is the sign of salvation for the transformation of the world. The church humble and hospitable, generous and full of love, is not just a comforting thing to have in society but points to the Kingdom of Heaven. The church, salt and light, courageous in prophetic utterance, gracious yet clear, is not another NGO: it is God's chosen means of shining light in the darkness.

That is why we began these three addresses by looking at God's world. It is the world that was made through Jesus Christ, spoiled by human sin. The second address looked at the church and described how even in its human weakness it is still the bride of Christ – every day, every moment, everywhere. And we are those reconciled in order to be reconcilers, that all things may come together in Christ – all nationalities, all men and women, rich and poor, strong and weak, and with all humanity, all of creation (Colossians 1).

The darkness of the world around us too often swirls with the smoke of hell. The church staggers and coughs in fear of the future. We argue and divide. But we should act, above all in loving relationship with God and one another. That is the first and greatest Call – the one we haven't listed, but it is the greatest Call because it is the gospel Call.

And through the conversations around the Calls, this week has become a time of intense ecclesiological thinking and reflection for the Anglican Communion. We have rediscovered that we are a communion of churches catholic and reformed, autonomous and interdependent. The scriptures are at the core of our reformed tradition. Our Catholic tradition is expressed not just by the historic episcopacy but also by the principles of Catholic Social Teaching. One of these is subsidiarity – that we should always work at the most local level possible. This resists centralisation which is the habit of control and the exercise of power. It is a very difficult habit to break. But we are a Communion of churches, not one church, and so we must. Another principle is that of solidarity, by which we express interdependence. And then there is the seeking of the common good, a third key principle of Catholic Social Teaching, in which we accept a level of mutual accountability without mutual control.

What, then, is our task? Many of the Calls have referred to the Five Marks of Mission, so let us go through each of them to see the actions to which we are called.

## Tell – to proclaim the Good News of the Kingdom of God

The practical reality is that we can only tell what we know and explain what we understand. We cannot give what we haven't got or, for those of you who like Latin legal tags, 'nemo dat qui habet' (it is the only Latin legal tag I know so I use it on every possible occasion). So we need to know and understand the gospel if we are to tell it to others. The strength of many churches that grow deeper and grow in number is that everyone knows the gospel and can say something about their own love and meeting with Jesus Christ. They may not be eloquent, the theology may be slightly crude, but when they speak from the heart others listen. And their transformed lives illustrate their words.

It is essential, throughout the churches of the Communion, that everyone understands themselves to be witnesses because they are baptised and filled with the Holy Spirit. And in those provinces that for generations forgot much of this or where the importance of culturally appropriate evangelism has been forgotten, evangelists must be discerned, trained and sent out. In many of the churches represented here this is taken for granted, but in many others it has been forgotten. So let every Anglican know they are a witness, and let them be caught up in worship. For they are the foundations of the health of the church. Do we have simple and useful courses that teach people how to explain the gospel? They exist in profusion but not every church is using them. Are our services so boring that people feel they have done their duty to God for the week when the service ends? Or are they so full of the life of the Spirit that those who leave the church long for those they love most to discover God and his love?

## Teach – to teach, baptise and nurture new believers

Ellen Davis (from her book *Opening Israel's Scriptures*, 2019) writes that '[Teaching/Exegesis] is necessary for the ongoing life of church and synagogue – whose identities, and even existence as communities with a common story and language – depends on the recurrent experience of hearing these texts and of speaking of and to contemporary lives with these texts.' Furthermore, 'while that experience is not predictable, it is contingent on the regular practice of exegesis – of unpacking the scriptures – by members of the communities of faith, generation by generation'. In other words, have confidence in the Bible, and if we have confidence we will enable our hearers to have the tools to think, and pray, and to decide.

Teaching is not simply saying what the text says but a prophetic task of reflecting on the world around us in the light of the scriptures and the life of Christ. This is why bodies like the Anglican Communion Science Commission and the Anglican Communion Health Network are so important – because they are about engagement with the world through letting the scriptures help us understand what is happening in the world. It is not about retreating from the world.

I came across a network of schools in which the only thing being taught is their scriptures. They do not teach science or languages or literature, or politics or maths – they do not teach anything except their scriptures. But that is not a Christian view of scripture. Scripture, like the Christian church, goes out into the world. It goes out and transforms and changes those around. To teach is to enable the hearers to have the tools to think and pray and see and decide, to explain the scriptures, but in explaining to demonstrate exegesis, so that the community sees, in culturally appropriate ways, not just the 'what' of what the Bible says, but the 'how' of understanding it for themselves. This is our reformed tradition.

As is well known, Richard Hooker, possibly the greatest of all Anglican theologians, who lived in the 16th century, rested Anglican theological method on three foundations. The first was scripture, with a decisive primacy. The second was human reason and the third Christian tradition. All three matter, and must be taught. Why, in Deuteronomy, is the youngest child taught to ask questions? Why do we continue to do this? The answer is because the world around must be questioned by scripture. Traditions must be questioned by scripture and reason. Traditions that are healthy grow and develop. Traditions that do not change and become irrelevant will die, because they lose contact with their roots.

Remembering is deep in the very nature of God, and so it is essential for God's people to be those who remember. The Israelites remembered God's actions at the Passover in order to make sense of their Jewish identity, as we do in the Eucharist, the Lord's Supper, to make sense of our identity in Christ. We remember the Ugandan martyrs at the end of the 19th century, for example, in order to help us understand what it is to be Anglican. I once heard an Old Testament scholar remark in a lecture that 'What God forgets ceases to exist; what we forget opens the way to error.'

Teaching is equipping. The farmer needs to know what it is to be a Christian farmer – whether they are running 10,000 acres on the prairies of North America or 3 acres in a clearing in a forest in Congo. The banker needs to know right from wrong. The cabinet minister or the soldier needs to recognise that Christ is their first Lord.

Anglican universities that are growing up in many provinces are one of the most important developments we are seeing in the Communion.

Even in places of war like South Sudan they are growing. Schools for girls and boys are essential. Churches that invest in teaching children, as All Saints Cathedral in Nairobi is doing, enables them to grow into mature Christians, able to read the Bible and listen carefully to what it is saying, comforted to know that they follow the truth who is Christ.

Most of all, we the shepherds must teach and explain the scriptures and make sure that every seminary teaches and explains the scriptures and prepares students for the challenges that the next 40 years will bring.

## Tend – to respond to human need by loving service

At the very beginning of the Covid-19 epidemic, one night I woke with a very clear thought in my head (and that is unusual) that I ought to offer help to the huge London hospital that is next to Lambeth Palace where I live, because we were in lockdown and I could not go anywhere. I emailed the chaplain and found out that most of her volunteers had gone because they were over 70 years old and were compelled to shelter at home by law. And so for the next 18 months I went into the hospital one evening a week, often or usually to critical care units, to pray with people, many of whom were dying.

Often the patients were unconscious and all I could do was commit them to the Lord. They were of all faiths and none in all probability. I had to pass exams in how to put on and take off protective clothing – what is known as your donning and doffing test – and to be able to do it within a certain amount of time and in the right order so you did not spread infection. The chaplain and I prayed with nurses and doctors with no religious background who were overwhelmed by the level of tragedy. And we listened to people as they told us their stories. None of it was complicated. Most of it was kneeling by a bed, holding the hand of someone who knew little or nothing about what was going on. The chaplain accompanied me – she would not quite trust me wandering around the hospital on my own – and wherever she accompanied me she would introduce me by saying, 'This is the Archbishop of Canterbury, I am his line manager.' Which indeed she was! The evening would end at some point with my returning home, a very hot shower and all clothes in a hot wash, as we did not know then, at the beginning of the pandemic, how easily or not the virus could be transmitted on surfaces. None of this was any more than millions of others did or experienced during that time. Yet the fact that the church kept showing up in this way was noticed in the hospital.

We are to tend, not for gain, not for advantage in evangelism, but just because the people we tend are people for whom Christ died and they are infinitely valuable.

## Transform – to seek to transform unjust structures of society, to challenge violence of every kind, and to pursue peace and reconciliation

I once listened to a Primate at the beginning of his ministry as a Primate address the president and cabinet of his country, in the Cathedral, about corruption and failure to care for the people.

It was a risky thing to do. Unfortunately, the history of the churches is so often – and tragically – not one of challenging unjust structures.

The Church of England is embedded in establishment. I am not against establishment, but the church is sometimes tempted to be too close to it. Not so much nowadays, but in history, in Empire, in politics, all too often all churches, not only Anglicans, have become sucked into supporting governments, colluding with injustice, and upholding oppression at any and every level.

To stand up against oppression is frightening, because it is costly. And so many of you know that so well. We do not like it when governments speak forcefully against us, or do worse than that in some parts of the Anglican Communion, yet we must speak, and we must act. We cannot be silent on the climate emergency and its implications for the economy today. We cannot be silent on the unethical treatment of migrants or on war or oppression, or the abuse of human rights, or persecution, otherwise we become one of the oppressors. And we live in solidarity with the victims because the person who has a gun pointing at them – and I have been there – often cannot say anything. One of the expressions in the days when I was doing a lot of work in places like that, every month, was that the man with the gun – and it is always a man – is always right.

It was half joking. But those in solidarity with victims in other countries can speak with power, can gather support, can take risks.

## Treasure – to strive to safeguard the integrity of creation and sustain and renew the life of the earth

Climate change, better called the climate crisis, or better still the climate emergency, as we know, is the result of the wealthier countries of the world having declared war on God's creation, unknowingly, unthinkingly, starting in the 19th century. The symptoms of that war now are that the wealthy dump refuse in the oceans, tell the poor not to use carbon-generating fuels, and say to the world too often, not by their words but by their actions, 'we will keep our wealth, and you, the poor, must discover new paths'.

It is an undeclared war with huge consequences. I have already spoken of the number of refugees rising to between 800 million and 1.2 billion. We cannot foresee the impact they will have on the world but we do know the results will be tragic beyond anything in human history, overwhelming beyond anything we can imagine, and devastating for so many people.

Our campaigns for urgent action on climate change are having an impact. Archbishop Julio is clear about that, and they are having great impact through working with others. I have had the huge privilege of working with Pope Francis and Ecumenical Patriarch Bartholomew in this way, through an approach springing from scripture. This is not the church getting involved in politics – it is the church getting involved in God. As Colossians 1 says, Jesus

> is the image of the invisible God, the firstborn of all creation; for in him all things in heaven and on earth were created, things visible and invisible, whether thrones or dominions or rulers or powers – all things have been created through him and for him ... through him God was pleased to reconcile to himself all things, whether on earth or in heaven, by making peace through the blood of his cross. (Colossians 1:15–23)

Notice that it says 'all things', not just 'all people'. So where do we go? How do we turn vision, ideas, strategy, plans into actions? How do we get away from that devastating sense of the church being a failed institution? We know it is wrong but what must we do about it? Each church, each diocese, each province needs to address this.

Over the next three years, a group facilitated through the Anglican Communion Office, under Bishop Anthony Poggo's leadership, will follow up this conference with further shared learning, as we have done over the last 18 months. I hope as many of you will participate in that as possible. This will be all about deepening relationships through Bible studies and conversations, deepening our love for one another. So it is not to say, 'What are we going to do?' It is not an action list, but a relationship approach. But we will have the aim of seeing how we can put into practice contextually, in our local area and in the right way, those things we have agreed.

And I urge you to share in this three years of follow-up. It will continue to deepen mutual understanding, it will reveal issues and errors, and it will enable us supremely to pray for and love one another. Most of all it will keep us facing outwards, going outwards, to enable our relationships to draw us towards greater holiness and unity. This vision – our Christian vision – is different from any other vision in the world, because we trust the God who raised Jesus Christ from the dead. We trust the God who says to us: 'go'. In John 20, when Jesus breathes on his disciples, and says 'receive the Holy Spirit', another translation of the word 'receive' is 'welcome'. But it is an imperative in a continuous present – it means to welcome the Holy Spirit every day, every moment, in every church, at every level. It is also plural and therefore it applies to everyone together.

When we welcome the Spirit, furthermore, we welcome God, we welcome life, we welcome learning; the Holy Spirit will lead us into all wisdom, all knowledge. And we trust that as the Holy Spirit is being welcomed, the Holy Spirit is sending, and when we are obedient to being sent, we will see transformation as hearts are changed.

We have a vision that is a picture of the Kingdom, not one of greater darkness but of spreading light. This includes science and technology not captured by the powerful but shared and developed for the common good of all human beings; not masses of desperate people vainly seeking shelter from climate disaster, but of peoples working together with generosity, hospitality, effectively tackling the climate emergency led by those who see our world as God's gift and who take seriously the reconciliation of all things to their Creator.

This is a time of hope, because hope is of God (1 Peter 1). This is a time of revelation to a world where many forget the gift of God's love. Dear brothers and sisters in Christ, we have received that gift of God's love. And our hearts rejoice. So let us share it with one another.

For each of you, I give thanks to God. I pray for you. And we pray for one another – I know you pray for me. I love you – as neighbours, as a family, as those who have been brought together in Christ. God's love is seen in this world through a countless multitude of people of every race and nation, a great multitude that is 'a royal priesthood, a holy nation, God's own people, who declare the wonderful works of the God who has called us out of darkness into his marvellous light'. It is a multitude of those who have received mercy. The Anglican Communion is one part of that multitude. Is it argumentative? Oh yes. Is it diverse? Immensely. Is it God's holy people? Certainly.

Let us go out together in obedience – sent out, as God's Church for God's World.

# 18

# Mission and Evangelism

## Archbishop Stephen Cottrell

1 Peter 3:14: 'Do not fear what they fear and do not be intimidated. But in your hearts, sanctify Christ as Lord and always be ready to give a reason for the hope that is in you.' So, dear friends, I want to start with a few things that most of us will know. We know that McDonald's make hamburgers. Those golden arches appear all over the world. I rather wish they didn't because they're ruining the world as well. But McDonald's make hamburgers. Cadbury's make chocolate, Starbucks make extremely unexceptional coffee (frankly, I don't know how they get away with it). It is as if they have invented a new drink, a hot brown liquid that calls itself coffee. I have visited Kenya many times where you can get decent coffee, but it has not found its way to Starbucks. McDonald's make hamburgers, Cadbury's make chocolate, Starbucks make coffee, the Simon Bolivar Youth Orchestra of Venezuela make music, Heineken make beer, Toyota make cars, Rolex make watches, Safaricom (across most of Africa) make connections and, sisters and brothers, the church of Jesus Christ makes disciples. That is our core business. That is what we are about. Not just converts: Jesus does not say go into all the world and make converts. He does not say go into all the world and make churchgoers. He says, 'make disciples', followers of Jesus. And what do disciples make? Well, disciples make peace; disciples make justice; disciples, quoting from the book of Revelation, make the 'kingdoms of this world, the kingdom of our God, and of his Christ'. You see, sisters and brothers, we are not trying to build the earthly empire of an institution called the church. What we are about is this, 'Thy Kingdom come, thy will be done'. That is our prayer. And that is our motivation. Disciples make disciples, which is the intentional, joyful, heart-changing, world-changing ministry of sharing with others the Good News that we have received.

We call this evangelism, and evangelism can be a bit of a scary word. But inside the scary word 'evangelism' you will find the lovely, beautiful word 'angel'. And this tells you what the word means. My grandma came from the northeast of England, and she would always call me an angel. She would say, 'Stephen, be an angel, put the kettle on', 'Stephen, be an angel, would you run up the shops for me?' And I want to say to the bishops of the Anglican Communion: 'Be angels, be messengers of the good news that God has lavished upon us in Jesus Christ. Share with others what you have received.' Bishops, evangelism is our core business. We are called to lead evangelising churches, in a world where there is so much need and so much confusion. What the world needs is what God has lavished upon us in Christ. The world needs humility, for we are destroying the earth itself. The world needs reconciliation, because of the misuse of power and the vainglory of too many tinpot tyrants causing too much pain. And the world needs hope. As Archbishop Justin has already spoken to us so movingly, what the world needs is the knowledge that peace can be found even with disagreement. And, dear sisters and brothers, is not this a particular opportunity before us this week? We could show the world that, despite profound disagreement, what we have in Christ is larger and deeper. And I want to say this: water is thicker than blood. It is our baptism that binds us together across the nations and tribes of our world. And that through our baptism we have an unbreakable belonging, because it is made for us in Christ through his dying, and his rising, a treasure stored up in heaven itself. We must therefore do the work of evangelists. We bishops must be people who always have the name of Jesus on our lips, able to give a reason for the hope that is in us.

A few years ago, I was at Paddington Station in West London, and I was buying a coffee (not Starbucks) from the kiosk on the platform. As I was waiting for my coffee to be given to me, there was a young woman standing next to me and she looks me up and down. I would love to tell you at this point that I was not in uniform and it was my natural aura of holiness that made her realise that I was a priest and a bishop in God's Church. Sadly, no, I was in uniform. She looked me up and down and said, 'Why did you become a priest?' I did not bother to tell her I was a bishop. So I said, 'I've got two answers for you. One short answer, one slightly longer answer.' The short answer is God. I thought I would not mess about with a long story but go straight to the chase. I said, 'The short answer is God.' I said to her that I believed in God and that I believed that God believed in me, that even though I was not brought up going to church, somewhere on the pathway of my life I had come to encounter God. And it was not for me a thunderbolt conversion. And it did not mean that I did not also have, many times, doubt and darkness. It is just that I had arrived at a point where the world made no sense, except it made sense with God. Moreover, I told her that as a Christian when I said the word 'God' I saw in my heart and in my imagination the person of Jesus, because for Christians we know God because we know

Jesus. Jesus is the human face of God and that Jesus *is God* speaking to us, in the only language that we really understand, which is the language of another human life and speaking to us in our human flesh and blood.

I have to tell you, sisters and brothers, that if I had been in charge on the Day of Pentecost I would have done it differently. I would have got everybody in the world to speak the same language, so there would be no need for translators. We would all speak a kind of holy Esperanto. But, thank the Lord, I was not in charge at Pentecost. And you see, it is not our speaking one language, it is the church of Jesus Christ speaking every language and God loves our diversity. That was the short answer: God, God as revealed in Jesus Christ. I said that the slightly longer answer is that I want to change the world. And I said to her, 'I don't know what you think when you look at the world – I look at the world, I see confusion, I see pain. I want to change it. I've got a diagnosis. I think what is wrong with the world lies in the human heart. My diagnosis is this: the world needs a heart transplant, the world has got a seriously bad heart condition. 'Also,' I said to her, 'I need a heart transplant. I believe that I would be a better person, and the world would be a better place, if I received the heart of Jesus. So that is why I am a Christian. I believe in God, as God is seen in Jesus, and I believe that God and only God can change our hearts.' I also shared with her that when I say I believe in God, I do not mean I believe in God like I believe the sky is blue. I believe the sun rises in the east. I said I believe in God in the way that I believe that love is real, and in the way that a piece of music like Chopin's Nocturnes makes me cry. It is a different kind of reality. In fact, it is more real. It is the heart of the matter. And this is evangelism.

She then said something to me, for often in evangelism when you are talking with somebody you are having a dialogue, not a monologue. She said, 'When I meet people of faith, they seem to fall into two categories. It seems that either their faith is like their hobby and they go to church on Sunday, but it does not seem to make much of a difference to the life they live on Monday. Or,' she continued, 'they embrace their faith so tightly that it frightens everybody else away.' She then asked me, 'Is there another way?' And I said to her, 'Yes, there is. It is the way of Jesus Christ. It is the way of true humanity.' I said to her that God does want to change her but not into somebody else. God wants to change her into the person that she is meant to be. And when I look in scripture I see how what Paul said in Athens is different to what he said in Corinth, and I notice that what Jesus says to one person is different to what he says to another person. I notice that what I must do is not have a formula in my back pocket to share the Christian faith but I must engage with people. At this point in the conversation I had to catch my train and she had to catch her train and we went our different ways, but I still remember her in my prayers.

With my whole heart, my hope for the Anglican Communion and the call that I hope we make today, is that the local church – and every Christian believer in every local church gathered and sent out a community of women and men who follow Jesus – will be a place where the thousands and thousands and thousands of people growing up in our world today who do not yet know Christ can learn and receive from him and follow in his way. But as with that conversation in Paddington Station, and with all evangelism, in the end people have to make their own decisions about whether to follow Christ or not. But evangelism itself, the actual business of bringing people to faith, is the work of the Holy Spirit. Maybe I should have said this right at the beginning, because I find this enormously reassuring: God is the evangelist. God is the one who brings people to faith in Christ. It is our responsibility, as the evangelising church, to participate with God in God's work of bringing people to faith, and helping all the people we serve understand that they have a part to play and that they are called to be witnesses to Christ. So this is the heart of our call today, to be intentional in the work of evangelism, that evangelism is the core business of the church, that we understand evangelism as disciple-making, and therefore part of the whole mission of God to bring the whole creation to fulfilment in Christ, to change the heart of the world. So although I cannot make someone follow Christ, I can tell them, as I told that young woman, why following Jesus has made a difference in my life and how I believe it can and will make a difference in our world.

As bishops, we need to lead on this and help people to do it themselves. We need to remember that probably the best definition of evangelism is simply this: one beggar telling another beggar where to get bread. So, I can be a living signpost pointing people to Jesus, I can be a good companion as Jesus was on the Emmaus Road, listening to people's questions, explaining to them the true meaning of scripture, and its relevance for their lives. I can be the compelling storyteller, telling the story of Christ, but also, as we have just done in pairs, the story of how God has been at work in our lives. I can be like a midwife, ensuring that all the right conditions are in place for someone to come to faith in Christ, so that the church itself is a safe place and so we understand the different ways in which different people, in different contexts, come to faith. The evangelising church will know and understand this, working with the Spirit in the different ways the Spirit is at work. And we have so much to learn from one another across our Communion. But, and there is a 'but', the most important thing for us to learn is this, something we need to learn afresh every single day, that in order to share the gospel of Christ, in order to be an instrument of Christ's peace in the world today, each one of us, myself included, has to receive the gospel afresh.

Being a bishop is a spiritually dangerous business. We say a lot of prayers, we preach a lot of sermons, we lead a lot of services, and people treat us as if we are very important. People carry our bags, drive our cars, defer to us endlessly, usher us to the top seats at the top tables. And, if we allow ourselves, we can be taken in by this. Then, after a while, we will stop looking like the beggars that need the bread ourselves, just as much as anyone else, and we will start imagining that we are the bakers who make the bread. We are not! We can only share what we have received. So I am not standing here telling you how to do evangelism in your context, or telling you the latest techniques to adopt. Nor am I going to try and impress you with stories of growth or scare you with stories of decline. But I do and must speak about the heart and spirit of evangelism, which is this: *Am I receiving the gospel of Jesus Christ as Good News for my life?* Is it the desire of my heart to share it with others? And am I in a place where all my titles and entitlements, and the baggage that goes with being a bishop, can be swept away and I am just Stephen, before God. Sisters and brothers, if I am not in that place where I know my need of God, and that God's Spirit evangelises me afresh, then I am in trouble.

The renewal of the church always flows from the spiritual renewal of our life in Christ. We must therefore pay attention to the spiritual disciplines that shape and sustain the Christian life: the life of prayer, the reading of scripture, the sacramental life, and begin from the overflow of what we have received. Therefore, if as bishops we want to lead our church in evangelism, we must also lead its people in prayer and lead them to a deeper encounter with God. But I do not mean we have to do one before the other. The best way to grow in your faith is to share it with someone else. But I do mean that we must understand the intimate relationship between spirituality, evangelism and discipleship. They belong together, and if they get separated our evangelism simply evaporates away. So, I invite you in your diocese to lead your people to a deeper encounter with God so that they will have something to share and that it will overflow into witnessing in their daily lives. It will overflow into building places in our churches where people can learn and understand the faith and it will always lead to word and sacraments.

We also need to understand the different ways in which different people come to faith. Some people have Damascus Road experiences where they come to faith suddenly and dramatically, but other people have Emmaus Road experiences where they come to faith gradually. The evangelising church will accompany people on these different ways. And leading by example, as bishops we must know ourselves to be the beloved of Christ, his disciples, before we are his bishops. We must teach and preach and give time for evangelistic mission across our diocese, but also lead its spiritual renewal.

Let me finish with my advice to myself about evangelism: Stephen, receive the gospel each day. Let it transform your life. Remember that you are a sinner in need of God's grace, today and every day. Then share that with others. Point the way to Christ, and be humble before him. Build a church where those who are formed in Christ are also sent out to live and proclaim the gospel, a truly apostolic church. And finally, remember that the gospel needs to be shared with cultures and tribes and nations as well as with individuals, because our core business is making disciples, people whose lives are conformed to Christ, and are participating in God's mission of love to the world. Then, the other things that concern us at this Lambeth Conference, like living with disagreement, like seeking carbon net zero, these may turn out to be the very best things that we do for evangelism. Because if we can do these things, the world will look at us and say 'these followers of Jesus, they live differently and the lives they lead align with the words they say. They love one another. They care for the earth. They seek peace. Please, please, show us this Jesus you follow.' Inside the slightly scary word 'evangelism' hides the beautiful word 'angel'. Let us release that word and be messengers of the gospel of Jesus Christ, in our diocese, and across our world. Tyrants make trouble. Vagabonds make mischief. The devil likes nothing better than making mayhem and chaos, but the church of Jesus Christ declares the praises of him who brought us out of darkness into his marvellous light. We make disciples and disciples make peace, amen.

I have one little story to end with and then an invitation. When our youngest son Sam was three or four years old he got locked in his bedroom. I do not know how he managed to lock the door, but it was certainly locked. He was panicking inside the bedroom. My wife and I were outside the bedroom wondering what to do. Let me tell you what I did. I did not say to him, 'Sam, you should not have got yourself locked in the bedroom. Let this be a punishment to you.' I did not say that. I did not say to him, 'Sam, you have been very foolish, locking yourself inside the bedroom, you are just going to have to work out how to get out. That might take a bit of time, but you got yourself into this mess and you can get yourself out of it.' I did not say to him, 'Sam, unless you say sorry and that you are really sorry that you have locked yourself inside the bedroom, I am afraid there is nothing I can do.' I did not do any of that. What I did was that I kicked the door down. I said to him, 'Sam, stand back from the door.' It is a great feeling actually kicking a door down. I kicked the door down. And, sisters and brothers, that is what Jesus has done for us. While we were still sinners, Christ died for us. While we were still locked away in our sinfulness and misery when everything was going wrong, he did not say, 'Work it out for yourselves.' He did not say, 'When you are truly, truly penitent, I will die on the cross for you.' He came and rescued us. This is such good news. Sometimes, particularly in the North and the West, we have been too good in keeping it to ourselves. Let us resolve today to change that. We are here because we have received God's grace. Let us keep on receiving it. And now let us share it with others.

## Archbishop Tito Zavala, Archbishop of Chile

My passion is church planting. I am going to talk to you about that because our Lord God, Father, Son and Holy Spirit, is a God of mission. And I have a question for all of you and for all of us. Do you know what is the only thing we are not going to do in heaven? Evangelism and church planting! No, it is not needed in heaven but it is our goal to do that now while we are here on earth.

In my diocese, about 25 or 30 years ago, we began to talk about maintenance and mission. And then when we were talking in our pastoral meetings, or even when I visited some churches, normally the question was: 'Are you a mission-minded person or a maintenance-minded person?' I want to raise the same question for all of us today. Are you a mission-minded bishop, or a maintenance-minded bishop?

I did some research about ten years ago on church planting and I interviewed Primates, archbishops, bishops and church planters. In response to the question about maintenance, all of them – 100 per cent of them – said, 'The Anglican Communion is in maintenance-minded mode, the Anglican Communion is in maintenance.' I was so sad to hear that. By maintenance I mean having the same church, same people, same activities, same preaching, nothing new, everything being predictable. But we have been called by God to change our manner of thinking from maintenance into mission.

I want to share with you my journey as the diocesan bishop, how I lead the church in Chile from maintenance into mission, because we want to be a mission-minded people in every place where we are. First, we need to change our way of thinking. This is very, very important. Second, to change our vision for mission, but also leadership. We have to work on leadership. We began to develop seminars, talking with pastors, with leaders in the church about church planting. We taught them how to do it and even developed a manual or guide on how to plant a church in different areas. We have been working with pastors and deacons, but the most important thing is that we have been talking to and teaching lay people. We have discovered that, in the end, the work is done by laity. They are the real church planters in our church. We as ordained people, priests, deacons, bishops, we are leaders who are behind them, mobilising them in order to do the work. We have learned how to mobilise laity for church planting.

I see my role as diocesan bishop, then, as one of mobilising my pastors and people for church planting. When I visit a church, even when I go for a confirmation service, normally in my preaching I will say, 'Brothers and sisters, what will be your next church planting project?' And some of the churches said, 'But we are a new church.' 'Yes,' I replied, 'I know you are a new church. But you have to start from now, from the beginning thinking about another new church, where you are going to grow in the next stage of the life of your church.' I said to my pastors, 'Think about what you received from the Lord, and then think what you are going to pass on to the next pastor. What kind of church are you going to pass him?' That is a very important question. 'If you receive the church, for example, with 30 people, good. Now, you have to work in order to grow to 40, 50 or 100.'

One of the churches in Santiago, the capital city, was facing a very depressed time and previously had been told to take the decision to close the church. This was before I was a bishop. And then when I heard about it, I thought to myself that we have not been called by God to close churches. We have been called to plant new churches. And I said to my wife, 'Let's go and we will take on leadership of that church', and we did it. We received that church with seven adults and five children and, after four years, we were almost 300 people worshipping in that church for God's glory. And then I was elected bishop, and Bishop Nelson, who is here, took over the church. He continued with the same mind around church planting. And from that church, which had been ready to be closed, Bishop Nelson planted a new church. Now that new church is hoping to plant another church, a daughter church, and now a grand-daughter church. Bishop Alfred Cooper, who is also here today, has more than 1,000 people every Sunday in the church, in different services. And in 2000–1 I called and said, 'Alf, I want to move you from the church to another place to do a church planting.' And so we began to talk about that. Then we thought that we would use a different model. We decided that his current church could become the mother church for church plant-ing. And from that church, for example, Alfred sent 100 people to plant a new church in a new area. This meant he lost 100 people from the mother church but, in God's economy, he received 200 more who have come into that church. Using this system, we have planted seven new churches in Santiago, plus other churches around the country using a mother church to plant new churches. It is very important to have a mission-minded mode with church planting.

Brothers and sisters, to finish let me say the following: 'If you do not talk, and if you do not pray about what you want in your diocese, nothing will happen in the end. If you want to lead your church or your diocese into growth, start talking. I want the church to grow, I want to plant new churches, I want more people to be converted to Jesus. Start talking, talking, then pray, and you will see the work of the Holy Spirit come alive to you, come into your church and come into your diocese.

# 19

# Safe Church

## Garth Blake, Chair of the Anglican Communion Safe Church Commission

What is safe church? Safe church and safeguarding are interchangeable words that refer to creating a culture of safety for everyone in the church by preventing and responding to abuse.

Why have a focus on safe church? People in many provinces, especially women and children, have experienced abuse perpetrated by some clergy and church workers. They have suffered harm and continue to suffer harm.

By way of context, what safe church or safeguarding initiatives have the Instruments of Communion recently taken? In 2008, at the Lambeth Conference, the abuse of power within society and the church, and its disproportionate impact on women and children, was an important theme. In 2012, the Anglican Consultative Council requested all provinces to adopt the Charter for the Safety of People within the churches of the Anglican Communion. This charter has five commitments: provide support where there is abuse; implement effective responses to abuse; adopt and promote standards for the practice of pastoral ministry; assess suitability for ministry; and promote a culture of safety. In 2016, the Anglican Consultative Council requested the establishment of a Safe Church Commission and requested all provinces to implement the 'Protocol for disclosure of ministry suitability information' between the churches of the Anglican Communion. This Protocol establishes a system for the provision of information about alleged and proven criminal conduct and sexual misconduct of clergy and lay leaders who move between, or within, provinces. In 2019, the Anglican Consultative Council approved Guidelines developed by the Safe Church Commission and requested each province to adopt the Charter and to implement the Protocol and the Guidelines.

The Guidelines have an introduction that contains information about their purpose, some theological foundations, and notes on format, presentation and implementation. There are five sections that contain background information and specific guidelines for implementing the five commitments of the Charter, and three schedules, a dictionary of terms, the Charter and the Protocol. The key word in the Guidelines is 'abuse', which can include bullying, concealment of abuse, cyber abuse, emotional abuse, financial abuse, gender-based violence, harassment, neglect, physical abuse, sexual abuse, and spiritual abuse. Each of these types of abuse is defined in the Guidelines. Abuse often occurs and continues because of the unequal power relationship between the abuser and their victim. In the church, other forms of abuse can be accompanied by spiritual abuse, such as when an abuser silences their victim by threatening punishment by God, or exclusion from the church, if the abuse is disclosed.

In the Guidelines the first section deals with providing support where there is abuse. The background information discusses the nature of abuse, the harmful effects of abuse, care for victims of abuse, forgiveness, and support for those providing care to victims of abuse. Specific guidelines explain how to establish systems for offering care to victims of abuse and support for those providing care to victims of abuse. They will be both primary and secondary victims where abuse occurs. Secondary victims include family members of the primary victim or the abuser, other church workers, and members of the church. The harmful effects of abuse are commonly not understood. Victims may experience harmful emotional and psychological effects, harmful effects on their relationships with others, and spiritual difficulties.

The second section deals with implementing effective responses to abuse. Background information discusses misuse of power and authority by those who abuse, concealment of abuse in the church, procedures to determine the truth of complaints, outcomes of complaints and support for church communities affected by complaints. Specific guidelines explain how to establish systems for fairly dealing with complaints, support for complainants and respondents, and support for affected parishes and church organisations. All church workers have power and authority by virtue of their role and are in a position of trust. Abusers have commonly betrayed this trust by misusing their power to groom their victim and others close to the victim. Some church leaders have covered up allegations of abuse by ignoring complaints or minimising their seriousness, or by moving the alleged abuser to another position. These actions have further harmed victims and damaged the reputation of the church when the concealment has been publicly exposed.

The need for adopting and promoting standards for the practice of ministry is the subject of the third section. Background information discusses ministry in the church, the imbalance of power in ministry relationships, standards for the practice of ministry in our code of conduct, and the importance of ministry support for church workers. The specific guidelines indicate the areas to be addressed by a code of conduct, and explain the nature of training for the code, and for ministry support. The experience of several provinces has shown that the scriptures and the ordinal have been insufficient to ensure ethical behaviour by clergy. Those provinces have responded by developing a code of conduct with clear standards for the practice of ministry.

The need to assess suitability for ministry is dealt with in the fourth section. Background information discusses the occurrence of abuse, where there has been no background checking, the importance of background checking, and the circumstances in which a risk assessment is required. Specific guidelines explain how to establish systems for the assessment of the suitability of persons to be church workers and the disclosure of ministry suitability information. Some church workers with a prior history of abusing others have been appointed to positions, or ordained without background checking, and have subsequently committed abuse in their ministry. Background checking is an essential means to prevent abuse in the church as past conduct is an important indicator of present and future behaviour.

The promotion of a culture of safety is the subject of the fifth section. Background information discusses how the culture of the church has contributed to abuse, how ineffective governance in the church has contributed to abuse, the challenge of known and suspected abusers in the church, and creating and maintaining a culture of safety in the church. Specific guidelines explain how to establish systems for the formation and ongoing development of clergy, educating parishes and church organisations, ministry to those known or suspected of perpetrating abuse, monitoring compliance with safe church rules and policies, and the review of safe church rules and policies.

I hope that each of you will read the Guidelines carefully. They have been translated into French, Korean, Portuguese and Spanish. Creating and maintaining a culture of safety in your province requires more than the adoption of the Guidelines. They will need to be effectively implemented and undergirded by a theology of safe church or safeguarding, which prioritises the safety of all those who participate in the life of the church. They are intended to be adapted to fit the context of your province and may be implemented in stages. I encourage your province to establish a group consisting of those who have skills in theology, canon law, training, pastoral care and administration to assist in the implementation of the Guidelines.

# Meditation on the Story of the Woman who Touched Jesus' Cloak

## *Kim Barker, South Africa*

This work that we have been hearing about is difficult to hear about and heavy to hold. It is painful work to do. So as people of faith we turn to one of the resources that we have, which is scripture, as a resource, to equip and strengthen us to do the work. And so, for a few moments, I want to reflect on Mark 5:21–34, which is not without its own complexities and power dynamics. But I do believe it has much to offer as we think about our responses to those who disclose abuse within the context of the church.

As Jesus is hurrying along with Jairus to his daughter, who is very ill, the story unfolds. Jairus has begged Jesus to come and heal his daughter. The crowd surrounds him and they are moving, but Jesus suddenly stops and searches the faces of the people pressing up against him. A hush descends, and Jesus speaks with authority and compassion. 'Who touched my clothes?' The disciples find the question very strange. Any number of people have touched Jesus in just the last minute, what can he mean? But there is one woman who knows exactly what he means. The woman has been bleeding for 12 years. The physical suffering and inconvenience of the illness is not the worst of her story. As a result of her condition, she has been considered ritually unclean and excluded from her place of worship and from her community. The woman has also been exploited and abused. We hear that she has been to doctor after doctor. They have taken her money but she still has no cure. In fact, she is getting worse. This is a woman who has reached the end of her own resources.

But she knows what Jesus means when he asked who touched him. She had gathered her remaining strength and courage to force her way through the crowds just to get close enough to Jesus, to touch his cloak, in a desperate hope that she would be healed. And she was. As incredible as it seems, she knows that her body was fully restored in the moment that her fingers touched the cloth, but now she is afraid. She knows that she has challenged taboos and her touch has made Jesus unclean and so she expects condemnation. She considers slipping away into the crowd. But perhaps something in the gentleness of his voice, the softness of his gaze, the faint smile playing on his lips, gives her the courage she needs to stay, and she cowers in front of him hiding her face.

The crowd is now silent, mesmerised by what is unfolding in front of them. How will Jesus deal with this nobody, this outcast, this woman? But there is no rebuke and no harsh words. Perhaps Jesus reaches down and takes the woman's hand, raising her to her feet. Perhaps he asks again, gazing into her eyes, with love and delight. Who is it that touched my cloak, and perhaps she gives her name. And we can imagine that moment of being seen with love. At his encouragement, she tells him her whole story, not just about her physical affliction, but what has been done to her, how she has responded, the whole awful truth, as Jesus listens. In the presence of the community, which would have marginalised her, he listens, and in his listening presence Jesus restores far more than her body. He restores her dignity and her place in society and removes her shame. And without saying a word, he exposes the injustices of those who listen with him. Then Jesus speaks. He calls the woman 'daughter', a term of intimacy and kinship, that tells us she belongs and she is loved. He affirms her faith, a faith that has endured despite being excluded from the faith community for more than a decade. He speaks words of blessing, and vocation: 'Go in peace', and restores her to wholeness in every aspect of her life. 'Be freed from your suffering'.

One of the things that strikes me again and again about this story is that Jesus did not need to stop, for the woman's body was healed when she touched his cloak. But Jesus knew that the woman's need for healing was much deeper and much broader than the woman's body, or even of just her as an individual in that society. It needed to include the community that surrounded her as well.

As we step back from the immediacy of the story, I am going to ask what the encounter of Jesus with this woman offers us as we think about responding to victims, the victims who disclose abuse within the context of the church?

## Justin Welby, Archbishop of Canterbury

When I became Archbishop, almost ten years ago, I knew some of the challenges that we would face. What I did not know was the challenge of Safe Church, of safeguarding. It has had a huge effect on me. It has been the biggest, most painful burden of this role that I have faced over the last ten years. There have been lots of reasons for this, but first of all I had to lose all my assumptions. These problems of safeguarding, of being a safe church, are not at heart to do with human sexuality. The biggest scandal I have been dealing with has been from a married conservative evangelical. It affects every part of the church, from evangelical through to liberal, from low church to high church. It is largely a problem of men, in the vast majority of cases. The biggest challenge has been to try and get the institution of the church to be serious about it, and never to cover up in any way at all.

The fundamental challenge to being a safe church is the misuse of power. It is not even normally particularly about sex, it is about power, the ability of someone to do what they like with someone who is weaker, whether bullying them or having sex when they want it. And when the victim tells someone else, the church says, 'Oh, we can't let that be known', or, 'Oh, a bishop would never do that'. Well, we have discovered that that is not true. So, I know that for me the experience of these years has been agonisingly painful. And over a long period, but certainly over the last 40 or 50 years, we have covered up what went wrong, until about the mid-1990s and early 2000s. And it has terribly damaged the church.

What I would say to all of you, whatever circumstances you are in, are the words of 1 John 1:9: 'If we say we have no sin, we lie, and the truth is not in us.' That, for me, is of first importance. So when someone says to me they have been abused I always take them very seriously indeed. In 99 out of 100 cases the victim is telling the truth. In 1 out of 100 cases, perhaps not. I remember someone hinting at, and then telling me about, abuse by a priest. So we sat down, where people could see us, not going into a closed office, and I said, 'I will make one promise to you, that I will follow this up every week and that I take you totally seriously', and that is what we did. The result was that the person who had abused was removed from their role. So that is my lesson, to be transparent and to walk in the light.

I carry a little card in my wallet that tells me some basic things to do, keeping it very simple. One of these things is who I need to call to report something that goes wrong. Every clergy person, and especially every bishop, should have these details. The worst part for us was a public inquiry, called the Independent Inquiry into Child Sexual Abuse, which looked at a number of churches including the Church of England. They said to us, 'You are marking your own homework'. And we were! When I gave evidence they asked me at the end what I felt and I broke down in tears on television because I was so ashamed of the church. And I would say to people, to clergy, that however few the resources, always take people seriously, always report it. And never try to deal with it yourself. This is because it needs to be someone independent.

# 20

# Anglican Identity

## Archbishop Kay Goldsworthy, Anglican Church of Australia

I come to this reflection on Anglican identity bringing the experience of Australia and especially the Diocese of Perth. Perth is one of the 23 dioceses of the Anglican Church of Australia. Like every diocese, we face challenges to the identity we Anglicans have had and enjoyed and become comfortable with, of who we think we are, and of who God is calling us to be. We need the wisdom and love of our partner churches in the Anglican Communion to help us navigate these challenges.

We face challenges of changing community attitudes to the privileges of Anglicanism, changes to the way in which we are viewed in the community, after scrutiny that has exposed us to the harsh light of unfolding truths. We must trust Jesus even as we repent and lament and seek God's Holy Spirit in the work of building a community of hope, and healing and transformation, a community as hospitable as the love of Jesus. These challenges are not new. They are uncomfortable and they are disruptive. It is their season. And it is our season to meet them head-on for the sake of the gospel. They are causing us to look afresh alongside others around the Communion at how we are being called to live into the future of God's new day in Christ here and now. I want to speak of 4 Rs: reconciliation, redress, refugees and relationships. These are four realities that have made an impact on our Anglican identity. I want to say something about the Anglican Consultative Council and how it helps to shape our identity in Perth.

Earlier I prayed a prayer from our Prayer Book, a prayer of thanksgiving for Australia. It was written by an Aboriginal woman called Lenore Parker and it is a prayer that speaks to the heart of who we know we are. It tells something of the very sad and awful history of our story. The Diocese of Perth covers more than 300,000 square kilometres with most of the population on the coastal fringe, while the rest is rural, remote and regional. The city of Perth sits on the traditional lands of Aboriginal people of the Noongar Nation. They are one of five First Nations groups in the diocese and across the country there are hundreds of Aboriginal languages, as well as the languages of the Torres Strait Islands off Australia's northeast coast. Some languages have been lost and others are increasing once more. The First Nations peoples of Australia and the Torres Strait are the oldest unbroken cultures in the world, with traditions going as far back as 60,000 years. At my installation as Archbishop, the congregation and I were welcomed by a group of Noongar elders, who accompanied me and members of the diocese from which I had come, one of whom was a priest. She is a Noongar woman and one of the thousands of Aboriginal people stolen from her family as a child as part of a long-running government assimilation policy. She was, in the cathedral, a visible sign of the new day into which Jesus is calling us, standing in that cathedral on her traditional lands alongside elders. Those children who were forcibly removed from their families are now known as the Stolen Generations. Australia's history in relation to this is shameful.

In Perth, the work of reconciliation goes on in church, in schools and in caring agencies and across business and community. As a diocese, we are working to respond to this history through a Diocesan Reconciliation Action Plan. It will be another step in taking responsibility. As we acknowledge and lament the hurt and pain of the past and especially the church's part in it, it will help us move into the future with new peace and changed relationships. This ministry of reconciliation that lies at the heart of God's loving faithfulness is costly, and some prejudices lie close to the surface of our common life. We are learning *with* and *from* Anglicans in other parts of the Communion who are also taking their next steps. We are learning from the Anglican Peace and Justice Network and the Living Reconciliation initiative. We are praying that our next steps will be gentle on the ancient land in which most of us are recent arrivals. We are thankful for the grace and the patience of elders, the members of indigenous networks in our country, both those locally, nationally and in the wider Communion.

Garth Blake and others have spoken about the Safe Church Commission, which has been underway for just a few years, and the cooperative work of many across our churches. He mentioned a public hearing in Australia that took place from 2013 to 2017. The abuse that was uncovered was simply awful. It has been a significant contributor to the erosion of trust in churches in Australia. The abuse is not the only factor but is a huge contributor to attitudes reported earlier this year by the 2021 Australian census, which shows that 43 per cent of people say they are Christian, a decline from 50 per cent in 2016, while 40 per cent of people in Australia said they had no religion. That was 10 per cent more than in 2016. Commentators have said that people think churches abuse children, that we hate the LGBTQI+ community, and that we are hypocritical when we speak of Jesus' love. We are facing questions of identity, our identity in Christ; our blindness; our shame about the ease with which many church members were groomed by those who abused the vulnerable, about the pain of knowing that a priest, a lay minister, a trusted spiritual leader, has committed such crimes. Redress is one part of the response. We hope that our Australian Commission may be able to assist others in vastly different contexts and cultures to keep safe the most vulnerable in our churches.

Around the Communion, leaders are also being raised up to care for the vulnerable and to change and transform our life as the Communion. There is the International Anglican Women's Network and the work that they are doing; the International Anglican Family Network and the commitments that they have; and, of course, the work of the Mothers' Union, to ensure that the pandemic of gender-based violence has no place in our churches. We pray for an end to it.

A few years ago in Perth we prayed to have more children in our churches and now some of the biggest parish communities in the diocese are South Sudanese refugee communities. God provided for us in ways we had not quite foreseen. These congregations have people from the cultural and language groups of Dinka, Bari, Nuer and Juba Arabic. The members of these communities live in the shadow of war in South Sudan, of ongoing bursts of conflict in their homeland, alongside the challenges of being first- and second-generation migrants in a completely new world. They are people who look back and forward and that is sometimes exhausting and difficult. Yet every service begins with the refrain 'God is good all the time. And all the time, God is good'. The clergy and people of these communities speak of the injuries of war – physical, psychological, moral, spiritual. They keep educating us bishops. They are helping us grow as leaders. We are slowly listening and learning, taking counsel and praying, seeking wisdom and then shepherding, as we teach and encourage within a community that feels so keenly the tensions of being a diaspora.

We have learned that as bishops we cannot be in a host/guest relationship with refugee groups. We cannot be like welfare providers perpetuating dependency. We are learning how to be *alongside* as co-workers, living together into God's future. There is looking back, there is trauma and pain and sadness, and there is also hope. I see how the first – and now second – generation of children and young people are shaping a new Anglican identity as they live into the future, in what for them is a new world, and how they make their home in this new place, never forgetting their roots, never forgetting their heritage. We are looking to the bishops and churches around the Communion who can help us with questions that are raised by diaspora communities, living in new and very different cultural contexts. We are listening very gently with the clergy about matters like purity codes and the shape of family as it was lived at 'home' but are not usual practices in Australia.

All of this is alongside sisters and brothers around the Communion who are facing similar challenges to mission and pastoral ministry. We know the unity and communion of God's love is slowly revealing that pattern of love to the church. Relationships, in all these areas, are vital: praying for one another and with one another; looking to build a home together where all have a chance to flourish; holding on when it gets difficult and when we do not understand. In Perth, because of the work done in previous Lambeth Conferences, we have had partner dioceses in other parts of the Communion for a long time. We currently have a partner relationship with the Diocese of Eldoret in Kenya and are just beginning a hopeful development of another with the new Bishop of Lomega in South Sudan. Bishop Onesimo was an archdeacon in the Diocese of Perth. Our relationships are strong and we hope that they will grow further in mutual love and trust. Bishop Onesimo is so ably supported by Frida, who as a priest in the Diocese of Perth had a role in caring for women and families in the Sudanese and South Sudanese communities. She is a marvellous spouse and companion for him.

I am currently the Episcopal Representative for Australia on the Anglican Consultative Council (ACC), which was created by the Lambeth Conference in 1968. We know that the ACC facilitates the cooperative work of the churches of the Communion, and also the exchange information between provinces and churches, and it helps coordinate common action. I rejoice in the many astounding gifts and graces that the ACC offers for the life of the whole Anglican Communion. One of the images I have of the Commission's departments and networks, which the ACC facilitates, alongside the other Instruments of Communion, is that of a quilting group, or workroom. Each section of the quilt is worked on by individuals, and each different piece enriches the whole emerging work. Speaking on the Anglican Communion in 1999, at ACC-11, one bishop said that provinces have tremendous gifts to offer one another, precisely because of the different cultures and contexts through which the gospel is interpreted and lived within those contexts. He added that that very diversity opens us up to new ways of looking at the mystery of God, Father, Son and Holy Spirit and, even more, that provinces share a kind of holy intimacy, and this calls us to allegiance and interdependence. I love that image of holy intimacy, of the sense that we Anglicans in all our complexity reflect the holy intimacy of the Trinity.

So many people contribute to the unity and purposes of the churches of the Communion. Theologians, biblical scholars, experts in mission and evangelism, ecumenical relations, communication, administration and finance. Alongside ecumenical partners and friends, these all assist in the work of unity for which our Lord prayed. The Communion's tensions and conversations, the reports and debates and considerations from around the world, are important to us in Perth. They are important to us in Australia. We live in our own cultural context and it has particular challenges and opportunities, as do you. Yet we also share in the richness and depth of theological understanding and insights that come from Anglicans in every part of the world. And, for them, we say thanks be to God.

## Archbishop Maimbo Mndolwa of Tanzania

Brothers and sisters, for those who have never known where Tanzania is, it is in the East African region. The name Tanzania dates from 1964, when the two countries of Zanzibar and Tanganyika united to form what became known as Tanzania. In this country, though, we have three main traditions: we have the Anglo Catholics, a tradition that was brought by the University Mission to Central Africa (UMCA). I am sure many of you know that Anglo Catholics emphasise worship and the seven sacraments. In Tanzania, this tradition has emphasised the building of an indigenous church for indigenous people. It is known as the High Church. The second tradition is the Evangelical, planted from the UK by the Church Missionary Society. This particular tradition puts more emphasis on two sacraments, evangelism and church planting, and using John Venn's theology of the three selfs: that a church should be self-governing, self-propagating and self-supporting. This tradition is commonly known as Low Church. The third tradition, which normally is confused, is the Charismatic brand of the Tanzanian church. This emerged from the great East African Revival movement. It really shifted people away from the Anglo Catholics and the Evangelicals. It was never planted in the country by missionaries from abroad. It came from indigenous people who came and planted this kind of church; their main focus was on being born again, and personal salvation with prayers. For this tradition, if you are not born again, you are just a dead stone.

As can be noticed from these traditions, each one holds a different emphasis and opinion. They built three different churches but in one province. I am sure my fellow Primates who do not have such a rainbow kind of church in their own provinces might wonder how a Primate of Tanzania manages the House of Bishops as well as the Provincial Synod when they are called. It is challenging because bishops have different understandings of what it means to have seven sacraments, what it means to have two sacraments, what it means to be a Charismatic. Agreeing on issues has not been easy. For example, Christians from one tradition may not feel happy to worship with others from the other traditions. Sometimes when people from the Evangelical tradition come into an Anglo Catholic service they feel as if Anglo Catholics are highly elevated Catholics because they use all their senses in worship, and there are all types of elevation of the High Church. Our brothers and sisters from Kenya are well aware of the Kikuyu controversy in which Frank Weston, a bishop from the Anglo Catholic tradition, had to leave a meeting because his tradition's understanding of the sacraments was not respected. These differences were elevated to the extent that even when the CMS had decided to vacate their mission stations in Tanzania, they decided to leave their mission work to a non-Anglican mission that was commonly known as African Inland Mission. Bear in mind that UMCA was already in that particular country.

Now, what made it possible for these traditions to combine and become one province, irrespective of their differences and some internal disagreements? They were conscious that they were all Anglicans. But I must say this did not come easily. There were sacrifices. Second, there was an awareness among them that the differences that existed among them were God-given gifts for the building up of God's Kingdom. This inward and outward look within the Anglican Church of Tanzania has benefited the African church in various ways. Some may not be aware of it, but my brother Bishop Anthony Poggo mentioned the Council of Anglican Provinces in Africa. The fact that the different dioceses of the Anglican Church of Tanzania could work together motivated other Primates to meet in Nairobi and make the decision to create a body that would unite them. They were coming from their divided traditions, bringing a sense of unity and telling them that we are Africans though we have different traditions: we belong to Africa, so let us be Africans. The executive team of the Council of Anglican Provinces in Africa (CAPA), based in Nairobi, is doing a great job of bringing together the Anglican provinces and making African Anglicans one body. No other continent, as far as I know, has this type of council. The Anglican Church of Tanzania used most of its resources to bring unity not only into that sense of creating the Council of Anglican Provinces in Africa, but also played a role in the creation of the Province of East Africa in 1960. Our brothers from Uganda refused to unite with us because of the presence of Anglo Catholics in our province, but our brothers and sisters from Kenya came and joined us and we created the province. Finally, in 1970, it was divided into two. The Anglican Church of Tanzania, then, by looking inwards and outwards, and following the lead of the national government of Tanzania, especially its philosophy of Ujamaa (solidarity), promoted the self-governing of new Anglican provinces across the continent, including training their future leaders, to the extent that today many bishops and priests from those countries were trained in Tanzania. Archbishop Carlos from the Anglican Church of Mozambique and Angola province is here and can bear witness to that.

The Anglican Church of Tanzania also played a part in the evolution of the role of bishops' spouses in Africa. This may not be clear to many of the African bishops but, by using the Mothers' Union model (of women playing a key role in all aspects of the life of the church), the first Primate of Tanzania raised a concern about the gap in expectation, between African women and their own bishops. As a result, it was agreed in Johannesburg in 1973 that just as the bishop is the 'father' to the African church, so should their spouse be the 'mother' to the church. This is not the case elsewhere in the world, as I know. So when we see spouses of African bishops gathered here together in this conference it is not by chance, but was fashioned and mandated by the Tanzanian Anglican Church. The bishops' wives are bringing the women of their own diocese into this conference, just as the bishop is bringing his diocese.

What can a global church learn from this Tanzanian brand of Anglicanism? If you will take it metaphorically, we will say it in this way: many of you who have used trains during our travels in the UK are aware of a sign or announcement that we see or hear when we get on or off a train from the platform: it says, 'mind the gap'. In order to get on or off the train safely, we need to be careful of the gap that exists between the train and the platform. We live in a world that has so many differences: differences in culture, differences in continental issues, boundaries that divide countries, gender, you name it. If we do not mind the gaps that exist between ourselves, then we can destroy our relationships. The Tanzanian brand of Anglicanism teaches us that if we want to stay together as one, holy, catholic, and apostolic church, let us be mindful of the existing gaps. My brothers and sisters from the Global South Fellowship of Anglican Churches, 'mind the gap' that exists between the South and the North and respect the cultural norms of the global North. My brothers and sisters from the global North, 'mind the gap' that exists between the North and South and respect the cultural norms of the South: you have your own God-given gifts of living which should not be forced on those in the South. Let us keep in mind that we have many differences, and those differences that are created by God are here to save us, not to break our relationships. May God bless you.

## Archbishop Hosam Naoum of Jerusalem

Who am I? Who are we? What makes us Anglican Christians? What brings us together in the here and now? My short address will focus on the theme of identity. I will reflect upon the topic from three different, but related, perspectives. First, I will talk about our identity from the perspective of the Pauline image of the church – namely, the church as the body of Christ. Second, I will talk about identity from my own perspective, as a Christian Anglican who lives in Jerusalem. Lastly, I will present the theme of identity from our own Anglican understanding of the Instruments of Communion.

There are quite a few verses in the Bible that speak about identity. One of my favourites is from the prophet Isaiah, 'Do not fear for I have redeemed you. I have called you by name, you are mine.' Our God is a great God who knows us inside out. God loves us and cares for us. He has redeemed us for this reason. This deep and profound relationship reflects both the nature of God and our own nature as God's children. The famous Genesis story of creation tells us that we are born in the image and likeness of God. As God's holy people and God's adopted children, we are called to search for our true identity, rooted in the person of Jesus Christ through the power of the Holy Spirit. Another verse that speaks to us about the topic of identity is from 1 Peter: 'But you are a chosen race, a royal priesthood, a holy nation and the people of his own possession.' As Anglicans we are called to be God's Church for God's World, to walk in the light of Christ as his own beloved body, to be transformed, and to become agents of transformation. One of the most significant images of the church in scripture is the Pauline image of the body of Christ. Now, you are the body of Christ and, individually, members of it. This image presents to us significant and profound meanings that have contributed to the life of the church in so many ways over the last two millennia. One of the most essential features of this image is the fact that Jesus is the head of this body; he is the head of the church. The other important feature of this image is the way that this body functions. Different members have different rules, talents, charisms and functions. Yet the harmony of the body and the relational aspects of its well-being depends upon how different members respond to the state of other members. The Bible teaches us that if one member of the body suffers, the whole body suffers with it. Another important feature of the image of the body of Christ is that this body belongs to Christ, and Christ alone. No member should claim to possess or control it or to exploit other members of the body as a whole. We are united because we all have the mind of Christ, for Jesus is our true north and compass. We walk together because Christ unites us to himself, for he is the way, the truth and the life. That is true for the Anglican Communion, in which our identity as Christians is rooted in the person of Jesus Christ, and our unseen or invisible unity as Christians does not depend on any one of us. It is Christ's own gift to the world. In his priestly prayer in John 17, Jesus prayed for the manifest and visible unity of the church when he said, 'I pray that they all may be one, just as you and I are one.' The unity of the church is rooted in the unity of the Godhead: Father, Son and Holy Spirit.

Similarly, God's people are called to live in that unity and holiness. Our failure as Christians to achieve unity has not diminished these truths and it does not affect the invisible and unbroken unity of God's one holy catholic, and apostolic church. In fact, the earthly manifestation of the church's unity depends upon Christ being at the centre. The Diocese of Jerusalem, where I have the honour and privilege to serve the Lord, covers all places where Jesus lived and walked, died and rose again, and ascended. Throughout every day of my life and ministry there, I walk in the footsteps of Jesus, both literally and metaphorically. This encounter is unique, if not exclusive, to the Diocese of Jerusalem which includes places like Nazareth, Bethlehem, Jerusalem and many other places where the Bible tells us the story of God's salvation. These are not simply historic places but, rather, centres of living witness of Jesus Christ. Our small stories are only glimpses of the manifestation of *the* story, God's story. Walking in the footsteps of Jesus is like being united with Christ and God's story of salvation. This mission was entrusted to the first disciples when they were commanded not to leave Jerusalem until the outpouring of the Holy Spirit upon the church, as the fulfilment of God's promise. It is from Jerusalem that God's story was shared with the rest of the world through evangelism and discipleship. Jerusalem is the cradle of our Christian faith; Christians in Jerusalem and the Holy Lands share in both the geography and the history of the place. Therefore their identity is deeply rooted in the holy sites and ancient stones. As living stones, a term that Peter uses in his first letter, Christians in the Holy Land discover their identity through walking daily in pilgrimage. This is a journey of faith where, through both suffering and joy, they follow in the footsteps of their Lord and Saviour Jesus Christ. Christian churches and denominations all have a deep sense of their vocation as pilgrims and custodians of the holy places. Nevertheless, Jerusalem has a special character that no one can take away from it. It is God's holy city.

However, human failures, including greed and other shortcomings, have caused it in many ways to become a divided place instead of a place of unity and tranquillity. Quite often people's extreme love for Jerusalem denies Jerusalem of its true nature. Human love can be possessive rather than liberating, exclusive rather than inclusive, alienating rather than welcoming, embracing and sharing. Many of us in Jerusalem forget that it is the divine love, agape, that achieved redemption and salvation for us and for the whole world on the wood of the cross. This was the fulfilling act of reconciliation that restored our relationship with God. It was a heavenly gift that nurtures our own relationships with one another.

As we all know, the four Instruments of Communion are the Archbishop of Canterbury, the Lambeth Conference, the ACC and the Primates' Meeting. As Christians and Anglicans we all agree that Christ is the head of the church and the shepherd of our souls. Yet as Anglicans we are guided by these Instruments of Communion in order to govern and sustain our visible unity as member churches of the same Anglican Communion. In fact, these instruments are there structurally to serve the Communion and help fulfil its mission.

Theologically and ecumenically, Anglicans have agreed to walk in unity according to the Chicago-Lambeth Quadrilateral – that is, by the Holy Scriptures, the Apostles and Nicene Creed, the sacraments of Baptism and Holy Eucharist, and the historic episcopate as locally adapted. Together, these four affirmations contribute towards guiding us as Anglicans in walking in the footsteps of Jesus in unity, love and peace. In addition, the Five Marks of Mission were later developed to help us articulate and carry out our mission in and for the world. In this part of my address, I would like to focus on one Instrument of Communion: namely, the Archbishop of Canterbury. The Lambeth Conference of 1930 underlined the constitutive role of the Archbishop of Canterbury when it defined the Anglican Communion as a fellowship within one holy, catholic, and apostolic church of their sees, provinces and regional churches that are in communion with the See of Canterbury. The Archbishop of Canterbury, as we all well know, is the President of the ACC and Lambeth Conference and the *primus inter pares* – that is, the first among equals – within the Primates' Meetings. Indeed, the Archbishop of Canterbury is the spiritual leader of the Anglican Communion and, as described in the Virginia Report of 1997, a pastor in the service of unity. Since AD 597, and Augustine who was the first Archbishop of Canterbury, the See of Canterbury has been seen and regarded as a see of mission. Indeed, this was the original purpose for which St Augustine was sent by Pope Gregory the Great to England. I believe that the significance and importance of the ministry of the Archbishop of Canterbury comes from the importance and significance of Canterbury, of the See of Canterbury. As Anglicans we are in fellowship and unity because we are in communion, not with the Archbishop of Canterbury, but rather with the See of Canterbury. The visible unity of the Anglican Communion, as it stands today, is held together because of the See of Canterbury. As member churches and provinces, we all have had our metropolitan jurisdiction bequeathed to us in one way or another by the Archbishop of Canterbury, as he has exercised authority through the oversight of the See of Canterbury.

The one aspect of our Anglican identity that I pray does not change is our ongoing theological conversations that form part of our pilgrimage together. Listening and being listened to, in the light of scripture, are very important ways for us to continue building up and shaping and reshaping our identity as Anglicans. More important still is how we can be united and made stronger together in order to make a difference in the world. The four Instruments of Communion are products of a long history of giving and receiving and are a gift to us. Let us remember that we are the body of Christ and, individually, members of it. Our unity does not eliminate our individuality or autonomy as provinces and dioceses; instead, it enables us to be God's Church for God's World.

As a Christian from Jerusalem, I am proud to be an Anglican. I am blessed to have the opportunity and privilege to serve not only my people within my diocese, but also the wider Anglican Communion in a pilgrimage of sharing our faith journey, as we walk together in the footsteps of Jesus, a contribution to its unity and well-being. As St Paul wrote, 'so then you are no longer strangers and aliens, but you are fellow citizens, with the saints and members of the household of God'.

# 21

# Peace and Reconciliation

## Archbishop Carlos Matsinhe

I represent Igreja Anglicana de Moçambique e Angola (Anglican Church of Mozambique and Angola, known as IAMA). I bring a word that expresses reconciliation from our cultures, which is 'kurula'. This is a word that means 'peace' in the southern part of Mozambique. Literally, the word means 'take the burden off your head and put it on the ground and be free and happy'. Take the burden off your head, heart and body and put it on to the ground and be happy: Kurula. This is how we greet one another.

But what is our experience of living in a world without reconciliation? The reality of the absence of peace and reconciliation is present in our daily lives and in our history as individuals and as families and as nations and peoples. There are stories of pain, bitterness and fear. They overshadow the future of life. This is the reality in Mozambique in the southern part of Africa and, I believe, in other parts of the world. The factors causing this lack of peace and reconciliation are the same everywhere; they are common in many places and can be expressed in different scenarios and levels.

We have the experience of deep racism, characterised by oppression, domination, segregation and destruction of the dignity of the African and indigenous people of the entire world, and of the promotion of the culture and mindset of the oppressors. Earlier we looked at the reality of colonialism: its impact and the participation of our own church. In Africa we have the experience and wounds of colonialism, such as apartheid in South Africa and other painful forms of division. They are open wounds, despite the appearance of 'problem solved'. One of the examples is to compare what we are paid as black people working in our own countries, with what someone with a different skin colour, even with the same qualifications, level of education and experience, will be paid.

In Africa we still have wounds and scars from the slave trade. I come from a country where there were more than three slave routes and historic harbours to transport slaves for torturing and for selling our ancestors to Europe and the Americas. These are the ports of Inhambani, Sofala, the

Island of Mozambique, and Pemba. I am aware that there are many other ports and routes of slave trading around Africa, as in Uganda, Tanzania, and Congo. These wounds remain. We still see our brothers and sisters, Afro descendants, living in diaspora and being highly discriminated against, despised and segregated. This hurts. We would love not to have to live like this. The examples are abundant and we all know them, in the United States and other parts of the globe. The slavery has painful impacts on Africans because racism, contempt and marginalisation are being expressed in several ways.

We are also facing many military conflicts going on in independent countries. Some of those conflicts turn into civil wars where outsiders, from countries where there is Anglicanism, continue to influence African countries, fuelling the military conflicts. We also face internal eruptions of violence. For instance, in South Africa the xenophobia is very prevalent and increases internal conflicts, where black South Africans express their discontent at receiving African brothers and sisters from other countries, coming to South Africa to seek a better way of life. This is out of fear of them. We also face tribal conflicts all over the world, and in our own context. These realities show a wounded and broken world in need of reconciliation.

We are experiencing domestic terrorism in our contexts, in Mozambique, Nigeria, Congo, and in other parts of Africa as well as in the Americas and Europe. We never know when a community will face terrorism. We have Cabo Delgado as an example of terrorism, generated, from my perspective, from faceless people forcing local communities into conflict. About a million people have been displaced from the northern Cabo Delgado into the south of the country. This has created a chaotic situation in the places they have moved to. Lots of brutal murders have been committed in that region, damaging the infrastructure, dismembering people, polluting sources of water, etc. Thank God the current situation is improved, but it is uncertain for how long.

Today we have the Ukrainian war, killing the innocent people of Ukraine. This is a war between superpowers. As Africans, it is difficult to take sides. The same is true as Christians. We are aware that it is not the ordinary people who are to blame. The responsibility lies with those who promote destruction and human misery and profit from it.

I come from a country with a very high foreign debt. This is the reality of many African countries, as well as others from the global South. During colonial times the Western powers sold lots of natural resources from Africa and the global South. They also kidnapped people to work for them for their own benefit. But now those countries, politically independent, try to develop their economies and they acquire increasing debt, and this debt may never be paid. This is a very painful reality and hinders the possibility of moving forward towards reconciliation. This increases inequality, poverty and other issues that take away peace and possible reconciliation.

I also come from a country where there is gender-based violence. It is rooted in our cultures and systems. A colleague from Brazil has just received images and messages about an attack on a community with several wounded, on the order of the landowner. What was the reason? It was because that community refused to deliver their daughter to marry one of the landowners. This is happening elsewhere as well.

Analysis shows that the cause of absence of peace and reconciliation is, first, the lack of respect for the dignity of a person. There is theft of resources from those who have less power to stand and defend themselves. There is power abuse and a mentality that supports the idea that only the fittest will survive. Those are the lions mentioned by Archbishop Justin in his first Presidential address. The princes of darkness do not know God and do not even want to know; they do not know the value of human life and do not want to get to know Jesus Christ and his power of reconciliation. This is why the world is in the midst of pain, fear and trauma and an uncertain future.

The church is chosen and blessed because it knows God, the living God and his Son Jesus Christ our reconciler. This is why we must cultivate and have hope and follow the gospel requirement to be a signal of hope to the world in so far as we continue to teach love, peace, justice and reconciliation, including restoration. This same church needs to work to heal the wounds of all kinds of violence and develop processes of peace for the people of God. We have a huge challenge ahead. Also, we have in front of us the opportunity to teach this path of reconciliation and peace, so the world can become a better place to live.

Mozambique won its independence in 1975 but in 1979 a civil war started, which was a destabilisation war supported by the apartheid regime in South Africa. It lasted for 16 years. There was a process of negotiation and a peace treaty was signed in 1992 in Rome. Then a process of demobilisation and disarmament started, conducted by the United Nations, but the opposition demanded that a portion of the soldiers remained in post to guarantee the protection of the opposition leader. As a result of this request the number of soldiers increased in the country. Until last year, the combatants of this resistance (represented in parliament by the Renamo Party) were over 5,000. Now and then there is some resurgence of war in Mozambique but a treaty was signed in 2019 to have a full reintegration of those soldiers, including receiving compensation to be reintegrated into the local communities to live a life there.

This is one step in reintegration. It is the duty of the church to accompany those communities and teach them how to live together peacefully. Those soldiers who lived in the forests, fighting, living daily with violence, a destructive life, need the church to plant seeds of peace in their lives and to be a light of reconciliation and love.

## Bishop Te Kitohi Wiremu Pikaahu of Aotearoa New Zealand

This presentation is primarily about the struggle of indigenous people in the Anglican Communion. It comes from the gathered indigenous voices present here at this Lambeth Conference. Unfolding before us is the vision of God, of the Kingdom of God that seeks reconciliation in a world where God is sovereign, where God is supreme, a world where Jesus Christ is Lord and Saviour. There is much attention being given to indigenous peoples, to First Nations people and their traditional and tribal lands. This presentation looks first at the experience of reconciliation in the context of the people of Aotearoa New Zealand, in terms of Maori and Pakeha relations, and in the Anglican Church of Aotearoa New Zealand and Polynesia in terms of Maori and Pacifica relations. Second, it offers theological reflection on the subject of reconciliation, drawing on the texts of the second epistle of St Paul to the Corinthians. Finally, it offers some thoughts on the unique contribution that indigenous peoples can offer the Anglican Communion when we seek to journey towards true reconciliation, throughout the Communion, especially of indigenous communities where the Anglican Church has been present, and continues to be.

You will have seen images of people touching noses. Those are images of what it means to embrace a person in my culture. It is the final stage in our rituals of encounter. For example, Archbishop Winston Halapua made an apology and he asked me to accept this apology. I had to go from New Zealand to Samoa to fulfil the ritual obligation to receive the apology. Archbishop Winston Halapua was covered with a fine mat and he had to wait with it on until I released him. I had the power to release him or leave him there. You will be pleased to know that I released him after a couple of minutes. That is a good place for me to start: at the end, with imagining transformation and reconciliation before we begin the journey towards it.

I will soon invite you to an act of generosity. For me to talk about reconciliation outside of this conference is one thing, but to acknowledge our need to be reconciled with one another here and now is another. In a heartfelt way I want to mention that we will have an opportunity to seek reconciliation while we are sitting next to, and alongside, one another. This will require trust and for us to be optimistic in our intent. I will ask you to consider exchanging your pectoral cross with the person next to you as a symbol of such trust. I want to highlight the giving away of something of value, knowing that it will return to you. The willingness to exchange your pectoral cross is important. For spouses who do not have a pectoral cross, you may wish to exchange some other item of value. At the end of this session you will be invited to return the gift you have received for the purpose of this exercise.

Archbishop Justin Welby has identified the theme of reconciliation as a priority for the Anglican Communion. He has challenged us all to be a community of reconcilers. Bishop Brian Castle describes reconciliation as a journey of a lifetime. I do not think he meant it as a journey that takes a lifetime, or that it takes more than a lifetime, but that it does require a lot of work and effort. He was speaking about the journey, the experience, and I have to agree. Our lives are filled with needing to be reconciled over and over again. I have an inkling he was pointing towards stages in the journey towards reconciliation, where you can look forward to arrival and departure, as with airport arrivals and departures. I have to say to you the stages are important and the process is equally important. We have to imagine having arrived at the destination and reconciliation from the beginning to the end, from departure to arrival, from isolation to belonging, from struggle to joy, from darkness to light, from doubt to faith, from despair to hope, from sin to redemption, from death to life, to arrive at resurrection joy, resurrection peace, resurrection hope and resurrection love. Christians, like anyone else, for a variety of reasons, are prone to fall in and out of friendships and relationships that tear at the fabric of our society and the communities we live in. This vulnerability and fragility is what we require to be rescued from. If we see reconciliation as a gift from God, then it is a gift of God, from God to the whole world. Christians then have a duty and a responsibility to share the gift of reconciliation, to offer this gift to our neighbour, to live our lives built on a foundation that continuously seeks reconciliation.

Indigenous peoples have been subjected to colonisation for generations. We have seen great suffering, including intergenerational trauma. First Nations people around the world know what it is to suffer. What is your custom when engaging with indigenous people? You may not have heard them say what is needed because they may not have said it in the way you expect. But I can say that it will run through their minds. It is for the dominant culture to ask of themselves, 'What is my custom when addressing indigenous people? What language do I use? What words do I use to begin what is usually a different and difficult conversation?'

A simple question such as 'What is your custom?' is an invitation to learn about a worldview probably foreign and incomprehensible at first. However, it is a generous invitation and it is critical if the conversation is to begin in the right way. More specifically, the rituals of encounter must be understood and performed properly. In my context, when a visitor arrives, there are three challenges that are put to the person. The first one is 'Who are you?' which means 'What is your name and where are you from?' The second one is, 'What is your purpose?', which means 'Why are you here?' The third one is 'Who sent you?' which means 'How many warriors do you have? What is your strength?' These are traditional customs of indigenous peoples. You are either welcomed to come forward or you will be turned back. There is no chance contact, no random opportunity to be embraced. It is either deliberate embrace or exclusion, depending on a person's response at the first contact. If reconciliation is sought, the result, depending on how matters progress, is either going to end in restoration or in being turned back.

At Archbishop Justin's enthronement there was a young woman at the door. These are the words she put to him: 'We greet you in the name of Christ. Who are you? Why do you request entry here?' This was similar to our rituals of encounter: 'Why have you been sent to us? And how do you come among us, with what confidence? Let us humble ourselves before God and together seek his mercy and love.' This was in the liturgy and it was a powerful symbol because the power dynamic was right. In my view, the custom was right. Archbishop Justin gave the right answer, so she let him in. Without such rituals we cannot take another step. We must stay where we are. The custom was correct.

During his visit to Canada earlier this year, Archbishop Justin apologised to the First Nations people of Canada. Pope Francis has done a similar thing. The point I want to make here is that indigenous peoples have been apologised to and there was a need for that to occur. Many indigenous people would agree that through our multiple tiered relationships are to be found the deepest expression of our customs and our traditions. The primary reason is because we have responsibilities and duties with our own relatives, in the sacred circle, through sacred talking, sacred conversations, and also sacred healing. That is the right custom. I believe in the power of reconciliation; that is the power of the reconciling love of God. True reconciliation has its own inherent power, a power that lies in intent and in action. If we intend to be reconciled to our neighbour, then we are on the right pathway. If we put our intention into practice, then we have moved farther along the journey.

Reconciliation is a gift from God and a gift from God to the whole world. It is about the gift of the love of God. It is about the power of love as opposed to the love of power. At the heart of reconciliation is the love of God, the extraordinary love of God, the unconditional love of God and the extravagant love of God. I have seen and witnessed the power of God's reconciling love to the world and for humanity. The reconciling love of God is in constant action in the world wherever God is present. It is both in the now and in the yet to come. Indigenous reconciliation requires more listening than speaking. That is the right custom. The listening process demands open hearts and open minds to wait patiently. To hear the other is an indigenous custom.

Sir Paul Reeves, a previous Archbishop of Aotearoa New Zealand, had the right custom. He declared forgiveness to the government before the government offered apology. That is because he is a Christian. He knew that the custom for him as a Christian was to forgive. He knew he could, and he knew he must. Archbishop Winston Halapua also knew, as a Christian, that he must make his apology and that he must wait for forgiveness. We are ambassadors for Christ in the ministry of reconciliation and in that way I see myself also as a navigator for reconciliation, through the person of Jesus Christ, his sacrificial life and his power to redeem and save: this is who we lift our gaze to. The pathway is in his teaching and preaching and miracles, in his healing, in his death, resurrection and ascension.

*At the Lambeth Conference bishops then exchanged their pectoral crosses as a sign of reconciliation.*

## Sheran Harper, President of the Mothers' Union

We have seen the suffering and we have seen what has been happening in our beloved world, God's world. Indeed, women and families are often powerful forces for reconciliation right across the world, and may I say in the same breath that women and families suffer most in times of division and conflict and also on the long journey towards reconciliation. Women and girls always seem to be on the front line of the harshest and most violent of circumstances. At one of the most difficult times for God's world in the past 100 years, this is the day-to-day reality we face in a changing world. It is against this backdrop that I share two stories of Mothers' Union's responses to situations of conflict and division.

The first story is from the Province of South Sudan. We were excited to engage 160 women from South Sudan, all diocesan leaders, in our consultation process, 'Mothers' Union Listens, Observes, Acts' (MULOA). We were in session but we sensed the atmosphere was not quite right.

Quietly, we could feel the restlessness and hear the almost silent whispers of some about others in the room: 'they are the ones who killed our children'. We stopped. The baggage was heavy, the burden was unbearable. Being in close proximity with those who caused years and years of pain and agony was not conducive to interacting or learning. As organisers we had to take quick action. We stopped and we consulted with the One who gave us this work: we fell to our knees and we prayed to him and positioned ourselves to hear from him. Then we started again. We used Bible studies that touched our hearts and we could feel the fresh pain that came with a willingness to let go. Participants wanted to surrender and they wanted to feel the power of God's forgiveness and to forgive one another. They willingly laid down their burdens, asked one another's forgiveness, and prayed for God's healing. As they laid down their burdens they recognised that they are one family, one body in Christ: they lit candles at the beginning of each day, signifying the light of Christ in their midst, bringing healing and hope as they laid them down. The Bible studies spoke volumes as they studied them together in their different languages. The Genesis story spoke of men and women being made in the image of Christ. The story of Mary Sumner helped to prevent early marriages. The story of Esther laying down her life for her people encouraged people to make the necessary sacrifices to bring peace, and the story of the woman who touched Jesus' cloak, reaching out when all else failed, gave immense hope and new life. Everything became clear to them. They said, 'We thought we were the only ones hurting, but in our sharing we realised that we are all hurting, and there is need for healing, if we are to move forward.' Today, three years later, laying down burdens is an integral part of their Mothers' Union community work and the women take the light of Christ and the Bible studies to every community they visit, whether it is to the refugee camps, or their own local communities. They want to take everyone on the journey of hope, and spread the good news of peace and reconciliation.

There is a story from a settlement in the Province of Formosa, Argentina, where men and families are engaged in an amazing work of peace in areas of conflict and division. A crowd of men and women were walking towards the police station, which put the entire police force on high alert. The situation was an everyday occurrence, as the police often had to take action against young people who continued to break the law. They were very accustomed to crowds of angry mothers bombarding the police station and protesting (you know how we mothers can be). As usual, the police approached the women and asked them to declare their intention and they were shocked this time when the women said, 'We have come to pray for you and for your job.' The police were deeply moved when the women began to pray for them and ask them for forgiveness. This was so different to the confusion that they used to cause before. They publicly prayed for God's blessing on the police, men and women doing their jobs in maintaining the law. This was the beginning of healing, peace and transformation in this community. Several years have gone by and the police continue to call the women of Amare (Agrupación de Mujeres Anglicanas Renovadas en el Espíritu – Anglican Women Renewed in the Spirit). Amare Mothers' Union help to resolve division and conflict in a community in which the politicians and local leaders cannot do so.

My brothers and sisters, the role of women and families is clear in these stories, and so important in a fractured world. We are all called and equipped by God to work together, have the necessary dialogue, and promote a culture of peace and hope that is transformative. In the dark moments, women prayed deeply seeking light, humility and forgiveness, a gift that only Christ can give. They go to extremes, serving as advocates for conflict prevention, reconciliation and peace, building in order to protect the most vulnerable and those at risk. My friends, in a world that is divided, conflicted and hurting, it is more important than ever for us to learn how to handle conflict and disagreement. Put the process of reconciliation into action and embrace the new course that brings opportunities for peace and reconciliation.

## Bishop Pradeep Kumar Samantaroy

My sisters and brothers in Christ, as an Indian I say 'Namaste'. Namaste is a combination of two words, 'Nama' and 'te', and we say it with joined hands to keep our thumbs close to our heart. 'Te' is 'you', 'namaste' means 'I honour you, I adore you and I worship you because I recognise God in you'. Namaste.

Almost every day all of us pray for peace in this world but we know that peace is not possible in this world of conflict unless there is reconciliation. We thank God for the gift that God is offering to us: his own peace, which is beyond human understanding. Reconciliation is not optional. Why? Because as we read in the scriptures, it is part of our identity. God through Christ has given us the ministry of reconciliation. Therefore, we are ambassadors for Christ because our purpose is to engage in a ministry of reconciliation, and to deny the work of reconciliation is to deny our own identity. We have an option to say no; many have said no before us, but reconciliation is a gift that gives joy, joy in our heart and, therefore, the ministry of reconciliation is a business of the heart. If we have that joy, which God has given, we cannot contain that joy in our heart: it has to overflow and, in this way, it will give hope to people who are without hope. It will give a message of life to people who are dying. Our spirit cannot be bound because we have received the Holy Spirit. That does not mean that we can do anything that we want, but it means that being empowered by the Holy Spirit we can go beyond our human boundaries to serve our God.

We need, then, passion to deeply and meaningfully engage in the ministry of reconciliation given to us. On 11 September 2018 when the Archbishop of Canterbury Justin Welby visited Amritsar, it was the centenary of the massacre at Jallianwala Bagh, when more than 1,000 people who were protesting were massacred. It was 43 degrees, and even as an Indian living in Amritsar I found it extremely difficult to stand without shoes at the memorial. But this man of God went around and prayed at different places and at the memorial. He prostrated himself on the ground and I thought, 'Well, 1, 2, 3, 4, 5 … he will not last for more than 10 seconds.' But it felt as if he was in a trance; he had forgotten himself because he was feeling the pain of the people, for even after 100 years the pain is still there. He made a confession of repentance and asked forgiveness, not on behalf of the government of the United Kingdom, but on behalf of the church. It was appreciated by everyone in my country.

Passion is, I think, something that we are called to offer. I encourage us to look within and see how deeply we are really engaged in the ministry of reconciliation. We appreciate someone else doing it, but am I doing it? Is the family of the Anglican world deeply engaged? Do we affirm that as disciples of Jesus Christ it is mandatory for us to engage in this ministry and to be willing, happily, to pay the price, whatever it takes, whatever it takes even unto death? That is the main concern. It is not just about what mechanism we are going to adopt, though that is necessary, but the need to act. Time is running out.

My dear friends, with joined hands, on behalf of our wider family, I appeal to you. Let us be honest before God, let us look within ourselves, within myself, within my family, what have I done to date? If I have survived Covid-19 I am alive. Why? What is the purpose of God in keeping me alive? Our life has to be purposeful and I feel it is to bring smiles to the faces of people who are struggling and to engage in the ministry of peace and reconciliation.

# 22

# Christian Unity

## Cardinal Kurt Koch of the Pontifical Council for Promoting Christian Unity, Rome, presented by Father Anthony Currer

This Lambeth Conference should have been held on the centenary of the 1920 Lambeth Conference's Appeal to all Christian people, a charter for the Anglican Communion's ecumenical efforts and a landmark moment for the whole ecumenical movement. It is a movement that the Catholic Church proved reluctant to join. But when we did join you in seeking to overcome the divisions among Christians, in the foundational ecumenical declaration *Unitatis redintegratio*, we echoed many of the convictions already set out in the Appeal. First, that all Christians are bound together with one another through baptism, and through the fundamentals of faith and tradition that all share and that are articulated in the scriptures and the ancient creeds; second, that division is caused by sin, and that Christians are therefore called to acknowledge guilt for sins that cause division and to do penance; that God intends his church to be a sign for the world; and that its unity must therefore be visible. *Unitas read de gratia* echoes all these convictions. And so the centenary of the Appeal seems an appropriate moment to say that we are sorry for being so late to join the ecumenical movement. But thank you for showing us the way.

The bishops of the 1920 Lambeth Conference described themselves as being inspired by the vision and hope of a visible unity of the whole church. And they describe the goal of humanity as that of a church genuinely Catholic, loyal to all truth and gathering into its fellowship all who profess and call themselves Christians, whose visible unity all the treasures of faith and order bequeath a heritage by the past to the present, which shall be possessed in common. This citation brings us neatly to the theme of Cardinal Koch's address. We need a common vision, because we shall grow further apart if we do not aim towards a common goal. 'If we have conflicting views of this goal we shall, if we are consistent, move in opposite directions.' These are the words of the Lutheran Roman Catholic Unity Commission in its 1980 document *Ways to Community*. Even 40 years later, these words have lost none of their relevance. The danger diagnosed here has not decreased, since it has not so far been possible for the various dialogues in Christian communities to achieve a really stable agreement on the goal of the ecumenical movement. That brings the main difficulty of the present ecumenical situation to light. On the one hand, it was possible in previous phases of the ecumenical movement to reach an extensive consensus on many hitherto controversial individual questions around the understanding of faith and the theological structure of the church. On the other hand, most of the still existing points of difference continue to make themselves felt in the different understandings of the ecumenical unity of the church.

In this double context, I perceive the most elementary challenge in the ecumenical situation today as being what the late Bishop of Wurzberg, the eminent ecumenist Paul-Werner Scheele, diagnosed as follows: 'Regarding Unity, we agree that we want unity, but not on what kind.' Why, then, this lack of agreement? Conrad Raiser, a former secretary general of the World Council of Churches, used to stress that strongly insisting on unity ran the risk of endangering unity itself, which is why he recommended doing without the category of unity altogether:

> Again and again, during the history of the church, those with other ideas have been excluded or suffered violent persecution in the name of church unity. Indeed, you can argue that most divisions in church history were the consequence of an overthrow of an overstated idea of unity. In any case, diversity only becomes a problem when it is measured against a normative form of unity. So the question is whether the ecumenical discussion should not refrain from using the notion of the unity of the church due to the misleading and static, even abstract, character of the concept.

With these critical statements, Conrad Raiser probably primarily had the Catholic Church in mind, which to this day holds to the originally common goal of visible unity in faith in the sacraments and in church ministry. This strong insistence on visible church unity is certainly also founded in the fact that the Catholic Church is a world faith community, living in interaction between the plurality of local churches and the unity of the universal church, striving to regain unity in its own sphere of life, and thus to transfer the Catholic ideal of unity on to the ecumenical movement, making its own internal model of unity the ecumenical goal.

On the other hand, we can only understand the sharpness of Conrad Raiser's judgement on the Catholic view of the ecumenical goal if we note the alternative he postulates, by contrast with the earlier paradigm, which was, he says, unashamedly vertical in its talk of church unity. Now, a horizontal understanding of unity should assert itself along the lines of mediating between differing traditions and positions, so that reconciliation, the balance of diversity between the church traditions, is realistically the maximum ecumenical unity that can be achieved. If you contemplate this definition of the goal of the ecumenical movement, you will quickly discover that it is not neutral, any more than the Catholic one is, but clearly reflects the history of the Reformation. This is because the great schisms in the Western church of the 16th century always lead to further divisions, so that the churches and ecclesial communities that emerged from the 16th-century reformations have developed into a plural- ist universe that is anything but straightforward. It is probably the result of these historical developments that quite a number of the churches and ecclesial communities that arose during the Reformation strongly pro- mote diversity and difference, and consequently have largely abandoned the original goal of visible unity, a visible unity in faith, the sacraments and church ministries, replacing it with the postulate of mutual recogni- tion of the varied church realities as churches, and thus as parts of the one church of Jesus Christ. That is not, in principle, postulating the invisibil- ity of church unity. Visible unity, however, merely consists largely in the sum of all available church reality.

This example was intended to make clear that asking questions about the goal of the ecumenical movement, and consequently of a more precise understanding of church unity, cannot be done in an abstract neutral way. This questioning is always directed and informed by prior ecclesiological decisions of a confessional nature. The reason for the different ecumen- ical goals is that the differing ecumenical arguments are more in favour either of unity on the Catholic side, or of plurality on the Reformed side. As every Christian community has and practises its specific idea of its being church and its unity, it also aspires to transfer this confessional conception on to the level of the ecumenical movement as well. There are basically as many different ecumenical goals as the raw confessional ecclesiologies. This means that the lack of agreement on the goal of the ecumenical movement is rooted in a lack of ecumenical agreement on the nature of the church and its unity.

We find a helpful way forward to a deeper common understanding of the church and its unity in the study of the Commission for Faith and Order of the World Council of Churches entitled *The Church: Towards a Common Vision*. This study aspires to an ecumenical view of the nature, definition and mission of the church. And it can therefore be regarded as a step on the way, and a valuable ecclesiological statement from an ecumenical viewpoint. However, this creditable study is not able to take most of the controversial topics on ecclesiology and the theology of min- istry beyond the framing of further open questions. And, consequently, there is much work to do in this direction, with the basic questions of what, who and where the church is, and what absolutely pertains to its unity, being the main items on the ecumenical agenda.

In its endeavour to regain the unity of the church, ecumenism today faces another great challenge about which we cannot keep silent. In the pluralist and relativist *zeitgeist* that is widespread nowadays, it is running into a strong headwind. The reason is that in contrast with traditional Christian thinking that regarded unity as the meaning and reason for being, pluralism has today become the decisive term for designating what is called the postmodern experience of reality. To quote the famous essay by Jean-François Lyotard, postmodernism means admitting and favouring the plural as a matter of principle, and being suspicious of everything singular, also as a matter of principle. The basic conviction of the postmodern mentality says that there is no thinking backwards from the plurality of reality. And we must not do so if we want to avoid the suspicion of a totalitarian approach. Instead, plurality is said to be the only way to reflect the whole of reality, as far as this is possible at all. It is, therefore, characteristic of postmodernism to abandon unitary thinking on principle, which means not only tolerating and accepting pluralism, but fundamentally opting for it. With this postmodern mindset, any quest for unity seems pre-modern and antiquated.

We have to know that the postmodern mentality is present and effective in ecumenical thinking as well. It is expressed in an ecclesiological pluralism that has become plausible to a large extent, according to which precisely having multiple diverse churches is regarded as a positive reality. And any attempt to regain the unity of the church appears suspicious. It appears that people have not only learned to live with the historical and present pluralism, but also basically to welcome it so that the ecumenical search for a way to restore church unity appears unrealistic, and is regarded as undesirable. This conviction is mostly expressed by using the phrase 'reconciled diversity' to describe the current ecumenical situation. From a Catholic angle, too, there is a positive point to using this phrase. However, it is understood as defining the goal of the ecumenical pathway on which we seek the unity to reconcile differences that are no longer church dividing. Hence, again and again, the question arises as to how much unity is necessary, and how much diversity is possible, or desired. The French thinker Blaise Pascal helpfully showed the way in his *Pensées*: 'unity that does not depend on plurality is dictatorship and plurality that does not depend on unity is anarchy'. In humanism, too, we have to constantly seek and take a middle way between dictatorship and anarchy.

If we orientate our ecumenical efforts to Jesus' high priestly prayer, in which he prayed for the unity of his disciples, the search for unity belongs to the essence of Christian faith, and is expressed with desirable clarity in the letter of the Apostle Paul to the Ephesians: 'There is one body and one Spirit, just as you were called to the one hope of your calling, one Lord, one faith, one baptism, one God and Father of all, who is above all, and through all and in all.' Since unity is and remains a basic category of Christian faith, we Christians must have the courage and humility to face up to the still existing offence of a divided Christianity, and gently but firmly keep the question about unity on the agenda. The theme of this Lambeth Conference, 'God's Church for God's World', motivates us to do just that. This motto can only be true to its meaning if the church can undertake its global mission, in reconciled form, in the way that Jesus prayed for the unity of his disciples in his high priestly prayer with the specific intention, 'so that the world may know that you have sent me and have loved them, even as you have loved me'. This final sentence, 'so that ...', expresses the fact that the unity among the disciples is not an end in itself. Rather, it serves the credibility of the mission of Jesus Christ and his church in the world, and represents the indispensable precondition for a credible witness in the world.

The first World Mission Conference in Edinburgh in 1910 recalls this goal of the ecumenical quest for church unity in a specific way. The participants of this conference were concerned by the fact that the different Christian communions were competing with one another in mission work, and therefore harming the credible proclamation of the gospel of Jesus Christ, above all in distant continents, because alongside the gospel they also took European church divisions into other cultures. For this reason, they had become painfully aware that the lack of unity among Christians was threatening the credibility of Christian witness in the world. The divisions in Christianity then turned out to be strong barriers to evangelisation. And this is still true as Pope Francis recalls in clear terms in his apostolic exhortation *Evangelii Gaudium*. Given the seriousness of the counterwitness of division among Christians, particularly in Asia and Africa, the search for the path to unity becomes all the more urgent. The missionaries in those continents often mentioned the criticisms, complaints and ridicule to which the scandal of divided Christians gave rise. Consequently, in the eyes of Pope Francis, commitment to a unity that helps them to accept Jesus Christ can no longer be a matter of mere diplomacy or forced compliance, but rather an indispensable path to evangelisation.

This ecumenical emergency implies that a sincere and thus common ecumenical witness to Jesus Christ in the present world is only possible when the Christian churches overcome their divisions and can live in unity in reconciled diversity. Ecumenism and mission belong inseparably together, since that is the only way in which God's Church really is *for* God's world. It is my wish for you, dear Archbishop Justin Welby and esteemed bishops, that this theme of the Anglican Communion may not only give orientation at this conference, but also accompany you into a blessed future. The delegates of the Catholic Church join me in this wish, and we will be glad to include it in our prayers. Thank you.

## Archbishop Marinez Rosa Dos Santos Bassotto, Diocese of the Amazon, Igreja Episcopal Anglicana do Brasil

I thank you for this opportunity to be able to speak in the name of the Anglican Episcopal Church of Brazil and to tell you about our ecumenical actions in defence of life in Brazil. It is important to highlight that the original inspiration for unity in the church of Christ came from building up solidarity and fraternity in our world, which included justice and fullness of life not only for Christians but for all of humanity. The Anglican Episcopal Church of Brazil was present at the origins of this movement and within its ecumenical organisations, which promoted inter-religious dialogue in Brazil. The experience of ecumenism led Christian churches to be involved in social and political issues, to struggle for democracy, acting in various forms, defending life and defending the environment and indigenous peoples. In response to the struggles for justice, fairness and for the ending of religious intolerance in Brazilian society, many walls have been built, among them the walls of racism, of economic inequality, of violence, of polarisation, of political intolerance, and also religious intolerance and the attack on democratic institutions. The church is a witness that only through unconditional respect is it possible to live according to Christ. It does this in unity and dialogue. Unity cannot be carried out without communion and respect for plurality as part of a creative design; of course, to love and create diversity, to dialogue, is to establish respectful dialogue, sharing in solidarity, and it comes together with humility and trust.

I would like to share with you an ecumenical action in defence of the indigenous people in which I participated just before coming here. There is the ecumenical campaign to support and be in solidarity with the indigenous Guarani people in the west of Brazil – to provide international and national visibility to the violation of their rights from pressure from the government – to bring solutions to the conflicts that exist in the region and reaffirm the ecumenical commitment to defend human rights and environmental and social rights. Eight indigenous reservations were created in the state of Mato Grosso early in the 20th century, around

1925. The aim was to confine indigenous people who were occupying the whole of that region and to free the land for settlement. Today, these reservations concentrate around 80 per cent of the whole of the Guarani and Kaiowa population in Brazil. Over the last 100 years, agribusiness continued to invade and abuse them. The indigenous people were pushed into a sliver of this land. However, their burial lands are in the wider reservations and are evidence that this land belongs to them. And that is why they carry on taking back their lands and occupying their ancestral lands, called 'tekoha'. Therefore, there is a lot of conflict in this region and the history of violence against the Guarani has become worse. In May and June of this year [2022] we have seen ambushes, murders and even a massacre in two of the recoveries of land, which means the serious violation of the rights of the people. Young people and children were the target of armed shootings, and children are not being allowed to go to school because they are in occupied lands. Women, old people and children are suffering from threats of being raped. The ecumenical campaign included churches, social movements, faith organisations and international non-government agencies. A campaign incorporated all the attacked villages and carried out public conferences and press conferences as a way to provide visibility to the situation and express unconditional support to the Guarani, and committed to denounce in international and national forums the crimes perpetrated against these indigenous peoples of Brazil.

I participate in this ecumenical action that is carried out to defend the environment and indigenous people, and I also denounce the violation against these people. I can testify that the unity of the church is relevant and necessary so that we can all be one and so the Kingdom of God can be revealed. And I wish to deliver to this Lambeth Conference the request of this ecumenical campaign to make visible the crimes perpetrated against indigenous people in Brazil to the global family. I conclude by sharing with utmost urgency some Guarani and Kaiowa prayers (called Ñanderus and Ñandesys). They use the 'maracas' to pray. It is an instrument to spiritually help the prayers. I want to invite you to listen to sung prayer in the Guarani language: [Marinez sings the Guarani Kyrie]

Oré poriaju verekó; Ñandeyara.
Oré poriaju verekó; Ñandeyara.

Oré poriaju verekó; Jesu Cristo.
Oré poriaju verekó; Jesu Cristo.

Oré poriaju verekó; Ñandeyara.
Oré poriaju verekó; Ñandeyara.

## His Eminence, Archbishop Nikitas of Thyateira and Great Britain, Greek Orthodox under the Ecumenical Patriarchate of Constantinople

It is with pleasure and in the spirit of unity and cooperation that I come before this esteemed body to share some thoughts with you on peace and justice, touching especially on the issues of human trafficking, and modern-day slavery. Each day newspapers, radio commentators and television personalities bring to our attention the events and challenges of our times. In their words and commentaries, we repeatedly hear about the abomination of human trafficking and modern slavery. We listen to stories of young women forced into prostitution, domestic helpers who are tied or chained so as not to escape, of beggars on the streets who work for some boss, of children who are abducted and sold as simple commodities, and the list goes on and on. The sins of the past are alive and thriving in a modern world that dares to speak of human rights, justice and truth.

While our politicians and world leaders speak out against these injustices, laws and other measures are rarely enacted to stop the abomination and evil. It is therefore time for us as Christians to unify our efforts and to do what is required by God, to speak out against injustice and every evil. If this does not happen, and we do not act as one, then we are not living to the fullest Christian potential. And we have failed in our calling not only as Christians, but also as human beings. The apocryphal words taken from the Wisdom of Solomon remind us of our responsibilities in life:

> Listen therefore, O kings, and understand; learn, O judges of the ends of the earth. Give ear, you that rule over multitudes, and boast of many nations. For your dominion was given you from the Lord, and your sovereignty from the Most High; he will search out your works and inquire into your plans. Because as servants of his kingdom you did not rule rightly, or keep the law, or walk according to the purpose of God, he will come upon you terribly and swiftly, because severe judgment falls on those in high places. (Wisdom 6:1–5)

As Christian leaders, we are those in high places of responsibility for the caring of souls, and the judgement of God will come upon us if we do not act. After all, indifference may be the greatest of all sins. If we as individuals and church leaders, people in high positions, failed to labour, then we are indifferent not only to those held in bondage and slavery but also to Christ and his message of truth and liberation. Christianity is not a faith tradition solely of meditation and philosophy; rather, it is a religion of action and violent resistance to evil. Though first and foremost it is about our own spiritual conversion and transformation, I might dare to say that in our days, and times, it has become *vogue* to speak about human trafficking and modern slavery. And on occasion, we tend to toss out these phrases into our statements about social justice, human dignity and other catchy expressions. But, in reality, what have we done to heal a broken world? I might also dare to quote from the Liturgy of St Basil the Great, who says, 'we have done nothing good upon the earth'. If we had acted and done what is good, right, true and just, some of these things may have changed. It is so sad that, as Christians, we so often focus on what separates us that we have forgotten the very essence of all things, Jesus Christ, the one Christ who belongs to all, and who is the source of all things. It is Christ who demands and commands that we come together now and act as a body, as the body of believers in him.

We were anointed at Pentecost and empowered with grace by the Holy Spirit. And now we must seek justice and correct oppression, as we are reminded by the prophet Isaiah. And this must be done not to fulfil a moral code but to transform and transfigure society and this world in Christ Jesus, crucified and risen from the dead, having always within us a strong desire to move from image to the likeness of God, as we were created. If this happens, then we can understand that overcoming the differences, including our theological ones, is indeed a possibility. And we can walk together in faith with hope and with love in our hearts.

## The Reverend Dr David Wells, Vice Chair of the Pentecostal World Fellowship and General Superintendent of the Pentecostal Assemblies of Canada

Christian greetings, brothers and sisters of the Anglican Communion, from your brothers and sisters in the Pentecostal World Fellowship. It is my privilege to be here with you.

The Pentecostal community, of course, is on a journey related to ecumenical activity and spiritual ecumenism has assisted us in coming more and more to the table. Let me explain. Within the Christian community we have families that we belong to and with that connectedness come many benefits, including a shared sense of belonging, common beliefs, rituals, practices and a mutual history that links our story with that faith community. So my faith story is linked to the Pentecostal family, because my aunt and uncle were Pentecostals and they didn't think it was right that the Wells kids were not going to Sunday school in the early 1960s.

So they took us to a Pentecostal Sunday school. As I pointed out once in an Anglican dinner, if it would have been an Anglican had it been my uncle, maybe I would have become an Anglican priest. So there you go. Sometimes that is how it works.

However, there are limitations to our knowledge, our perspective and faith development. If we only know the relationships, histories and insights found exclusively within our own community, we can end up with a fixed identity and it can lead to a myopic view of the family of God, and from it sometimes arises arrogance and judgement, things that Pentecostals at times have been accused of (not by yourselves I'm sure). But there is a need for us to think more along the lines, as missiologists would describe it, of having a centre-set identity. And I also heard Cardinal Koch referring somewhat to that in his presentation. Related to how we hold these core senses of truth, core senses of those things that we are about, we may even become more and more convinced about them, as I am about a number of the distinctions related to the Pentecostal community. But we also understand that there is so much more to learn from our other brothers and sisters. So let me give you a quick summary of what I think Pentecostals bring to the ecumenical table as a result of clarity about having a centre-set of identity with an openness to the broader body of Christ. This is somewhat based on an outline from Dr James K. Smith in his excellent book, *Thinking in Tongues*.

One aspect is of being open for God to do new things; the passion of Pentecostals to see renewal, to see revival, to see restoration, to be creative. Sometimes this can be a little frustrating for the more historic churches. But I think we all agree that we serve a God who renews, refreshes and is creative.

The second aspect is recognising spiritual realities in every area of the natural world. Smith calls it an enchanted worldview. And it is the Pentecostal, and also the broader family of God, understanding of the continual sense of God's presence, of keeping in step with the spirit of openness to the Spirit's voice, and experiencing the Spirit's leadership and direction. And this can lead to divine appointments, and moments of the operation of the giftings of the Spirit.

Third, it is Jesus' work on the cross that provides for both spiritual and physical restoration. It is sufficient for our wholeness, in the complete person, body, soul and spirit. And though Pentecostals are criticised at times for being heavenly minded, the reality is that we take the physical world and the physical nature of a person very seriously.

Fourth, high value is placed on faith stories of salvation in the miraculous. And this is where I appreciate the initiatives that have taken place in the Global Christian forum through my friend Casely Essamuah, who is here today, and other efforts to invite Pentecostals to the table, where our sharing of our faith stories is an important part of our shared unity. Mistrust really breaks down fast when you are in a room in Bogota and hearing your Syrian Orthodox friend express what it means to be a church of martyrdom, and of the stories of them walking through times of great trial in the name of Christ, and you learn to honour your brothers and sisters who are not of the same tradition or background.

Mission is taken very seriously, which is point five, especially to the poor, the broken, and those who have never heard the Good News. It is expected that all the followers of Jesus will be involved in the mission of God, because the Spirit of the Lord is upon us. And he has anointed us. We thank you that we share this gospel together; and please welcome us as we come to the table and share with you working for Christ to be known in the world today. God bless you.

## The Revd Anne Burghardt, General Secretary of the Lutheran World Federation

Honourable bishops, participants, guests, sisters and brothers in Christ. Please allow me to start with a word of gratitude to Archbishop Justin and to the whole Anglican Communion for extending this invitation to the Lutheran World Federation. Indeed, as the psalmist says in Psalm 133, 'how very good and pleasant it is when kindred live together in unity'. Just over 100 years ago, in 1920, the Lambeth Appeal was made public, calling for a united Christendom. We employ a different language today, though the search for the visible unity of the church remains the same. It requires, in the words of the Lambeth Appeal, a new discovery of the creative resources of God. We at the Lutheran World Federation are grateful that our two communions have been able to join together through many decades of theological discussions, pastoral and spiritual partnership, joint proclamation, and joint service in the midst of a suffering world. I praise God for this Lambeth Conference and its theme of God's Church for God's World, for your honest searching and discernment, your heartfelt listening to one another, honourable bishops of the Anglican Communion. You provide a strong example of listening to scripture, in dialogue with the cries of humanity and creation. My colleague, Assistant General Secretary for Ecumenical Relations, Professor Dirk Lange, is also very grateful for the ecumenical welcome extended to him throughout this conference, a welcome that already embodies that unity for which we yearn. I am also thankful for the contributions of this panel who have each presented important perspectives on our ecumenical journey, from the doctrinal to the spiritual, to social justice and renewal, to the cry of the environment, and the call to solidarity as one human family.

Allow me to respond in a more general way, highlighting some aspects that caught my attention. The unity for which we yearn, a unity not always easy to define, has taken shape through decades of dialogues. The World Council of Churches has formulated a number of unity statements, one of the classic ones being in 1961 from the New Delhi assembly. The statement highlighted that unity in faith, sacraments, baptism and Holy Communion, prayer, mutual recognition of ministry, and witness through service to the neighbour are needed for the visible unity of the church. One could say that these elements mentioned in the New Delhi unity statement have also offered a certain guidance to the choice of topics that have been handled in various ecumenical dialogues. Is the New Delhi statement the guiding principle of the ecumenical movement?

His Eminence, Cardinal Koch, sets a challenge before us. How would we today define visible unity? Perhaps an initial step is for each of us to ask ourselves, as Christian world communions, first and foremost, how do we define visible unity? What does it look like for my own communion? Can we share that vision with one another? And in the sharing perhaps find a way forward? Or do we simply fall back and expect the other to look like us? Getting up and walking together is hard work, as David Wells states. Spiritual ecumenism, that first step of inner conversion and conversation, is challenging as we let go of preferences that may have guided our faith journey up until this point. So is it possible for each of us to get up and walk a new path together? Great ecumenists through the decades have reminded us that prayer is at the heart of our ecumenical work. Spiritual ecumenism is a starting place.

But, in a certain way, our common worship is also a beginning. The liturgy and prayer can turn us around, shape us anew, reorient us differently towards one another and the suffering world, so that we can hear the cry of the world. In his letters from prison, Dietrich Bonhoeffer wrote that the future of the church will be in prayer and action. Our vision of the church and therefore of unity, I believe, will be shaped by this fervent prayer and solidarity with others. Cardinal Koch mentioned the Faith and Order document *The Church: Towards a Common Vision* in his presentation. This document indeed offers important insights for our quest to define unity. Visible unity does not necessarily mean institutional unity, but *koinonia* between churches. There are several examples among post-Reformation church families where we have churches being in such *koinonia* with one another. In this context here, I particularly think of the many full communion agreements between Lutherans and Anglicans, such as Porvoo, which my own home church – the Estonian Evangelical Lutheran Church – is part of, as well as Waterloo's *Call to Common Mission*.

Unity is expressed in various ways, through bishops mutually participating in laying on of hands at episcopal installations and ordinations, through church members mutually participating in Holy Communion, through joint theological working groups, through expressions of spiritual and receptive ecumenism. Through all this, living traditions are shared among different church families that are in communion with one another, while having kept their special spiritual and theological accents. The notion of *differentiating consensus* developed in the Lutheran–Roman Catholic dialogues points in the same direction. It led to the signing of the Joint Declaration of the Doctrine of Justification, which is now a shared consensus between five Christian world communions – Anglican, Methodist, Reformed, Catholic and Lutheran. The statement seeks implementation at the local level, as local neighbouring parishes who, rather than living in isolation or occupied only with themselves, turn to one another to proclaim Jesus, to share Jesus, to engage in the world out of love for Jesus, and to do so together. In that ecumenical dynamic we evangelise (to use a word you have been exploring) but we do it together not for the sake of the church but so that God's immeasurable goodness and God's good intent for all people and all creation will be known. We already have the tools to do this work. We already have the consensus statements that allow us to start the journey.

Evangelisation, as an ecumenical dynamic, addresses the suffering world. His Eminence Archbishop Nikitas and Bishop Bassotto have sought to concentrate on different aspects of serving the neighbour and creation while also emphasising the importance of spiritual ecumenism. His Eminence Nikitas urgently calls us to our baptismal vocation. We are called urgently to respond to the cry of God's people, especially those suffering the abomination of human trafficking, not simply to fulfil a moral code but to transform and transfigure society and world in Jesus Christ.

Our prayer and action rooted in Christ transforms and transfigures. When talking about the message of the truth of the gospel, and joint ecumenical engagement, one often encounters two different approaches. In one case, the starting point is human being with his or her experiences within context, spiritual or physical. In the other case, the starting point of engagement is, rather, settling doctrinal truth. In our ecumenical endeavour, we must keep theological reflection, prayer, service to the neighbour and public witness closely connected. Yet is this a time when our solidarity with the suffering neighbour and the distressed creation may open up new hermeneutical frameworks for our doctrinal and theological reflection as well? I see this as one of the big tasks of the ecumenical movement in our time: how to ensure that 'faith and order' and 'life and work', when talking in older terminology of the ecumenical movement, are holistically kept together and mutually shaping each other. The cry of indigenous people in Brazil, as Bishop Bassotto points out, or the cry of the indigenous peoples of Canada, highlighted by both the visit of Archbishop Justin and this past week by Pope Francis, cannot but shape our ecclesiology. For, as we have discovered, a certain theological framing, in collaboration with political self-interest and economic greed, has created those cries: so how can we together engage in an ecumenical campaign that not only dismantles the power structures of our world, but also the power structures within our own churches, and within our very own ecclesiologies? Is this part of our task to be God's Church for God's World?

From that angle I am then, as a Lutheran, not afraid of pluralism or postmodernism. I will use a rather old image, but very effective one I believe, to describe what I mean. When the churches place Christ at the centre of their theological reflections and search for unity, and the centre is surrounded by concentric circles through which churches start to move towards Christ, the centre, the churches obviously do not only get closer to Christ but they also get closer to one another. And on this journey towards Christ, the churches will discover different aspects about Christ and God's liberating grace, and they are able to share these with one another. The postmodern world has much to share with us as churches. Perhaps most notably it has helped us engage in a critique of all systems that believed themselves to be self-contained and that too often hold us captive. The process of deconstruction is, perhaps, as some think, what is required today of the ecumenical movement, in engaging critical self-reflection occasioned precisely by the cry of wounded peoples, and the suffering of creation.

Again my thankfulness to Archbishop Justin and the whole Anglican Communion. As Lutherans, we are very grateful for all the full communion agreements that exist between our two communions, but also for agreements that facilitate mutual recognition and reconciliation, such as Common Ground, Meissen and Reuilly; and we are now excited about launching the Anglican Lutheran International Commission on unity and mission, a commission that will seek to implement many theological consensus statements, but also listen to the cries of the neighbourhood, and environment. Together let us find ways of making the new creation, the trustworthy world God intends, a little more visible in the world.

# 23

# Hospitality and Generosity (Inter Faith)

## Bishop Guli Francis-Dehqani

The subject of inter faith relationships touches most if not all of us, in some shape or form, because we live in a pluralist society, with people of all faiths and none; but our vastly varied contexts mean that our own thinking and responses will probably be very different from one another. I speak out of my own particular context and experience, which relates especially to Christian–Muslim relations, but I hope that some of the themes that I am going to touch on will be helpful to others in stimulating thinking and discussion.

Let me begin with my own life story, so that what I present can be placed within this context. Although I am now a bishop in the Church of England, I started life in Iran where I was born and grew up. It was in the tiny Anglican community there that the seeds of my early faith were planted. My father was a Muslim convert from a small village in the middle of the country and by the time that I was born he was already Bishop of the fledgling Diocese of Iran. My mother, the daughter and granddaughter of British missionaries, was herself born and raised in Iran so I lived an unusual life, between and betwixt the worlds of Islam and Christianity, Persian and English, and Eastern and Western influences. This unusual childhood was what I considered normal and, for the most part, my two worlds of school and wider society on the one hand, and home and church life on the other, coexisted reasonably peaceably, and there was some occasional overlap. But all of that changed as the events that led eventually to the Islamic Revolution of 1979 began to unfold. At school, I began to be ostracised, both by friends and by teachers, and at home the church was coming under increasing pressure. Over a period of around 18 months, our institutions such as hospitals and schools were forcibly taken over or closed. Church offices and the bishop's house were ransacked, raided and confiscated. The church's financial assets were frozen. One of our clergy was found murdered in his study, and my father was briefly imprisoned before an attack on his life, which he survived, but my mother was injured. For us as a family, events culminated in the murder of my brother in the spring of 1980. When he was 24 years old his car was ambushed on his way back from work, and he was shot in the head and died instantly. My father was out of the country at the time for meetings. Although no one was ever brought to justice, we have always understood that my brother was targeted because of his association with the church and simply because he was his father's son. After the funeral, my mother, my sister and I joined my father here in England, assuming that we would be back home within a few weeks or months. Of course, that was not to be and so, having arrived here originally as a refugee aged 14, I am still here over 40 years later and a British citizen.

My father continued working as Bishop in Iran in exile until his retirement, and he dedicated his life to supporting and encouraging Christians still in Iran and working with Persians, both Christian and Muslim, in this country. In particular, he dedicated his time to writing and translating Christian literature in Persian. During his episcopate he attended three Lambeth Conferences. Both my parents have now died and the diocese in Iran is extremely isolated and currently without a bishop. So these formative experiences have shaped my thinking and they continue to inform my understanding of how we as Christians engage with other faiths, especially when elements within those faiths wish us harm. It is not easy and it has not been straightforward, but for me it has involved embracing the concept of paradox, that ability to hold together apparent contradictions, to help us navigate a way faithfully through what is often rough terrain. For example, I have known Islam both as a great civilisation, which over the centuries has gifted to the world some of the greatest scientific advances, architectural designs, poetic and literary masterpieces, and spiritual insights. My grandfather was a godly and wonderful Muslim man of deep faith. But I have also known Islam as a force that has done my family and the church in Iran great harm. It is difficult but necessary, somehow, to hold both these threads together and to remember that the evils that have befallen the church are not a reflection on the whole Islamic faith. In the words of the late great Kenneth Cragg, while 'certainly *an* "Islam" was guilty', nevertheless 'the Islam that is indicated in what befell the [Persian] Church might have stayed its hand by counsels no less claiming its name'.

What impact, then, has this way of thinking had on my encounters with Muslims in the West? I try to see the best, to be respectful, to learn and understand more deeply. Alongside this, I have also sought to be honest, to tell the story of the church in Iran, and to ask Muslims respectfully and gently if they are willing to condemn this element of their faith, even as we condemn the Christianity that fought the Crusades, for example, or that shows itself in some of the far right politics of the Western world today? These are attempts to hold together intention, both the Christian call to forgiveness and to justice. These are immense and complex themes, which there is no space to engage with more fully now. But let me just say that my story and experiences, indeed those of all of us, sit today within the context of the theme of this chapter, which is hospitality and generosity, and against the backdrop of 1 Peter 4, which itself holds the importance of hospitality and generosity alongside the reality of suffering and persecution. It is important to note that Peter does not glorify suffering for its own sake and neither does he suggest that it should be endured passively. Again, this relates to the call for Christians to act and speak for justice, wherever and whenever possible. Nevertheless, Peter also reminds his small community that they should not be surprised by the suffering that they are undergoing, because Christ himself suffered and, in that sense, suffering is the default for any Christian community. Indeed, perhaps the norm for Christianity is that it should be persecuted and we should be worried when we are not experiencing persecution. Peter encourages his community and all of us to associate any suffering we undergo, because of faith, with the suffering of Christ, thereby finding comfort and even joy in its midst. In a mysterious way, suffering can take us closer to Christ. This is how my father described it, at the height of the revolution in Iran: 'The way of the cross has suddenly become so meaningful that we have willingly walked in it with our Lord near us. Our numbers have become smaller, our earthly supports have gone, but we are learning the meaning of faith in a new and deeper way.'

This is therefore part of our thinking as Christians, and should permeate our practice, when we are seeking to relate to people of other faiths, even when they may be wishing us harm. The paradox is that while there is injustice, which must be spoken out against, the suffering is also taking us closer to Christ and is part of our calling as people of faith. This is to be put, then, alongside the themes of hospitality and generosity in 1 Peter 4, but in much developed Anglican theology around inter faith relations, especially in the document *Generous Love* that was endorsed by the Lambeth Conference of 2008. While 1 Peter 4 relates specifically to hospitality within the church family, there are many scriptural passages and theological traditions that help us expand this familial imperative to one that Christians, through the church, extend to the wider world. God's love and generous hospitality, demonstrated through the inner life of the Trinity, draws us in and sends us forth to do likewise.

This is how *Generous Love* expresses it:

Our pressing need to renew our relationships with people of different faiths must be grounded theologically in our understanding of the reality of the God who is Trinity. Father, Son and Spirit abide in one another in a life which is 'a dynamic, eternal and unending movement of self-giving'. In our meeting with people of different faiths, we are called to mirror, however imperfectly, this dynamic of sending and abiding. So our encounters lead us deeper into the very heart of God and strengthen our resolve for inter faith engagement.

This has resonances with Kenneth Cragg's life and work in which he emphasised the need for Christians to learn to be both hosts and guests, with all the power imbalances and paradoxes which that involves. Cragg wrote, 'We find ourselves guests at God's banquet. "You spread a table for me" was how a psalmist saw it, speaking of the very landscape as a scene of hospitality.' We, then, have a pattern of relating where the church can be both host and guest, 'shaped and embraced within the hospitality of the Godhead'.

The wide diversity of engagements with other religious traditions that are represented at the Lambeth Conference emphasise different elements of inter faith relations, including dialogue, work for the common good, witness and evangelism. Each bishop and spouse will have important insights that somehow need to be held in tension together for the fullest and richest understanding. For some, the priority will be dialogue that seeks deeper understanding and works towards the common good – people of faith, seeking peace and reconciliation and looking to make the world a better place.

For others, this may be a far cry from your experience. Under the Islam of present-day Iran, Persian Christians are guilty of apostasy and their legal status as a church is unrecognised. How can a body that doesn't even exist engage in dialogue? Christians are charged with the mission to share their faith with their neighbours. This means that they cannot be closed communities but instead ones that reach outwards. But how to do this when you are in a minority who is fearful for your existence? Is it possible to dialogue with those who persecute you? Well, yes and no. If dialogue means conversation between equal partners based on mutual respect and understanding, then 'no'. But if the urge to dialogue is a Christian impetus to be fully present, and Christ-like, then 'yes' – to have confidence in one's faith while continuing to try to understand the other more fully. That is a kind of dialogue. When the situation arises, by offering the hand of friendship based on generosity and forgiveness, that too is dialogue in action. It is the kind of dialogue that Anglicans in Iran have participated in for much of their history.

In other contexts, there are possibilities to work collaboratively for areas of shared concern, for the common good, and for the peace of the world. The Covid-19 pandemic, tackling climate change, and indeed the very cause of religious freedom, can provide huge opportunities for partnerships across faith communities. These are valuable and they should be pursued wherever possible. To those who are fortunate enough to live in relative safety and to be able to engage in such fruitful relationships, I would gently say, 'Always remember your brothers and sisters around the world who are suffering persecution. Do not forget them and do not be silent in the face of their reality.' I would like to share an excerpt (translated into English) from one of the many letters that I have received over the years from Iranian Christians who are fearful and desperate. Having described his plight and that of his son, this person writes:

> I am aghast at the Community of Christians, sitting on their hands, not raising a finger to act, but only observing and praying. They do not do anything in the face of the evil going on. They say there is nothing they can do apart from pray ... the only sympathetic phrase we keep hearing is, 'Oh dear, what a shame.' On hearing our stories such as those who are executed or imprisoned or tortured, they repeat the same phrase so often that it becomes normal. In the words of scripture, their hearts are hardened. The hard-hearted ones who have been saved! This is no salvation. I don't want to judge but the God who said, 'I was sick and you did not visit me' is unlikely to thank them for failing to act.

I feel helpless, powerless and impotent in response to this letter. What can I possibly say or do for the writer? I carry the letter around with me and I share it when I can, as a constant reminder not to become immune to the suffering of others, even as my context in Britain allows me the freedom to build good relationships with Muslims, and people of all faiths.

What of witness and evangelism? This too is a Christian calling to be lived out graciously, gently, authentically, both in words and actions. In my way of thinking, it has nothing to do with standing on street corners and shouting Bible verses at passers-by but is about the forging of meaningful relationships that cultivate the possibility of sharing faith through deep and honest engagement. Again, context is everything, and so witness and evangelism will look different in different places, and in some parts of the world may not be possible in the way that we fully understand them. But let us be honest and admit that for many of us in the West, at least, the barriers are nothing to do with safety or fear of persecution but more to do with our own embarrassment, our misplaced fear of offending others, and our lack of commitment in developing those deep relationships of trust.

Let our final thought be for those Christians who live as minorities in often hostile and dangerous environments. Many years ago I read an article by Bernhard Reitsma called 'Strangers in the Light', which has always remained with me. He suggests that there are generally two possibilities for those who are persecuted: to withdraw from the world, or to fight for the right to ring the church bells, as he puts it, and live with the consequences. Neither approach, he says, is quite in keeping with the gospel, so what is the alternative? Surviving as a threatened minority, claims Reitsma, is only possible in the context of a strong community. The challenge, then, is neither to fight nor flight, but to build a vibrant, living, true community that becomes God's new society and seeks to engage with the world around it as best it can. In words from 1 Peter 4:19, 'let those suffering in accordance with God's will entrust themselves to a faithful Creator, while continuing to do good'. This is something we would all do well to remember and to live by, no matter what our context.

## Bishop Joseph Wandera of Kenya

I come from the Diocese of Mumias in Kenya to share stories around engagement with peoples of other faiths. How can we be a church that works together with sisters and brothers from other faiths? How can we learn from and engage in constructive dialogue? How might we cooperate in the common issues we face? I speak from my context, a largely rural diocese, where engagements with Muslims are shaped by historical but also contemporary paradigms. Mumias diocese has one of the earliest encounters with Islam in the interior of Kenya. This goes back to the 18th century when Arab traders travelling from the coast of Mombasa, on their way to Uganda, paid homage to an African monarch at the time called Nabongo Mumia. The Arab traders knew that by paying homage they would get protection and probably also some slaves and ivory and, in turn, the king would get guns to fight off his enemies – especially from within his own tribe.

In that context, therefore, the Arabs settled in Mumias and intermarried with local women and this gave Islam a stronghold. In the diocese where I serve 50 per cent of the people around us are Muslims and the remaining 50 per cent are Christians. Yet God is calling us to serve in that specific context and the way we respond is really shaped by it, which includes mutual suspicion from time to time and occasional violence. How can we work together? When I became bishop five years ago, one of the first things I did was to visit the local Jamia mosque in Mumias town and to be welcomed by the imam for a cup of coffee. It was on the day of Eid al-Fitr, the day of breaking the fast, and that has opened immense doors in terms of my ministry with, and alongside, my Muslim brothers and sisters in the context of Mumias. We continue to work with them. In the context of Covid-19, we had joint work of advocacy around safety, and called upon our Christian communities to wash their hands and to use masks in their marketplaces, and this has proved a very, very fruitful form of engagement with them. We have been involved in joint clean-up exercises in our small town of Mumias. Muslim youth and Christian youth joined together to clean our markets. In Nairobi where I served at St Paul's University, I co-founded the Centre for Christian-Muslim Relations in Eastleigh, an area that is largely occupied by Somali Muslims. We have had very productive engagements, whereby Muslim and Christian young people have come together to share one another's stories of faith.

The Nigerian novelist Chimamanda Ngozi Adichie has warned against the danger of having just one story, so I now share a second story, that of mutual suspicion and conflict. The popular assumptions about Muslim politics as inflexible, authoritarian and under-achieving, which in a sense is a global story about Islam and Muslims, plays out in our local villages as they look at us as Christians. In Kenya, where I come from, our neighbour is Somalia and our story is one of occupation in Somalia and many years of war. Kenya and other East African countries have suffered terror over the years, including the attacks on the American Embassy, Garissa University, Dusit and in many other places. All these happenings, on the global scale and at the local level, impact how we relate to Muslims and sometimes it makes it extremely difficult for us to be faithful witnesses of the story of Jesus in that context. It is a story of polemics, street preaching, and castigating what others believe. In one particular case, a Seventh Day Adventist was preaching in Mumias and he said that the reason why Muslims do not eat pork is because when the Prophet Muhammad was buried, a pig dug up his body and ate it. When the Muslims in Mumias came to the Jamia mosque for their Friday Salah prayers, they were saying to one another that there was someone in the town who was abusing them. They decided to go and teach him a lesson and marched towards the space where the preaching was taking place. One person was murdered, Bibles were torn into pieces, and bicycles were destroyed. Our story, then, is also a story of some serious conflict side by side with peaceful coexistence in Kenya. A phobia against Islam is manifested in many other ways in our thoughts and ideas and expressions. Islamic courts are seen as only being about amputating the hands of petty thieves. The story is not just our story. It is an image that plays out in our global world. Prejudice has persistently contributed to historical antagonisms and animosity, making working together with Muslims in Mumias very difficult. We slip into a different mode of existence, from the peace of coexistence and harmony and sharing one another's story, to mutual distrust and protectionism.

My invitation to each one of us is to look at the positive possibilities around working together with Muslims. It is true that we want to tell the story of Jesus. But how? How can we tell it if we are not also building positive relationships and friendships? We must all look out for opportunities, for platforms, for spaces to extend generosity, because 1 Peter invites us to do so. In those spaces we shall develop confidence in telling the amazing story of grace, how Jesus has saved us, and how he invites all others around us into the building of his Kingdom.

## Archbishop Linda Nicholls of Canada

Through her personal story, Bishop Guli has shared some of the complexities of inter faith relationships, where political and social dynamics challenge such relationships. Over the past 125 years, waves of immigrants and refugees have brought the religions of the world into Canada. Our large urban centres are highly multicultural and multifaith. My landlord during my curacy was Muslim, neighbours in my last parish were Orthodox Jews, and within a few kilometres of my home can be found a Zoroastrian temple, a mosque, several synagogues and a Hindu temple. In recognition that loving our neighbour includes every neighbour near and far, it is essential to respect and understand the values and beliefs of those with whom we share our communities and our world. It is also essential to examine ourselves to ask whether our own expressions of faith are consistent with the gospel and the call to hospitality. Christians have a long history of antisemitism in our relationship with our Jewish neighbours. From a too-quick blaming of Jews for the crucifixion, to the scapegoating of Jewish peoples in ways that contributed to the Holocaust, the Christian community is called to repentance.

In Canada, Christian–Jewish dialogue has sometimes struggled as Christian communities criticise the actions of the State of Israel yet also desire a relationship with Judaism that supports Jewish people in the face of recurring antisemitism and violence, both at home and abroad. In the face of strained relationships, the Anglican Church of Canada in 1992 revised our Book of Common Prayer, removing the third collect for Good Friday for the conversion of the Jews, recognising that God has a particular and special relationship with the Jewish people through the Abrahamic covenant that is not ended by the coming of Jesus. However, we missed the opportunity to remove a similar prayer from a selection of occasional prayers at our General Synod in 2019. So, after careful preparation and consultation with Jewish scholars and rabbis, a resolution to replace this prayer with a more appropriate one was proposed. We invited a local rabbi, Adam Stein, to address the General Synod, which he did with humour, grace and honesty. The first reading of the resolution passed easily. It will come for a second reading and hopefully final affirmation at our next General Synod in 2023. The prayer now reads, 'O God, who did choose Israel to be thine inheritance, have mercy upon us and forgive us for violence and wickedness against our brother Jacob. The arrogance of our hearts and minds have deceived us, and shame has covered our face. Take away all pride and prejudice in us and grant that we, together with the people whom thou didst first make thy own, may attain to the fullness of redemption which thou has promised to the honour and glory of thy most holy name. Amen.' Rabbi Stein commented, 'I think it is such a wonderful thing and a really wonderful feeling for us. That a prayer that certainly made the Jewish community feel uncomfortable might soon be replaced with one that's so beautiful and so positive.' Rabbi Reuben Poupko of Montreal, speaking on behalf of the Canadian rabbinic caucus, commended the Synod for its principled decision which represents a milestone in Anglican–Jewish relations, and further said that it has sent a strong signal to the Jewish community that we stand with them against antisemitism both past and present.

Extending hospitality to our neighbour requires us to offer respect and dignity, to treat them as we wish to be treated in all things, upholding freedom and safety and recognising them as part of the family of God in which all humanity shares. This is one small example of extending hospitality to an inter faith partner through self-examination, recognising where our words and actions create barriers to welcome and sharing. As Bishop Guli mentioned, another arena for direct cooperation is in actions for the common good of our communities. The needs of the homeless and poor cross all religious lines, inviting joint responses; inter faith cooperation for housing projects, community gardens and food banks extend hospitality through one another, to the whole community. These actions happen right across Canada wherever people of faith choose to act together for the common good, encounters in which we serve others, deepen understanding and enrich our lives, helping us to witness to the generous hospitality of Christ.

## Archbishop Samy Fawzy of Egypt

Egyptian society is a very religious society and religion plays a very important role in the lives of Egyptians, both Muslims and Christians. The church and the mosque are a key presence in secular Egyptian society and cannot be separated from it. Egyptians have lived in a pluralistic society for 15 centuries, with all its joys and pains. Therefore, dialogue and inter faith relations are of paramount importance for all Egyptians. This led us to establish the new Christian–Muslim Partnership and Study Centre in April 2022. It is the first centre of its kind in any of the churches in Egypt.

Dialogue and inter faith relations first begin when people meet people of other faiths and sow seeds of friendship. This is its first principle: it is people meeting people rather than the creation of theoretical impersonal systems. It is a live dialogue that takes place between neighbours and friends. Our relationship with God and our mission to the world cannot be separated from our relationship to our neighbour, to their faith and my faith in the society of today, not simply to coexist but to interact and co-relate. Cultural centres in Cairo and Alexandria are instrumental in bringing together hundreds of young Muslims and Christian youth from the ages of 18 to 25 to share in cultural activities within the church walls, and in the arts: music, poetry and drama.

Second, dialogue depends upon mutual understanding and trust. This involves meeting people, listening carefully to their account of faith, and sharing with them an account of our faith. We live in a situation of permanent dialogue, we share the same land, we share the same history, and we share the same destiny. The daily encounter of Christians with Islam has greatly affected our theological outlook, our values and traditions, and our understanding of ourselves. Dialogue as an exchange of information about one another's religion, though it is valuable, does not seem very important. In Egypt, however, the understanding and the reputation of religion does change with contemporary economic, religious, political and social challenges. Inter faith dialogue includes dialogue between Muslims and Christian leaders. It is common to find pictures of Muslims and Christian leaders together in the pages of the newspapers and this removes barriers of misinterpretation and misunderstanding in the society in general. Religious institutions have a major role to play in reaching a common mind on crucial issues relating to the Christian community, such as issues of citizenship in an Islamic society, the right to reach senior positions in government, assurance of no persecution, and the freedom to build new churches. Forums are needed to provide encounter and fellowship between Christians and Muslim leaders.

Third, dialogue makes it possible to share and serve within the community. This kind of dialogue seeks to build the community. It is people from different faiths meeting together to address common problems. The church's entire existence is shaped by its living among Muslims. We need a coherent and relevant theology to make us more reliable partners with our neighbours. Now our common mission is one of building a new theology that is strong enough to allow mutual witness and, at the same time, to resist any temptation to compromise. Our mission is apparent: it is a call to renewal of the entire human community. This is essentially a transformation of human beings, community and the whole creation as together we develop Egypt and, as it were, plant a tree of hope. We want partnership to create harmony in society through seminars and workshops, by religious leaders, on how to live together to defuse tension in villages across Egypt. We bring young people from very difficult places to our hospitals and schools and give them two or three weeks of education on how Muslims and Christians can live together in harmony.

Finally, dialogue is a means of authentic witness if we enter dialogue with a firm commitment to our faith. Time and again dialogue gives an opportunity for authentic witness and with this kind of dialogue there is a possibility of authentic witness and spiritual encounter and mutual respect, in which each can testify to his or her own faith without fear of prejudice. Also, through dialogue each religion has the opportunity to find its own beliefs more clearly, which results in a mutual understanding with more clarity. The distinctiveness of each religion must be acknowledged and respected. Any attempt to pass judgement on another tradition has to be rejected. In conclusion, there is a need for dialogue on all levels, both in a personal capacity and by more formal means, to reach a point of acceptance that there are differences but also points of mutual agreement. This kind of dialogue needs to be formed and progressed from both religions.

# 24

# Discipleship

## Archbishop Howard Gregory of Jamaica and the West Indies

When the Lambeth Conference of 1988 indicated that there would be a Decade of Evangelism this never really worked in our diocese, because we could never agree on exactly what is meant by evangelism. There were some who just wanted to have a tent with a speaker on the platform, but the bishop at the time would have none of this. And so the Decade pretty much passed us by. This time around, then, it was clear that we would have to do better. I was very intentional about the way we approached intentional discipleship, as the Anglican Consultative Council had asked us to be. In its call it indicated that every province, diocese and parish in the Anglican Communion was to adopt a clear focus on intentional discipleship and produce resources to equip and enable the whole church to be effective in making new disciples of Jesus Christ. As in most parts of the Anglican Communion, discipleship has been understood in terms of initiation into the body of Christ, through the sacrament of holy baptism, which is most frequently administered in infancy. In this context, the term 'discipleship' can be used in an all-encompassing sense to embrace everyone in the church who has been baptised. So the question may be asked, 'What is different about our understanding of discipleship as inherent in our baptism in this focus on intentional discipleship, and why has this emphasis become necessary for us as Anglicans?'

I will speak from several perspectives but primarily from that of our diocese, and informed by a Roman Catholic, Sherry Waddell, in her book *Forming Intentional Disciples*, with which I believe many of us may be familiar. She argues, speaking from the Roman Catholic perspective, that many members of the church are essentially at a passive stage of spiritual development. I believe this is true of my context and you may feel it applies to yours. The fundamental problem, Waddell argues, is that most of our people are not yet disciples. She found that among Christians, baptised or not, there is a kind of pre-discipleship stage where many are located. This speaks to our situation here. Intentional discipleship, she argues, begins when people have the opportunity to hear the Good News of the gospel, renew their own baptismal covenant, consciously choose Christ as their own personal Lord and Saviour, and commit themselves actively in the life of their church. The prevailing milieu in many churches in our diocese has been a preoccupation with the care of the existing members, rather than trying to increase the membership of these churches. Our churches are facing a decline in membership, decline in finances, and increased costs for the maintenance of systems and structures. In our diocese, we have church buildings that are as old as 300 years. You can imagine what the maintenance of some of those can be.

The question therefore became 'How are we going to proceed?' Consequently, steps were taken to communicate to the faithful that the Season of Intentional Discipleship calls us back to a focus on our baptismal covenant and what it means to be disciples of Jesus Christ in every sphere of life. Intentional discipleship, then, is first of all a call to a sense of consciousness regarding our identity in Christ, to grow in our relationship with Christ, to allow the living Christ to shape our lives, and to be a witness to our faith in word and actions, in the family, in the workplace, in the community and, of course, within the fellowship of the church. The faithful exercise of intentional discipleship, then, will lead others to Christ – the discipling dimension – and to a living, growing and vibrant church.

The first step in proceeding with the diocesan thrust involves seeking access to resources available at the Communion level, resources that will help to spell out the programme and its primary focus. And, to this end, an invitation was extended to Canon John Kafwanka who was then responsible for the mission desk at the Anglican Communion Office and who willingly agreed to stage training events in Jamaica that would involve a group of potential leaders for the programme. He was accompanied by Canon Mark Oxbrow and Archbishop Nicholas Drayson. These initial sessions were well attended and had enthusiastic support from participants right across the diocese. These sessions were subsequently followed by seminars and workshops within the area of Kingston, one of the three regions within the diocese; and this aspect played the leading role in the programme. Attendance at the workshops far exceeded any previous experiences of such events. From the outset, there seemed to be high levels of enthusiasm for the programme. As a result of the workshops run by John Kafwanka and the other members of his team, it was determined that it would be a good idea to conclude the workshops with a service to launch the Season of Intentional Discipleship in the diocese. It was attended primarily by some of the clergy and laity who had participated in the initial workshops, or those who had expressed an interest in participating in subsequent activities.

Communicating this across the entire diocese to get their involvement for the next step of introducing the call to a Season of Intentional Discipleship would be the job of the annual Diocesan Synod, when the clerical and lay leadership of the diocese were gathered together as a forum for delving into the nature of the call and what it meant for us as a diocese. The Synod theme for 2018 was 'Intentional Disciples Called and Empowered'. This was subsequently followed up by regional seminars and workshops within the region of Kingston (one of the three regions) as well as in other regions. Kingston itself played a key role in all of this.

As a result of these initial seminars, the decision was made to produce a series of Bible studies in a publication that could be used during the upcoming Lenten season by both individuals and congregations, but that could also be used at other times in the liturgical year. The enthusiasm for this Bible study material was unprecedented. *The Bible Study Guide* was a direct response to the call for the Season of Intentional Discipleship and was written by a team of committed Anglicans that included ordained and lay persons under the oversight of the then suffragan Bishop of Kingston, the Right Reverend Robert Thompson. The Bible study material was shared with the House of Bishops of the province, and was subsequently used by some of the dioceses within the province as a Lenten study. Being that the Bible studies material was intended for use throughout the year and not just for the Lenten period, it appealed to a wide readership and was used by individuals in various Bible study groups, fulfilling our hope that the material would be used extensively across the diocese. In fact, we had to do several reprintings because we ran out of copies. There had not been any material of a similar nature in recent years that was used by congregations across the diocese.

Various activities took place to get the 300 congregations in the Diocese of Jamaica involved. There were deanery and parish days when congregations could come together and focus on intentional discipleship. We had residential workshops, and intentional discipleship prayer was formulated across the diocese, such as an intentional discipleship prayer that is now used in congregations every Sunday and at other times. As we reported to the Anglican Communion Office, we were also asked to share a video of what was happening in the Diocese of Jamaica and the Cayman Islands.

What is the impact on the diocese? What have we been noticing from this engagement with the Season of Intentional Discipleship? We have seen a significant increase in lay involvement in ministry and mission and the Covid-19 pandemic did not really hinder this. In fact, what the pandemic did was to reveal an enthusiasm that manifested itself in things like care packages, telephone ministries to persons who were unable to come to church, and the recognition that the clergy cannot do all of the pastoral care – and demonstrating that lay people were key in sustaining us through the pandemic. We have also seen unparalleled registrations for lay reader training. I have been pushing for the development of lay readers within our diocese for a while and under the current programme we have had 200 lay people register for this, which has been online. We have never before had such numbers registering for a lay leadership programme. There has also been increased interest in the Bible studies and teaching activities online. I believe some of you will have experienced this in your own diocese. People are tuning in and sharing information about where Bible studies are to be found online as well as other teaching activities, all of which demonstrate the level of enthusiasm and interest arising out of this programme.

As in most places, Covid-19 has had its impact, with the pandemic curtailing many of the activities planned for the future. Inevitably, this has changed some aspects of the focus for the discipleship programme. At the same time, it has served to highlight the option of using technology in promoting activities associated with a Season of Intentional Discipleship, just as it has served to empower many members of the laity to deepen their involvement in the mission and ministry of the church, and respond to the needs and challenges that have been evident during the pandemic. There are many ongoing ministries in the diocese, many of which have been in existence for a number of years. For example, we still operate 200 schools, we have children's homes, and we have a hospital, and some of those were established in previous generations.

Therefore, the intentional discipleship programme is directed at motivating, engaging and energising the present generation in their discipleship, and not just continuing with what we have inherited from past generations. We are comfortable that, yes, we are doing discipleship and being intentional. This basically sums up our approach at this point in the Diocese of Jamaica and the Cayman Islands.


## Bishop Eleanor Sanderson of Aotearoa New Zealand

Greetings, brothers and sisters in the name of Christ. From Bishop Justin and Jenny Duckworth, and from my husband Tim and myself, greetings from the Diocese of Wellington. It is my joy to share some of our adventures with Jesus together over the last 20 years or so, concluding with a period of shared episcopal ministry. We began this week in Canterbury with a call for evangelism and stood together in commitment that we would make disciple-making our priority. So today, as we come towards the end of the week, I want to bring us back to that moment and the fire that was within us that made us want to make disciple-making the priority of our ministry. I want to help us not to let go of that fire by illustrating what is at stake when we choose to make disciple-making our priority, but also to share and encourage you with some examples of the joy of life in the Diocese of Wellington as my colleagues and I have lived into that call, based on a decision made many years ago in the diocese that this would be our central call.

I want to begin with the big picture. When God renews the church, God often does so by a fire and a passion from a radical edge. This then reminds the rest of the church what a Jesus-shaped life looks like. It has been seen throughout history, and right now, within our secular and often nominally believing context, we are experiencing renewal by the Holy Spirit who is initiating a broad act of renewal through our experience of church life at a radical edge. In the diocese this is seen in a whole range of intentional residential missional communities, and new monastic orders, with all participants being deeply committed to the biblical priority of serving those who are last and least. These communities are shaped by a clearly focused missional discipleship culture.

As bishops and families in mission together, we felt called by the Holy Spirit to live, model, create and nurture this way of life ourselves, in different missional communities and, importantly, to minister a unifying and renewing missional discipleship call within, through and for our whole church. The seed of this renewal, I think, was already at the very heart of our Anglican ecclesiology and is part of our core Anglican DNA. This is because Anglican ecclesiology is based on place, connected by covenant. Every bishop here has made vows to be dedicated to particular people in particular places with a particular gospel purpose, and we have given our whole lives and our whole hearts to those calls and covenants. Now that same invitation, and challenge, is for every single follower of Jesus Christ to choose to give their life for particular people in a particular place for a particular gospel purpose.

One example of this is one of our young adult communities filled with young people who are doing just that. This is our Anglican Youth Movements – or YM, as we call them – which began in one house with Bishop Justin and Jenny who, when they stepped into leadership in our diocese, brought with them decades of on-the-ground experience of residential missional communities. They brought a vision of new monastic community life and of its multiplication across the lower North Island – and, more broadly, within Aotearoa New Zealand – of people dedicated to serving neighbourhoods in need. So when these young people arrived at the bishop's house it was converted from a normal house into a home for many, many youth workers. It began with seven of them but at one point there was 20 (but this is another story as to how it became 20). Each of those young adults was committed to the daily rhythms of prayer and to voluntary youth work in our parish and our diocese. Their lives were shaped by weekly team nights, where missional discipleship tools and contextual youth-work tools were taught. These young adults are supported to then lead broader youth ministry, and potentially to become leaders in new YM houses. This is because this model enables multiplication.

After initiating this community, Justin and Jenny handed over every-day leadership and growth to another amazing couple, Luke and Amelie. They led this YM work for many years, and they lived with their young family alongside 14 other young adults in a cluster of houses continuing the same rhythms. In these first years they ate every meal together, and everyone paid rent. Luke and Amelie then relocated, from what was a more suitable house for their family in a better area, to the cathedral area and a less suitable house, but also to pay more rent in order to renew our church. They are highly committed, highly sacrificial followers of Jesus who have amazing personal testimonies of their own transforma-tion in Jesus. And they are raising missional disciples who will model and then extend God's call to people who will go anywhere and do anything for Jesus, for the ordained priests, and for our diocese. Recently, Luke and Amelie have begun a new missional adventure in a rural part of our diocese.

Over the last 20 years some 14 new missional communities have been formed across the Anglican Diocese of Wellington. Inspired by the Spirit, each community carries a particular call within their particular context. While one is focused on Christian community development, others offer radical hospitality, prisoner reintegration, refugee support, shared com-munity, caring for the land, ministry among street communities, church planting and abandoned places. Initially, these were clustered in the inner city and surrounding suburbs of Wellington. Many of these communities have now multiplied and spread to outer suburbs and towns and also throughout the region as a whole. These missional edge communities provide discipleship and formation for young adults and are commonly formed by two or three neighbourhood homes where Christian mission and community can be lived out among those on the edge. All these com-munities share a common commitment to evangelism and, as missional movements, to live as disciples, as family and to follow the biblical call to prioritise those who are last and the least. In growth, energy and mission-ary zeal, these missional communities have blessed the church through the planting of new parish units and the renewing of local congregations.

They have clearly built within them discipleship training, implicitly, in daily, weekly and annual rhythms. This in particular includes one-on-one mentoring as they share life together, with a leadership structure tailored to multiplication and, in the vast majority of cases, have no reliance on outside sources for financial stability. They are resourced by the members themselves, who relocate for the gospel, who get local jobs, whatever they can do, to live and love the neighbourhoods that God calls them into.

In our theological college in Aotearoa New Zealand, St John's, there is a very, very narrow door that you have to enter to get into the chapel. Above the door, the words 'narrow the gate, not the city' are written in Greek. From my experience, it is clear that sometimes God gives us narrow-gate moments, times of focusing and pruning so that we can experience more fruitful times when Jesus asks us to let go of something, to not say 'yes' to an invitation, to give things away, not because those things are bad but because we need to do that out of faithful obedience to him. Right now, in our individualistic and self-consumed context, the invitation to covenant ourselves to a particular people and place in gospel purpose feels like that narrow-gate moment.

But such a community does not need to be a residential community, it can look very different. We have needed a common language and clear and simple discipleship tools that can be easily shared and easily copied and, most importantly, are easily accessible for everyone. In our parish ministry contexts, we have begun to speak of a discipleship pathway that follows the journey of faith from when the gospel is encountered, to when belief in Jesus leads to growth in faith, and then to making a commitment to some form of missional discipleship and community, which has within it the capacity to then release new expressions of discipleship, community and mission. In a parish setting, it can look something like this very simple model of missional community. These are missional communities that are embedded in the very life of our parishes, such as a men's group, a family games night, a gathering of parents supporting neurodiverse children. The possibilities are as big as your imagination. All kinds of mission can flow within the life of a parish. They all have the DNA of clear leadership by people who have been discipled and are confident to disciple others who can shape a pattern of activity around fellowship, service and encountering God, and can do so with a clear missional focus, called and invited by the Holy Spirit.

Just as communities grow best in the support of one another, so too we find that the central renewing of discipleship grows best in fellowship, and the encouragement of broader groupings of parishes, churches and denominations. People who said that they wanted to prioritise discipleship and journey together for four years, as a particular group for learning and practical community, encouraged one another on this journey to not become distracted but to place discipleship culture at their heart. I could talk for a very long time about what we have learned and what we are still learning on this journey. But here are some very brief headlines.

The first is that it works! People do come to faith, people grow in discipleship and lead multiplication. I do not see it fail but I do see it get frustrated, endlessly. Sometimes we can self-sabotage ourselves as the church. We have to confess that sometimes we have sat together and questioned the wisdom of God, to the extent of whether renewal is even possible. But it keeps going, it creeps on, it is happening.

Second, that these simple toolkits of discipleship have been immediately adopted and embraced by those who are fresh in faith, and also by those who already are in wholehearted expressions of missional discipleship, and who see these tools as something to explain what they are already doing. But they can often be rejected and critiqued by those who do not fall easily into those categories, particularly when it becomes an academic exercise and not about our lives being transformed. This makes me feel really sad and it makes me feel like that moment in the Gospels when Jesus is saying to the religious leaders, 'You are holding the keys to the kingdom in your hand, you are preventing other people from going in, and you are not even going in yourselves.' It is such a huge, significant shift in our context: to move away from a 'pick and mix' approach to spiritual self-growth, to submitting one to another in that DNA of 'people, place and gospel purpose'. But it is a necessary shift in our secular context, and it is a necessary shift for my generation, those who have no nominal church option left for them. In some places the Anglican expression of our church is simply ceasing to exist. We *have* to multiply missional discipleship to receive the treasures of the Kingdom, that which is old and that which is new, to be passed on to the next generation.

The missional discipleship of the edge communities can sometimes be characterised by vulnerability and volatility. Sometimes this is seen in frustration, dismissal, missional dilution. Holding both together is not for the faint-hearted. But there can be creative renewing tension when we do so. The Holy Spirit is genuinely renewing our church in this way. And we are so thankful for God's initiative.

I want to finish by giving you two images from our land, and one brief story, so that in a month or so, or in a year, when the inbox has piled up, and all the other things that can distract us from discipleship-making weaken our resolve, you can recall these images. First, we have witnessed this week the beginning of the 'communion forest'. Archbishop Don Tamihere of Aotearoa uses the language of the forest to best define discipleship. The word for 'forest' in Maori does not actually mean a neighbourhood of trees, but the abundant interconnected flourishing of life that a true forest generates. So, for example, a commercial pine plantation is not a forest. It has some impressive structures, but it has no biodiversity or ecological life that warrants the term. So, in a similar way, if disciples make peace, they do not make the sort of peace that you get when you turn off the television, a dead peace like the dead life of the commercial pine plantation. The sort of peace that disciples make is the abundant peace and fullness of life that the English language struggles to translate from the beautiful biblical word 'shalom'. Is the church that we give our lives for, then, the one that we serve in a neighbourhood, teeming with flourishing peace and life, of men, women and children from every walk of life, who come together as the extended family of God? Or are we standing amid some impressive structures that are seriously lacking in life?

The second example is the cultural process of welcoming in Aotearoa. This is the detailed process that happens when a person or a group is welcomed into the Maori meeting house. This process finishes with the *hongi*, the exchange of breath, when the noses are pressed together, and two separate people join as one. But at the start of the process of welcoming there is a very important moment when those who are welcoming extend a peace offering to those who are coming. This offering is laid down on the ground in the space between the peoples, and it is often a leaf or a small branch. This reminds me of our gospel and its invitation to be welcomed into the very heart of God, where divine and human breath once again flow as one. An invitation is offered, a peace offering laid down in the gap between us, which is the life of Jesus. Those entering have to choose to humble themselves to bend down to intentionally pick up this peace offering, as a sign that they have chosen the way of peace and that they come in peace. When we bend down and humble ourselves, and choose to learn continuously, and to live a Jesus-shaped life, a life of discipleship, we choose peace. But if those who are entering do not intentionally bend down to pick up this peace offering, they will intentionally or unintentionally tread upon it and, believe me, if that happens in Aotearoa during the ceremony the warriors rise up and all hell breaks loose. Brothers and sisters, too many of our people, and in too much of our other lives do we unintentionally tread upon the peace offering of Christ when we do not humble ourselves as learning disciples of a Jesus-shaped life, and heaven does not hold sway in our world as a result. This was why our Anglican Consultative Council called our church to a Season of Intentional Discipleship. It came from sadness at some of the particular shapes in our world that did not reflect a Jesus-shaped life: the shape of racial atrocities; the shape of complicit news and unjust economic systems; the shape of a normalised nominal church culture. Within the non-indigenous communities in New Zealand we bear witness to all of those, but it is the challenge of nominalism that is first and foremost: nominal belief and belonging that is a gateway not to heaven or hell, but to other kingdoms that do not bow their knee to the name of Jesus. This is what is at stake if our church culture is not passionately committed to whole-of-life discipleship-making; when we cannot continue to testify to our deliverance from the kingdom of darkness into the Kingdom of God's glorious light, which is actually at the heart of God's heart. What is at stake is that the people Jesus died for will not get to hear about it and will not have the opportunity to live the resurrected life as a co-heir with Jesus of his earthly and heavenly Kingdom.

Finally, a story to help you keep going if your context is one where nominalism has become normalised. When I was vicar of a parish I was visited by someone who had recently retired and wanted to do something with their life. I invited him to be part of one of our discipleship groups. Through that he then began to be one of the leaders in our church, in the vestry and organising community activities. On an away day we were each sharing what God was saying to us. This man, who had had a highly professional working life, began to cry. He sobbed and sobbed and then he said, 'I never knew that living without Jesus could be lifeless. And I'm so scared I have not got enough of my life left. Why did I not know this earlier?'

Friends, life, death, that is always the choice of God. May we choose to both live and share the abundant Jesus-shaped life.

# 25

# The Decade Ahead

## Cardinal Luis Antonio Tagle, Pro-Prefect of the Dicastery for Evangelization, Rome

Dear friends, sisters and brothers in the Lord Jesus. Greetings of joy and peace. I thank the Archbishop of Canterbury for inviting me to the Lambeth Conference and to contribute to the theme of the church of the first letter of Peter for the coming decade. I stand before you trembling with fear. I am neither an expert on 1 Peter, nor an expert reader of the future. So, please bear with my sharing, which relies heavily on images and narrative. I tried to imagine the first letter of Peter being addressed to me, to the church and the world of today, the world that I know in a limited way, and I was struck by the images used by the author of this letter, like sojourners of the Dispersion (1:1), aliens and sojourners (2:11), 'once you were not a people, but now you are God's people' (2:10), a chosen race, a royal priesthood, a holy nation, a people of God's own (2:9), living stones built into a spiritual house, in Jesus the living stone (2:4–5). And as God's people in Jesus, they will be called evildoers by non-believers (2:12), they will be vilified for not engaging in licentious behaviour (4:14), but by imitating Jesus they will maintain good conduct among non-Christians (2:12). They will not return insult for insult (2:22), nor evil for evil (3:8), they will be of one mind, sympathetic, loving, compassionate, humble (3:8); they will be ready to give an explanation for the reason for their hope, in the midst of persecution and suffering (3:15). And what is the reason for their hope? The resurrection of Jesus Christ from the dead (1:3). Observing their good works, their persecutors may hopefully glorify God (2:12). These are a few of the images that struck me now. Along with the original readers of the first letter of Peter, I also long for this spiritual house. I dream of this home for the church, for the human family and for creation. Let us dream together. And let the dream purify us today.

Allow me to offer some elements of that dream presented by 1 Peter. First, the letter is addressed to Christians in the diaspora (the Dispersion) where they were made to feel like strangers, and even exiled. Do we still feel like travellers or temporary settlers or guests moving towards a future homeland? I ask this question of myself and now all of you because sometimes we become so established in our ways and projects that we start thinking of ourselves as *owners* of lands, of peoples and of ideas. Pope Francis always talks of a church that goes forth, a pilgrim church. I imagine the church, which is a spiritual home, in constant encounter with people in very diverse conditions of life, a church that thinks of itself as a community on a journey.

Second, 1 Peter reminds me of the displaced peoples of today, the exiles, the travellers, those who are on the move today, like the forced migrants, the refugees, the victims of human trafficking, slavery, prejudice, systematic persecution, wars and environmental catastrophes. And when they reach a new place, their condition does not necessarily become better. As strangers, they are often avoided, marginalised and blamed for the ills in society. I hear the first letter of Peter asking, 'How are we as church and as a human family dealing with millions of homeless and dispersed people? Will they find hospitality and compassion?' One fundamental question is how do we see and relate with *the other*, with those who differ from us? We are brought once again to the question of diversity in building our common home, which is built from diverse peoples. We admit with sadness that even within the church ethnic and cultural issues ruin the spiritual home. Dreaming of a common human family is becoming difficult even for future generations because of traumatic memories caused by years of neglect, violence and wars. I do not know what will happen in this coming decade, when we already deal with children who have been traumatised by violence, by neglect, by abuse. Will they listen to the good news of constructing a common home?

We note that building relationships faces a contemporary challenge in populism. Pope Francis sees the use of populism as a key for interpreting society. Social media have influenced daily language by spreading this problematic use of the words 'populism' and 'populist'. As Pope Francis writes, 'In recent years, the words "populism" and "populist" have invaded the communications media and everyday conversation. As a result, they have lost whatever value they might have had, and have become another source of polarisation in an already divided society. Efforts are made to classify entire peoples, groups, societies and governments as "populist" or not' (*Fratelli Tutti*, 156). And it is sad to note that so-called populist demagogues use or misuse religion, for their interests, undermining efforts at developing relationships and forming a human family.

There is also another phenomenon of feeling strange to one another. We cannot ignore the intergenerational otherness, experienced even within the same family. One example is the digital technological matrix

DTM, constructed using artificial intelligence, that has been reshaping or redefining human identity, human work and human relationships. In Manila, when a group of young people saw me, they asked for a selfie. I said 'Sure', and one young girl said, 'Your Eminence, we are friends.' And I looked at her and said, 'Have we met before?' She said, 'On Facebook.' I say that my generation will not use the word 'friend' for someone that you bump into casually. So when your children or grandchildren use the word 'friend', beware. They do not mean the same thing as you do. What do they mean by it? And do we consider this in evangelisation? Or do we just presume that we are connecting? These are just a few examples of such strangeness.

The first letter of Peter says, 'Come to Jesus, the living stone, so that in him, we can become living stones of God's spiritual home.' Of the many examples that I have given, let me look at one: developing cultural intelligence and learning from Jesus. Now inviting people to walk and live together requires humility. People are diverse not only because of individual human freedom but also because of culture, which is second nature to us. We talk, we relate, we eat, we grieve, and celebrate according to our cultures. Now pastoral leadership in the church requires what some people call 'cultural intelligence'. What is that? As I grow in my knowledge of how my culture has shaped me, I also try to understand how other people express their humanity in their own cultures. In the process, all traces of cultural superiority and prejudice must be admitted and purified. Humanity is required to admit that while I lack knowledge of many cultures, I am quick to judge even what I am not familiar with. So I suggest that pastoral leaders develop their capacity to appreciate other cultures, not only through sociological studies, which are helpful, but also through simple observation. For example, we can learn much about a culture through the use and arrangement of space. So, when I arrived here, I said to myself, 'What does the space say about the culture?' The understanding of time is another example. When I attend a meeting in the Philippines, we say 'Okay, let us meet at nine o'clock' and they ask 'Filipino time?', which means 'whenever you are available now'!

We know our culture through its heroes or idols: who are your children's and grandchildren's idols? What of your culture's system of reward and punishment? How does it prepare and consume food? Let us open our eyes to these things. Intercultural walking together lessens the fear of the other and allows cultures to purify and draw the best from one another, to purify one another, and to make one another good. Jesus was very much a person of his culture but he also brought God's culture to human cultures by redefining space. The Jewish culture was very clear about space: it was to be clean and pure, but Jesus touched those afflicted with leprosy. He allowed the woman to bathe his feet with her tears. It was his Father who determined the concept of family, not by blood relations but obedience to the will of God. The Syro-Phoenician woman, the good Samaritan, the repentant criminal, the centurion: we know how much Jesus suffered for offering a home to outsiders, strangers and public sinners. He identified with the strangers. He was persecuted as a threat to the holiness of God's people and God's temple. He was crucified outside the city walls. From his wounded side was born a home for aliens, sojourners and exiles. And he wants his body, the church, to be that home in him as the living stone, for his disciples to find hope and a reason to rejoice.

Let me close by narrating a past experience of mine, one that reading the first letter of Peter brought back to my memory. In this memory I see the future, Jesus' future, of not just the coming decade but beyond. In my first diocese as a bishop there was a summer camp for young people. I gave a 30-minute talk on finding one's purpose in life, after which we opened the floor to questions. The first question came from a young girl: 'Bishop, will you sing for us?' I was caught off guard. I said, 'Nobody told me that I should sing. Please ask serious sensible questions. And afterwards, I will sing for you.' There were many good and difficult questions, and I regretted inviting them to ask questions. Then one young boy asked, 'So, bishop, will you now sing for us?' So I sang them a song that everyone knew. Then after the song they came to me to ask for a blessing, a selfie, an autograph, to sign their Bibles, their books, and even their T-shirts. While this was going on I was searching for its meaning. I asked myself, 'What do they see in me? Do they see a bishop? Do they see an actor? Am I behaving myself as a bishop?' The answer came a year later, in a similar youth summer camp. One young man said to me, 'Bishop, last year you autographed my T-shirt.' I said, 'Oh, so you are one of them.' And then he said, 'I have not washed it for a year, but every night I fold it and put it under my pillow. I have not seen my father in years. He is a migrant worker. But with that T-shirt signed by you, I know I have a family in the church and the Father.'

So the gospel is proclaimed in the form of a T-shirt signed by a bishop for a young boy longing for a family, a home and the Father. Seven years ago, I visited a refugee camp, a meeting point of many people who have left their home countries and have taken perilous journeys through land and seas. They brought their families and the little that they could carry. The refugee camp was a point of convergence of peoples of different cultures, religions, economic and educational backgrounds. What unified them was a journey from poverty and war towards a dream of safety and growth for their children. Suffering is a common path for refugees, and those who assist them assist them to walk on. The woman responsible for the distribution of food, medicines and clothing in that camp was extremely efficient. When there was a pause in the work I conversed with her and learned that she was a government official in that town. So I asked her if her responsibility in the refugee camp was part of her official duties as a government official. She said no, this was volunteer work for her. So I jokingly said, 'Don't you have enough work to do in your office?' She said, 'My ancestors were refugees so I have refugee DNA. These refugees are my brothers and sisters.' She was teaching me how to walk humbly with others. And when it was time for me to leave the camp I asked one of the guards where the exit was. He pointed to a sign right beside me. As I walked that way I carried with me the pains and hopes of many brothers and sisters whose journeys continue, and I knew God would walk with them always. We don't give them a home – we are the home that God wants to build.

# 26

# Closing Sermon

## Archbishop Justin in Canterbury Cathedral

'Do not be afraid, little flock.' 'Do not be afraid, Abram. The word of the Lord endureth forever.'

When we fear, we cling to what we know. We clutch at what makes us feel in control, be that the things we own, the possessions we have stored up for ourselves, the story we tell ourselves about who we are, what our power is, what our importance is and what is possible. We want, when we are afraid, to be comfortable with the familiar and familiar with the comfortable. And these things – our assumptions, our possessions – become a comfort blanket that ultimately smothers us. For they forbid us to engage with one another and with Christ. We make our worlds and our ambitions smaller because it feels safer, and they come to define and constrain us. So the institutions, the power, the status, positions that we hold on to out of fear – personal fear for ourselves, fear for the future of the church – end up fulfilling our fears.

Let us be clear, though, about the fact that in this broken world there are very real reasons to fear. The roar of the lions is real. And the reality is that there is so much suffering. We moaned collectively when we heard of the earthquake this morning. There is so much uncertainty. There are people here who will know the uncertainty of food supplies, the precarious nature of poverty, the insecurity of life in places of conflict and flux and natural disaster. People around the world live with the reality of these fears every day. For so many, it is very real indeed.

How can God tell us, 'Do not fear'? We do not like being told what to do. We think commands limit us. Not God's commands, though. God's commands set us free. They liberate us to step into a new world that he makes visible and known to us. We are continually being invited to begin a journey from fear to faith. When we slip from faith to fear, then Christ comes to us as he did to the fearful disciples in the upper room. He appears to us and says, 'Do not fear.' He comes to us, he does not call us to find him. We are liberated to look outwards, to imagine a new way of relating to the world around us, as well as among us, to imagine what it means to be given the Kingdom in his world. As Jesus said, the Kingdom of God is near us, the Kingdom of God is within us. It is found, as we heard so movingly yesterday, in a boy hugging a T-shirt under his pillow, signed by a bishop who made him remember that he had a father in God and an eternal Father.

Some years ago, in 2016, it was discovered, to my surprise, by a major daily newspaper in this country that the man I thought was my father was not my father. Someone else was. I am told it was the only time that the then senior legal adviser of the Church of England was seen to run. The Secretary General had said to him, 'The Archbishop has just rung up to say he is illegitimate. He said, "That is not a problem as we changed some years ago the canon regulation that said you could not be a bishop if you were illegitimate. At least I'm sure we changed the canon. Excuse me, I'm going to check!"' It had been changed in 1952 but, he said to me later on, that as he ran down the corridor he thought, 'If we have not changed it, he is not a bishop. And if he is not a bishop the priests he ordained are not priests. And if they are not priests, then the people they have married are not married!' But, again to my surprise, I found within me an unbreakable certainty that the God who knew me knows my true identity at the deepest level, at a far deeper level than just a DNA test.

There is a story that shows this was also the case for Cardinal Nguyễn Văn Thuận, the former Archbishop of Saigon, held for nine years in solitary confinement and a further four years in prison. He was eventually let out but kept in an area far from his home. He was out one day and near the forest. Three people came out of the forest and, meeting him, asked if he was a pastor. He said yes and they requested that he make a three-day journey to baptise their village. They were a people of a mountainous region. He went, and found a village that had converted to Christ by listening to a Pentecostal radio station. So he baptised them, some thousands, as Christians, certainly Catholic Christians, he said with a smile. But the Kingdom breaks down our denominational barriers and overrules our frontiers and our theological border guards.

The Kingdom is seen in how we set out as the revolutionary movement that is God's Church in Christ, for it leads us from tightly clutching to freely receiving the grace of God, from zero-sum scarcity to abundance, hospitality, generosity, because God dares us to join a whole new way of being and the Holy Spirit gives us the power to take up the dare.

What we gain is not what the world tells us we should want. What the world values is not what God values. So following God may not get us wealth or power. But it does guide us to riches beyond measure, treasure in heaven, and a world that looks just a bit more like the Kingdom, to a world where people do not suffer because of where they were born, where the scandal of poverty and huge inequality does not exist, where people are not persecuted for their faith, gender, sexuality, where we do not allow our brothers and sisters to be told that they matter by the wealthy but then are ignored materially.

In this command, 'Do not fear', our eyes are opened to God's promise. We are called again to conversion to life, a conversion that daily says to us that we should pray to God: 'I trust you to hear my prayers, my protests, my praises, my laments, to hear my heart crying out to you in anger'; that says, 'Whatever happens I trust that in some wonderful and mysterious way you feed me for eternity, with a wafer and wine over which a prayer has been said, and that in the host I see a crucified God.' This kind of conversion expands our world.

We have met, over the past weeks and days, with people from all the corners of the globe, from contexts and experiences that are totally alien to us. In these meetings we have found the antidote to fear, as we read in John's letters, that perfect love casts out fear. God's promises will be fulfilled. He will draw abundance out of barrenness and riches out of our poverty. That is his promise to us and this releases us to be radical, bold, courageous, revolutionary *today*, to have the courage to have faith in God, to be brave enough to defy the world, even to defy other Christians, by loving one another without ceasing, to have the courage shown by bishops and spouses here, clergy and laity around the Anglican Communion who make the Good News known to those who live in fear and who go to church in greater numbers the week after a suicide bomb attack has killed 160 of them, who fly with the Missionary Aviation Fellowship to a remote part of Papua New Guinea and then work for a week across mountains to do confirmations, who protest against civil rights abuses, against gerrymandering of votes, against shooting unarmed people of colour in a routine traffic stop. As we grow in love, our fear shrinks and the Kingdom of God finds space, finds its rule in our hearts and in our lives as God's people.

Dear sisters and brothers in Christ – no mere greeting, that – dear sisters and brothers in Christ, who to each other and to me have become dearer and dearer over the last ten days, as you, as I, go home, do not fear, take heart, take courage, because it is the Father's good pleasure to give you his Kingdom!

# PART 3

# Witnessing Together

## *The Lambeth Calls*

# 27

# Introducing the Lambeth Calls

Before the Lambeth Conference took place Archbishop Justin announced that this conference would adopt an innovative approach to its outcomes. Instead of passing resolutions, as had happened at previous conferences, it would adopt a process called 'Lambeth Calls'. These would be declarations and affirmations on themes discussed in the plenary sessions at the conference which bishops could consider and adopt. Each Call would have specific requests which they could enact themselves or call on others to reflect and act on. Each Lambeth Call would be finalised after bishops had given feedback on their content. The revised Calls would then be offered as a gift to the Anglican Communion, and member churches would be invited to consider the Calls in their own synods and other bodies if they wished. It was expected that several requests from them would be taken up by the Anglican Consultative Council and other agencies.

Drafting groups were convened with members from across the Anglican Communion, bringing together those with knowledge and expertise in the respective areas covered by the Calls. The groups were asked to produce a text which would include a link to the book of 1 Peter, usually including a quote from the letter and an indication of how it related to the topic or issue being discussed. There would be a declaration, a section that would declare what the Christian church had generally believed about this matter and include a summary of what Anglican churches have taught and believed about it. This would be followed by an affirmation, a section that would set out what the bishops of the Anglican Communion gathered together in Canterbury in 2022 wanted to say about this matter now. Finally, there would be specific Calls, a series of requests arising from the previous two sections which would call upon bishops or provinces or the wider world to reflect, pray and, if they chose, to take some action on this issue.

Some of the specific Calls or requests would include an indication of which body within the Anglican Communion could be responsible for taking it forward.

## The drafting process

Archbishop Justin asked a small working group to oversee the preparation of the Lambeth Calls. The group was convened by Bishop Tim
Thornton and it commissioned the drafting groups for each Call. Each
drafting group was comprised of Primates and senior bishops, representing member churches from around the Anglican Communion, and was
invited to include a youth representative in their discussions. The drafting
groups also had a staff member with them, either from Lambeth Palace
or the Anglican Communion Office, to support their work. Altogether
over 50 people were involved in the drafting and writing of the Calls. The
working group also provided some editorial oversight so that the Calls
would have a consistent format and likeness.

## How the Lambeth Calls were discussed at the Lambeth
Conference

On most days of the conference a plenary session looked at a key theme.
These plenary sessions included speakers from around the Anglican Communion who presented a range of views and information about the topic
or issue (all the key presentations are printed in this book). The Lambeth
Call discussion followed the plenary each day, at which each section of
the Lambeth Call text was discussed. Bishops were seated at round tables
in small groups, the same group as for the Bible study discussions. Some
members of the drafting groups were present to answer questions when
these arose at the tables.

Responses were received from the groups through a dedicated email
account. While an attempt had been made at the beginning of the week to
provide an electronic system of registering feedback, allowing the numer-
ical recording of different responses, this was quickly abandoned in
response to objections from many bishops. Verbal and non-verbal forms
of registering assent or dissent were also tried but again abandoned. In
the end, groups sent in their own detailed feedback by email.

## The Call on Human Dignity

While most of the Calls were received positively by bishops there was
deep division over the Call on Human Dignity and its upholding of
Resolution 1.10 of the Lambeth Conference of 1998 (which includes the
statement that homosexual practice is incompatible with scripture). This

division became apparent as soon as the Calls were published a few days before the conference. As bishops arrived in Canterbury it was clear that the division was not going to be bridged. Social media and other press outlets were busy with comment and a sense of consternation from both sides of the divide.

On the day of the tabling and discussion of the Call in plenary it became clear that the conference host, Archbishop Justin, needed to intervene in some way to allow the business of the day to be completed and the rest of the conference to proceed as planned. He tells the story of what happened in the following way: 'The Lambeth Conference was an extraordinary moment because, on the Tuesday, the first Tuesday we discussed this at length, knowing how deeply divided and knowing that there were very extensive groups outside the hall, and outside the bishops, who were using all kinds of really quite unpleasant methods to try and get people to split and divide, offering money and things – and so it was a really remarkable moment. The afternoon ended with people of entirely opposite views embracing each other, and spending the rest of that week in united prayer and agreement. It was a very remarkable thing' (Press Conference on Living in Love and Faith, 20.01.2023, Lambeth Palace Library).

Archbishop Justin's own role in this transformation needs to be recognised. His intervention took the form of a letter sent to the bishops earlier in the day and then some introductory remarks on the Call at the start of the session. These remarks need to be quoted in full:

This is one of the most important sessions of this conference. In it, we come to a question – of what we believe about human dignity, including sexuality – that is deeply dividing, not only for Anglicans but for every part of God's global church.

This conference is one of the few places that we can meet and be honest with each other about what we think, listen to others and pray together. In some churches, like the Anglican Communion, the disagreement is open. In others it is behind locked doors. But in all it is real. And in all, the subject is of the greatest importance.

Most of the Call on Human Dignity (including sexuality) is uncontentious. None of us would want to argue for sexual violence in conflict, abuse of the vulnerable or violence against minorities or women.

But paragraph 2.3 is very different [with its affirmation of Lambeth 1.10]. For some here it will be a great relief. There is no attempt being made to alter the historic teaching of the vast majority of churches of the Anglican Communion. For some, this paragraph will be hugely painful, agonising emotionally, for it is felt by many to state that who they are and who they love is wrong, that they are less than fully human.

So in this very brief address, please let me state some important principles. First, the Call is about Human Dignity and also about Sexuality. The reason the two are combined is that its central theological foundation is that all human beings are of equal worth, loved by God and are those for whom Jesus died on the cross and rose to life. As St Paul says again and again in Romans, 'there is no distinction'.

Second, as we discuss this, we are all vulnerable. For the large majority of the Anglican Communion the traditional understanding of marriage is something that is understood, accepted and without question, not only by bishops but their entire church, and the societies in which they live. For them, to question this teaching is unthinkable, and in many countries would make the church a victim of derision, contempt and even attack. For many churches to change traditional teaching challenges their very existence.

For a minority, we can say almost the same. They have not arrived lightly at their ideas that traditional teaching needs to change. They are not careless about scripture. They do not reject Christ. But they have come to a different view on sexuality after long prayer, deep study and reflection on understandings of human nature. For them, to question this different teaching is unthinkable, and in many countries is making the church a victim of derision, contempt and even attack. For these churches not to change traditional teaching challenges their very existence. So let us not treat each other lightly or carelessly. We are deeply divided. That will not end soon. We are called by Christ himself both to truth and unity.

Third, there is no attempt to change people's minds in this Call. It states as a fact that the vast majority of Anglicans in the large majority of provinces and dioceses do not believe that a change in teaching is right. Therefore, it is the case that the whole of Lambeth 1.10 1998 still exists. This Call does not in any way question the validity of that resolution. The Call states that many provinces – and I say again, I think we need to acknowledge it's the majority – continue to affirm that same-gender marriage is not permissible. The Call also states that other provinces have blessed and welcomed same-sex union or marriage, after careful theological reflection and a process of reception.

In that way, it states the reality of life in the Communion today. As I said in the letter [published earlier in the day], and I re-emphasise, there is no mention of sanctions, or exclusion, in 1.10 1998. There is much mention of pastoral care. As Lambeth 1.10 also states: 'all baptised, believing and faithful persons, regardless of sexual orientation are full members of the Body of Christ' and to be welcomed, cared for, and treated with respect (1.10 1998).

Fourth, many people are watching and listening, both inside and outside the church. But we bishops, you alone and I are responsible for what is decided on this Call. When we will all answer to God on the day of judgement, we will not be able to say – and there is no vote today, but when at some point if ever we make a decision on this – we will not be able to say that I voted this or that way because others told me to. Please therefore be present, in this room or online, today. Do not spend the time looking on your phone at what others outside the room are saying. You are the shepherds of your flock as I am the shepherd of the flock that I serve. Let us not act in a way that disgraces our witness. Speak frankly, but in love.

Finally, a short comment on my own thinking. I am very conscious that the Archbishop of Canterbury is to be a focus of unity and is an Instrument of Communion. That is a priority. Truth and unity must be held together, but church history also says that this sometimes takes a very long time to reach a point where different teaching is rejected or received. I neither have, nor do I seek, the authority to discipline or exclude a church of the Anglican Communion. I will not do so. I may comment in public on occasions, but that is all. We are a Communion of Churches, not a single church.

I want to end by repeating this line from the Call on Human Dignity: 'As Bishops we remain committed to listening and walking together to the maximum possible degree, despite our deep disagreement on these issues.'

Sister and brothers, may I thank you for your patience in listening to me.

It is important to record that these remarks were followed by a spontaneous and room-filling round of applause, with most bishops standing as they applauded. As suggested above, it was a remarkable and transformative moment in the conference and allowed the discussion and revision of the Call, and all the subsequent Calls, to proceed in an open and positive way throughout the rest of the conference.

## What comes next

Feedback from the sessions was received through a dedicated email address and then distributed to the relevant drafting groups. These groups have now revised the Calls in the light of that feedback, keeping the Calls as close to the collective thinking of the bishops as possible. The revised Calls have been released in the period around Pentecost 2023.

Phase 3 of the conference (from Pentecost 2023 to the end of 2025) includes the dissemination and promotion of the Calls to the member churches of the Anglican Communion. They are being offered as a gift which those churches can receive, discuss and, if accepted, act upon. The Calls are offered to provinces, dioceses, churches, groups, commissions, networks and agencies to adopt and use as they so choose.

They are being presented in a different order from the one at the conference, in order to tie them in more closely with the seasons of the Christian year and with major international events through the Phase 3 period. They are printed in the new order below.

# 28

# Lambeth Call 1
# Discipleship

## 1 Introduction

1.1 A disciple is a learner in mind, body and spirit. In the Call that follows the bishops assembled at the Lambeth Conference ask all Anglicans to learn and learn again the loving, liberating and life-giving way of Jesus Christ in every aspect of their lives and to follow him in this. The bishops are issuing this Call because 1 Peter calls all God's people to such disciplined and whole-of-life discipleship:

> *Therefore prepare your minds for action; discipline yourselves; set all your hope on the grace that Jesus Christ will bring you when he is revealed. Like obedient children, do not be conformed to the desires that you formerly had in ignorance. Instead, as he who called you is holy, be holy yourselves in all your conduct; for it is written, 'You shall be holy, for I am holy.'* (1 Peter 1:13–16)

1.2 This is a demanding Call because of the pressures that come upon us from society and the spiritual battle faced by all. But the letter shows that we can and should depend on God's help:

> *Whoever speaks must do so as one speaking the very words of God; whoever serves must do so with the strength that God supplies, so that God may be glorified in all things through Jesus Christ. To him belong the glory and the power for ever and ever. Amen.* (1 Peter 4:11)

This Call, then, is for all Anglicans in every aspect of their lives to learn and learn again the way of Jesus Christ 'with the strength that God supplies', a strength given by the Holy Spirit, and to follow him in this.

## 2 Declaration

2.1 Jesus taught his disciples to 'Go therefore and make disciples of all nations.' The size and extent of the Anglican Communion today shows that Anglicans around the world have been doing this throughout their history with enthusiasm and commitment.

2.2 Some have commented, however, that while Christian commitment 'is a mile wide it is only an inch deep'. For example, in many places Christian commitment has been seen as nominal. To address this a Season of Intentional Discipleship and Disciple-Making (Jesus shaped life) was launched at the Anglican Consultative Council in Lusaka in 2016:

> In light of the Gospel and theological imperative to make disciples, [we] recognise the need for every province, diocese and parish in the Anglican Communion to adopt a clear focus on intentional discipleship and to produce resources to equip and enable the whole church to be effective in making new disciples of Jesus Christ. (ACC-16 Resolution 16.01)

2.3 This was re-affirmed in 2019 at ACC-17 in Hong Kong. The Season will run until ACC-19 in 2026. Up to now well over 100 dioceses and many of the 42 provinces of the Anglican Communion have formally adopted intentional discipleship as a key priority and/or have hosted con-sultations and workshops on this subject. The use of small groups are central to it. The Anglican Communion has developed many resources to support the Season and Jesus shaped life (www.anglicancommunion.org/mission/intentional-discipleship.aspx).

2.4 Many other churches around the world are also responding to the need to deepen discipleship. The Arusha Call to Discipleship of 2018, from the World Council of Churches, to which Anglicans contributed, expressed this powerfully when it declared: 'We are called by our baptism to transforming discipleship: a Christ-connected way of life in a world where many face despair, rejection, loneliness, and worthlessness.'[1] Pope Francis has also called on all God's people to become missionary disciples and has placed this Call at the heart of his ministry.[2]

2.5 As Anglicans have entered into our Season of Intentional Discipleship many have found that the Five Marks of Mission provide an inspiring and unifying set of signposts for learning and following the way of Christ. The Calls that follow therefore invite Anglicans to be formed by these so that we may live and share a Jesus shaped life more and more.

## 3 Affirmation

We the bishops assembled at the Lambeth Conference, in this Season of Intentional Discipleship, commit ourselves to learn and learn again the loving, liberating and life-giving way of Jesus Christ in every aspect of our lives, through prayer, Word and sacrament, with the strength that God supplies, so that our following of him may be renewed by the Holy Spirit and that the people of our dioceses may be encouraged to do the same.

## 4 Specific Requests (The Calls)

4.1 We call on all Anglicans, in this Season of Intentional Discipleship, to learn and learn again the loving, liberating and life-giving way of Jesus Christ in every aspect of our lives, in everyday life, through prayer, Word and sacrament, and in small groups, with the strength that God supplies, so that our following of him may be renewed by the Holy Spirit and we make disciples of others. Life-long learning is needed for this, aware of our vocation. We especially call on Anglicans to be formed by the Five Marks of Mission, as an Anglican Communion Rule of Life, as habits to acquire through regular, thoughtful and contextually appropriate expression:

- Tell – to proclaim the Good News of the Kingdom of God.
- Teach – to teach, baptise and nurture new believers.
- Tend – to respond to human need by loving service including through healing ministries.
- Transform – to work to transform unjust structures of society, challenging violence of every kind and pursuing peace and reconciliation.
- Treasure – to strive to safeguard the integrity of creation and sustain and renew the life of the earth.

4.2 We call on all leaders, lay and ordained, to enable our worship and liturgies intentionally to be a place where we are formed and transformed in our mind, body and spirit to live a Jesus shaped life, focused especially in the baptismal covenant of the Baptism service, in which the newly baptised are assured of the support of the congregation in their new life in Christ.

4.3 We call on dioceses to help parishes establish and extend small groups also for formation in discipleship and to offer and support other 'gates' into discipleship in everyday life, online and in-person, appropriate for their context, including in the workplace, schools and communities. Resources for the faith development of young children are also needed.

4.4 We call on all in our churches intentionally to sustain deep relationship with young people, in schools, congregations and communities, and to learn from those who are senior in their discipleship, and from women, the marginalised and the poor, so that this learning and transformation can take place across the whole church and for everyone to discover their gifts from Christ, using them fruitfully as they follow him.

4.5 We call on our seminaries, theological colleges and training programmes to consider giving discipleship and disciple-making a central place, reframing programmes of learning and teaching around them, so that all ministers, ordained and lay, may be equipped to enable those they serve to learn these things, not least through preaching.

4.6 We call on the Secretary General of the Anglican Communion to encourage and support progress in these areas with the help of the Commission on Evangelism and Discipleship, including through promoting the Season of Intentional Discipleship across the Communion, and to report back to the next ACC and next Lambeth Conference on the ways provinces are actively promoting intentional discipleship.

## 5 Implementation

In receiving and implementing this Call, provinces and dioceses will need to do more work on specifics, e.g. which kind of small group formation works best in their context?, what are the possibilities for church planting?, and what are the competencies that colleges, seminaries, and programmes need to instil in their graduates?

### Notes

1 R. Jukko and J. Keum, *Moving in the Spirit*, Geneva: WCC 2019.
2 *Evangelii Gaudium*, 2017.

# 29

# Lambeth Call 2
# The Environment and
# Sustainable Development

## Lambeth Call 2A
## The Environment

## 1 Introduction

1.1 We have been gifted a world of breath-taking beauty, astounding abundance and intricate interconnection. It is a world God declared good and loves.

1.2 That world is now in crisis. Climate change, biodiversity loss and pollution threaten both people and planet. Alongside these environmental challenges, and often fuelled by them, lie poverty, inequality, injustice and conflict which each damage the lives of millions of people.

1.3 Yet, this is still God's world and God calls us to respond as Easter people: bearers of hope.

1.4 The Lambeth Conference studied the book of 1 Peter. In this scripture, we are called to 'have genuine mutual love' (1 Peter 1:22), expressed in hospitality, stewardship and mutual service (diaconia) (1 Peter 4:9–10). These are essential in our care for one another and our common home, the earth.

1.5 God so loved the world (*cosmos*) that he sent his only Son into the world (John 3:16). On earth, Jesus found peace and solace in the natural world as well as inspiration for his teaching. Jesus died on the cross to bring reconciliation to the whole of creation. In Christ, 'God was pleased to reconcile to himself all things, whether on earth or in heaven, by making peace through the blood of his cross' (Colossians 1:19–20).

1.6 While the environmental challenges are huge, the Christian story is one of redemption, resurrection, transformation and hope. Jesus calls his disciples to follow in the Way of reconciliation with all creation and, through the Holy Spirit, we are empowered do so.

## 2 Declaration

2.1 Anglicans hold to Scripture and the teachings of the church, reflected in the Five Marks of Mission. These provide a clear vision and holistic framework for intentional discipleship and for being God's Church for God's World. They call us to proclaim the Good News of the Kingdom, nurture disciples, and to express our concern for people and planet, for justice, peace and care for vulnerable people, as well as our duty to safeguard creation (Genesis 2:15) and to sustain and renew the life of the earth (Fifth Mark of Mission).

2.2 Anglicans therefore not only take human well-being and creation care seriously, but also see these as missional imperatives and how we share in the 'renewed creation of heaven and earth with justice' (2 Peter 3:13).

2.3 The integrity of creation is under threat and at risk of collapse. The need to make the Fifth Mark of Mission central to our life as Anglicans has never been greater. Theologies of dominion have been used to justify exploitative and extractive behaviours, which have contributed to the current environmental crises. We need to repent of the sinful damage done through these harmful theologies and commit to change – and to call others also to repentance.

2.4 The Anglican Communion is building on the legacy of the 2008 Lambeth Conference, which made a strong commitment to the UN Millennium Development Goals and gave birth to the Anglican Alliance. It is also building on ACC-17, which reaffirmed this commitment in light of the UN Sustainable Development Goals (https://sdgs.un.org/goals).

2.5 Provinces throughout the Communion continue to respond to local, national and global societal and environmental challenges. With crisis comes opportunity: for the church to listen to God's voice, to imagine how the world could be different, and to help build towards God's Kingdom.

2.6 But the triple environmental crisis of climate change, biodiversity loss and pollution is an existential threat to billions of people and species of plants and animals across the globe. The Intergovernmental Panel on Climate Change (IPCC) has warned that it is 'code red for humanity'; 'It's now or never, if we want to limit global warming to 1.5°C'.[1] Drastic action is needed in the next three years to bring down greenhouse gas emissions to achieve net zero targets.

2.7 As a global, connected body with a shared identity that transcends national borders, the Anglican Communion has a distinctive perspective. Member churches of the Anglican Communion are involved in every part of the environmental emergency. We are the people facing devastation in disaster-stricken communities. We are all the polluters, especially in wealthy countries. We are people living in poverty and on the margins. We wield power and political influence. We are experiencing loss and damage of our land, homes and livelihoods. We are investors with financial capital. We are first-responders to disasters and those who accompany communities on the journey of recovery and resilience.

2.8 We contribute to the problem. We contribute to the solution. We are both local and global. We connect with one another, share our experiences and can leverage our networks and Anglican identity to mobilise for action. We do not speak from just one position but from many. We do not only speak to others; we speak also to ourselves. We are all part of the web of God's creation for 'in God all things in heaven and earth were created, things visible and invisible' (Colossians 1:16). And we are called now to act together for the sake of all humanity, for all creation, and our shared home, planet earth.

2.9 By the next Lambeth Conference, increasing areas of the Communion will be uninhabitable, because of drought, rising sea levels and other impacts as we reach tipping points in climate change. Meanwhile, despite these terrible realities, carbon emissions continue to rise and there are over 50,000 new fossil fuel developments in the pipeline.[2] Our oceans and rivers are clogged with plastic and people are choking and dying from polluted air. The web of life is becoming so damaged by the loss of biodiversity, including through deforestation, over fishing and unsustainable agricultural practices, that the integrity of creation is under threat.

2.10 The global response has been wholly inadequate – both in the level of resources dedicated to the response and in the level of urgency with which those with most power to make radical changes are taking action.

## 3 Affirmation

3.1 For ourselves and for future generations we need to act now, urgently and at scale.

3.2 However, actions are difficult to sustain unless there is also the transformation of hearts and minds from which such action flows. The climate emergency is not just a physical crisis – it is also a spiritual one which is exacerbated by greed, apathy and selfishness.

3.3 Humanity needs a spiritual and cultural transformation. We must see the world differently: repenting of and rejecting an extractive world view, which regards the earth and all nature as something to be exploited, and embracing instead a relational worldview, at the heart of Christ's teaching. This is espoused especially by indigenous peoples, who see the profound interdependence of all creation.

## 4 Specific Requests (The Calls)

4.1 We call on ourselves as bishops and the people of our provinces, dioceses and parishes to:

4.1.1 Treasure God's marvellous creation, recognising the profound interdependence of all life on earth and repenting of actions and theologies of domination, which have caused great harm to the earth and injustices to its people.

4.1.2 Recognise the triple environmental crisis as a crisis of cultural and spiritual values and build on the reach and influence of the church to challenge ourselves and humanity to transform our mindset away from exploitation of the natural world to one of relationship and stewardship, as embodied by the wisdom of the Christian tradition and by indigenous peoples.

4.1.3 Integrate the Fifth Mark of Mission into the life of our churches by: bringing this Call to our diocesan and parish structures; teaching our people about issues of the environment; embracing creation liturgies, and responding in prayer and lament such as during the Season of Creation; raising up the prophetic voices of young people and women who are calling for climate justice; and forming partnerships of solidarity with dioceses on the frontline of climate change.

4.1.4 Equip communities to build resilience to help them withstand and recover from disasters, and promote the prophetic voice of young people and the key role of women as earth protectors, recognising that climate change impacts unequally on women and future generations.

4.1.5 Join in the Communion Forest initiative, to protect and restore forests and other ecosystems across our planet and commit to promoting tree growing at the time of confirmation, and other key life and faith moments, as a symbol of spiritual growth.

4.1.6 Ensure we use and invest our assets ethically to be good news for our planet and people and, as a matter of urgency, remove our funds from any new fossil fuel exploration, and seek to invest in renewable energy sources.

4.1.7 Acknowledge the impact on our lifestyles and commit to changes in the way we live, reducing our travel, consumption and energy use.

4.2 We call on the Instruments of Communion to:

4.2.1 Support commitments to tackle urgently the triple environmental crises of climate change, biodiversity loss and pollution, and help resource dioceses in their efforts.

4.2.2 Advocate with the international community to deliver, as a matter of justice, the required financial commitments for loss and damage due to climate change, and to speak and act prophetically within the Communion on the issue, to demonstrate solidarity.

4.3 We call on world leaders to:

4.3.1 Enact bold and urgent policy changes, including:
- Achieving net-zero carbon emissions as soon as possible to limit the global average temperature rise to 1.5 degrees above pre-industrial levels.
- Fulfilling and substantially increasing their commitments to climate finance, including for loss and damage due to climate change.
- Halting new gas and oil exploration, while at the same time enabling and financing emerging economies in a just transition to clean, renewable energy.
- Protecting and restoring biodiversity and tackling pollution.

4.3.2 Challenge wealthier nations and those with greatest responsibility for climate change to take the lead on climate action and just financing for other countries to reduce emissions.

4.3.3 Support international cooperation and ambitious targets to transition to clean energy and to sustainable land use practices and food systems.

4.3.4 Acknowledge that the scale and urgency of the climate emergency is such that politics must give way to action based on science and rooted in a moral call to recognise our interdependence with each other and the natural world.

4.3.5 Recognise the wisdom within faith communities about the value and care of creation and the role that the faithful, and their faith leaders, can bring in influencing change in communities across the world.

## Notes

1 2022 IPCC Report: https://unfccc.int/news/the-evidence-is-clear-the-time-for-action-is-now-we-can-halve-emissions-by-2030.
2 https://theconversation.com/how-treaties-protecting-fossil-fuel-investors-could-jeopardize-global-efforts-to-save-the-climateand-co.

# Lambeth Call 2B
# Sustainable Development

## 1 Introduction

1.1 Millions of people today live in communities and nations where extreme poverty and inequalities damage their lives and capacity to flourish. The Covid-19 pandemic has exacerbated inequalities and undermined the development gains of recent decades. Levels of extreme poverty rose during the pandemic crisis, with over 700 million people now estimated to be living on less than $1.90 per day.

1.2 Many Anglicans and other Christians are among these numbers. People face both chronic challenges in daily living and sudden disasters, often related to conflict, economic crises, and climate change causing drought, sea level rise, flooding and fires. These disasters take lives, destroy homes, devastate livelihoods, cause food insecurity, interrupt education, impact health, force migration, put people at risk of trafficking, increase gender-based violence, disrupt communities and break up families. They have a vastly disproportionate impact on women, young people and indigenous peoples. The impacts of these crises are costly, both financially and in terms of the trauma they cause. The pandemic worsened the situation, increasing poverty and inequalities, both within and between countries.

1.3 This situation can also be seen as a result of human sin, in that we have failed to love God, love our neighbour and care for creation. Yet, as expressed in 1 Peter, studied at the 2022 Lambeth Conference, we are called to 'have genuine mutual love' (1 Peter 1:22), expressed through hospitality, stewardship and mutual service (diaconia) (1 Peter 4:9–10). These are essential in our care for one another locally and globally.

1.4 Jesus called us all to follow his ministry seeking justice and giving loving service: 'to bring good news to the poor ... to proclaim release to the captives and recovery of sight to the blind, to set free those who are oppressed, to proclaim the year of the Lord's favour' (Luke 4:18–19).

## 2 Declaration

2.1 As Christians, our hope is in the Lord, who made heaven and earth. Our hope means that we are called into the adventure of participating in God's eternal story, taking us towards the way the world could be, should be and one day will be as God's Kingdom comes.

2.2 The UN Sustainable Development Goals (SDGs) are a vital vision for the mutual flourishing of people and planet, living together in peace and prosperity and in partnership as one humanity. Humanity is called to justice, compassion and solidarity with those who are poor, marginalised, and facing injustice, including gender injustice. The SDGs provide a vision and a framework through which all of us can play a part in working towards a more just world – a world in which all have the opportunity to flourish and where no one is left behind. The principles of the SDGs are reflected in the Five Anglican Marks of Mission.

## 3 Affirmation

3.1 In this spirit, we are in a season of action: a vital, urgent opportunity to re-imagine our world and address these injustices and threats. 2030 is the crucial target date for the SDGs. As Anglicans, the mission of the church – that is, the mission of Christ – is expressed in our Five Marks of Mission. These recall Jesus' mission to bring good news to the poor, release for the oppressed, fullness of life for all and renewal for all of creation (Luke 4:18; John 10:10; Mark 16:15). It is our call and our desire to follow in Jesus' footsteps. The SDGs are a tool to help inform our understanding and response, our call to action, to be part of a wider global movement for people and planet. We are called to be God's Church for God's World.

## 4 Specific Requests (The Calls)

4.1 We call on ourselves as bishops and the people of our provinces, dioceses and parishes to:

4.1.1 Pursue more fully the Five Marks of Mission in the life of our churches as we serve as God's Church for God's World.

4.1.2 Identify which SDGs are of the most relevance to our mission and embed them in our diocesan mission plan for action.

4.1.3 Engage and equip our churches to work together with their local and global neighbours for transformation, using our gifts and assets to build resilient, sustainable and just communities in line with the vision for the SDGs as reflected in the Five Marks of Mission.

4.1.4 Support and encourage one another across the Communion to work together towards achieving universal human dignity and flourishing (John 10:10) in a thriving planet.

4.2 We call on the Instruments of Communion to:

4.2.1 Uphold the Five Marks of Mission as integral to Anglican identity and our discipleship and holistic mission as God's Church for God's World.

4.2.2 Promote the Five Marks of Mission, including their vision for reimagining our world, responding to human need by loving service, challenging unjust structures of society and safeguarding creation, and thereby encourage and equip the Communion to make a significant contribution to achieving the ambitions of the SDGs. [Changed language from concept of a global 'campaign' to be more rooted in diocesan action.]

4.2.3 Collaborate in partnership with other faith communities and all people for the mutual well-being of people and planet. In particular, support women and young people's contributions and amplify their voices.

4.2.4 Challenge the unjust structures that perpetuate global economic and political systems driving injustice, inequality and instability within and between countries.

4.3 We call on world leaders to:

4.3.1 Commit to finance and action to enable all nations of the world to be able to fulfil the 2030 SDGs, including its vision to 'leave no one behind'.

4.3.2 Recognise the strategic importance of faith actors and faith-based organisations and include them as key partners in sustainable development and in disaster preparedness, resilience and response.

## 5 Implementation

Bishops are invited to follow up these Calls at a diocesan level, in diocesan synods and gatherings, in order to make them a living document, incorporating them as priorities in mission planning and delivery.

These Calls appeal to the bishops to give leadership and implement them within their own provinces and dioceses, with support from the Instruments of Communion along with mission and development agencies. The ACC and its standing committee will monitor the specific Calls and report on progress up to 2030, including at ACC-18 and ACC-19. Communion-level bodies, including the Anglican Office at the United Nations, the Anglican Alliance, ACO departments such as for Gender Justice, and the relevant Anglican Networks, Commissions and agencies will all collaborate to help connect, equip and inspire members' churches, as well as work with global bodies, towards fulfilling the actions laid out in these Calls for the Environment and Sustainable Development.

# 30

# Lambeth Call 3
# Anglican Identity

*... you are a chosen race, a royal priesthood, a holy nation, God's own people, in order that you may proclaim the mighty acts of him who called you out of darkness into his marvellous light.* (1 Peter 2:9)

## 1 Declaration

1.1 The church is the community of the risen Christ. Christians affirm that the Church of Christ is one, holy, catholic, and apostolic.[1] The church is the fruit of God's redemptive mission through the incarnate Word (Romans 12:5; Galatians 3:26–28). The church is alive in its discernment of the mission of God and in its participation in the mission of God.

## 2 Affirmation

2.1 The Anglican tradition has its roots in a shared history committed to catholicity, reform, international mission, and inter-cultural witness. Our unity, and hope for deeper Christian unity, is expressed in the Chicago-Lambeth Quadrilateral:

- The Holy Scripture of the Old and New Testaments, as 'containing all things necessary to salvation', and as being the rule and ultimate standard of faith.
- The Apostles' Creed, as the Baptismal Symbol; and the Nicene Creed, as the sufficient statement of the Christian faith.
- The two Sacraments ordained by Christ Himself – Baptism and the Supper of the Lord – ministered with unfailing use of Christ's words of Institution, and of the elements ordained by Him.
- The Historic Episcopate, locally adapted in the methods of its administration to the varying needs of the nations and peoples called of God into the Unity of His Church.[2]

2.2 Grounded in Scripture, and guided by tradition and reason, Anglicans seek faithfulness to God in richly diverse cultures and in distinct human experiences. In communion with the See of Canterbury, the Anglican Communion has grown into a family of interdependent churches and provinces in over 165 countries.

2.3 Anglicans, therefore, believe in the visible and institutional form of the church.[3] Each province of the Anglican Communion is autonomous and called to live interdependently. Four Instruments of Communion have developed to express Anglican interdependence.[4] These Instruments are:

• The Archbishop of Canterbury
• The Lambeth Conference
• The Anglican Consultative Council, and
• The Primates' Meeting.

Member churches of the Anglican Communion are defined in relation to their fellowship with each other and with the Instruments of Communion.

2.4 Our common baptism calls all God's people to a life of ministry in service of the Lord Jesus Christ. We affirm a common ordained ministry according to the threefold order of deacons, priests (presbyters), and bishops. Formed in liturgical community, fed by Word and sacrament, we turn outwards as witnesses to the Lordship of Christ in the world.[5]

2.5 Our witness is rooted in local communities and has global reach. The call to mission is expressed in Anglicanism's Five Marks of Mission.[6] The mission of the church is the mission of Christ:

• To proclaim the Good News of the Kingdom
• To teach, baptise and nurture new believers
• To respond to human need by loving service
• To transform unjust structures of society, to challenge violence of every kind and pursue peace and reconciliation
• To strive to safeguard the integrity of creation, and sustain and renew the life of the earth.

# 3 Specific Requests (The Calls)

The bishops gathered at the Lambeth Conference 2022 call on the Communion to:

## 3.1 *Reimagine the Vision and Practice of Communion*

Aware that shared traditions can narrow our vision of the world, that the gift of institutions can feed institutionalism, that the gift of authority can be sullied by abuses of power, and that the grace found in discernment amidst disagreement can be squandered by sectionalism – we desire a fresh vision of Communion. We call on the Archbishop of Canterbury and the Anglican Consultative Council to establish an independent research group to study the various ways in which Communion (*koinonia*) is understood and embodied across provinces and ecclesial traditions.[7] This inter-cultural research group will produce resources that reimagine, inspire, and renew theologies of Communion and ways of being in Communion. An initial design for this research (clarifying, for example, method, scope and outcomes) will be presented to the ACC standing committee in 2024. The research group will publish its first set of resources in 2025.

## 3.2 *Explore the Possibility of an International and Inter-Cultural Gathering in the Global South*

This is an era marked by authoritarianisms; both vulnerability and activism of indigenous peoples; inter-religious co-operation and conflict; mass migration; pluralism; the climate crisis; and enormous changes in science and technology. Amidst such challenges and opportunities, and in the distinct and diverse cultures that shape our Communion, we celebrate the presence of the risen Christ in the world and testify to the hope found in the gospel. Giving priority to the voices of indigenous leaders, women, young people, and the laity, we call on the broad Anglican family to gather together in joyful testimony to the rich expressions of the gospel in our many cultures expressed in the visual, literary and performing arts.[8] Such a cultural and inter-cultural celebration will provide a renewed approach to discerning the Holy Spirit and thus to the church renewing its vision and practice of Christian mission.

We call on the Standing Committee of the Anglican Consultative Council to set up an exploratory group to present a feasibility study for this international Anglican festival or congress.[9] An initial report, establishing the frame of reference for the feasibility study, should be presented by the Secretary General to the ACC standing committee in 2025. The final feasibility study should be presented by the exploratory group at ACC-19 in 2026. If appropriate, the Secretary General, in consultation with the Archbishop of Canterbury, would then call for an international Anglican gathering and set up a design group. This international gathering would take place before the next Lambeth Conference.

### 3.3 Review the Instruments of Communion

We call for a review of the current Instruments of Communion. We ask the Archbishop of Canterbury to set up an independent review group on the Instruments of Communion with special attention to how all the ministerial orders (including the laity) relate to the Instruments and/or are represented in the Instruments. To what extent are the Instruments fit for purpose? To what extent might some (or all) of the Instruments be reconfigured to serve the Communion of today and the future? Should there be a further Instrument of Communion in order to centre those voices too often marginalized – indigenous leaders, the laity, women and young people?[10] This review should be presented to ACC-19 at its meeting in 2026.

### 3.4 Revitalise Anglicanism's Commitment to the Five Marks of Mission

We call on all bishops to lead their dioceses in a reaffirmation and recommitment to the Five Marks of Mission.[11] The Standing Committee of the Anglican Consultative Council, in consultation with appropriate Communion networks and departments, should be tasked with convening an international group of Anglican missiologists to study the diverse ways this reaffirmation and recommitment to mission is embodied across the Communion. This study will be published by the end of 2026 as a renewed vision for mission in the Communion.[12]

### Notes

1 The Nicene Creed; The Inter-Anglican Standing Commission on Unity, Faith & Order (IASCUFO), *Towards a Symphony of Instruments: A Historical and Theological Consideration of the Instruments of the Anglican Communion* (2018), 1–2.

2 Lambeth Conference 1888, Resolution 11. See also the formularies enshrined in the Book of Common Prayer (1662).

3 Articles XIX–XXI, *Book of Common Prayer* (1662). See also the 'Principles of Church Order' set out in Encyclical Letter 1.5 (Lambeth Conference, 1878): https://www.anglicancommunion.org/resources/document-library/lambeth-

conference/1878/recommendation-1-union-among-the-churches-of-the-anglican-communion-encyclical-letter-15?language=english&year=1878, accessed 1 July 2022.

4 *Towards a Symphony of Instruments* (2018).

5 See The International Anglican Liturgical Consultation (IALC), *Report on Liturgical Formation of All the Baptised* (2021): https://www.anglicancommunion. org/media/493609/The-Liturgical-Formation-of-All-the-Baptised_ACC18_ IALC_2301.pdf.

6 See https://www.anglicancommunion.org/mission/marks-of-mission.aspx. The Marks of Mission began to emerge at the Anglican Consultative Council (ACC-6) in Badagry, Nigeria (1984). The 1988 Lambeth Conference affirmed this emerging sense of Anglican mission ('The Nature and Meaning of Mission') and at ACC-8 in 1990 a fifth mark addressing the ecological crisis was added. The Lambeth Conference 1998 endorsed the Five Marks of Mission. See Cathy Ross, 'Mission' in Mark D. Chapman, Sathianathan Clarke and Martyn Percy eds, *The Oxford Handbook of Anglican Studies* (Oxford, 2015), 504–515; Robert S. Heaney and John Kafwanka K., 'Discipleship in the Mission of God' in Robert S. Heaney, John Kafwanka K., and Hilda Kabia, *God's Church for God's World* (New York: Church Publishing, 2020), 1–19.

7 1 Cor. 10:16–17.

8 https://www.youtube.com/watch?v=o4k4vHR8nhY. This is one example of how young people have explored their Christian identity through an integrative approach that takes seriously the gospel in relation to culture and the creative process. This *Waiata* (song) is the result of spiritual, theological and artistic endeavour. Further, the performance *itself* is an act of theology and spiritual discernment. Such artistic-theological expression is, in part, what we have in view as the work and witness of an international and inter-cultural gathering.

9 Such an international gathering might find inspiration in the Anglican Congresses that met in London, UK in 1908; Minneapolis, USA in 1954; and in Toronto, Canada in 1963. For information on the last Anglican Congress in Toronto, Canada (1963) see https://www.episcopalarchives.org/e-archives/the_wit ness/pdf/1963_Watermarked/Witness_19630905.pdf.

10 On 2 May 2022 the Archbishop of Canterbury promised the First Nations peoples of Canada discussion on the rights of indigenous peoples. See Archbishop of Canterbury, 'Apology to the Indigenous peoples of Canada' (Press Release, 2 May 2022): https://www.archbishopofcanterbury.org/speaking-writing/speeches/read-archbishop-justins-apology-indigenous-peoples-canada, accessed 23 June 2022.

11 See also the Lambeth Call on Mission and Evangelism.

12 If it is judged that an international and inter-cultural gathering take place, the research and studies envisioned in this Call would be key documents in shaping that gathering.

# 31

# Lambeth Call 4
# Safe Church

## 1 Introduction

The theme of the Lambeth Conference was God's Church for God's World and bishops studied 1 Peter. In this letter, the apostle Peter wrote to the Christians scattered throughout Asia Minor reminding them of their identity in Christ as God's chosen people, sanctified by the Spirit for obedience to Jesus Christ (1 Peter 1:1-2). Both the Old and New Testaments express the call to be holy as the appropriate response to God's grace (1 Peter 1:15-16). Christians are therefore to live as servants of God and are to honour everyone and love the family of believers (1 Peter 2:16-17). Christian leaders are called to protect the people of God in their care (1 Peter 5:1-2).

## 2 Declaration

2.1 In making this Call we are deeply mindful of, and guided by:

- the voices of those who have experienced abuse within church contexts;
- the range of circumstances which can make persons or communities more vulnerable to violence, abuse and marginalisation such as race, gender, sexual orientation, ethnicity, religious belief, living with physical, cognitive or sensory disability, or economic vulnerability;
- the World Health Organization citing research which estimates that: globally, up to 1 billion children aged 2-17 years experienced physical, sexual or emotional violence (abuse) or neglect in the past year. Violence against children has lifelong impacts on their health and well-being;[1] 1 in 3 women worldwide have been subjected to physical and/or sexual intimate partner violence or non-partner violence in their lifetime. This violence can cause serious short- and long-term health

consequences as well as social and economic costs for women, their families and societies;[2]

- the 2030 Agenda for Sustainable Development (SDG) targets: 'to elim-inate all forms of violence against all women and girls in the public and private spheres, including trafficking and sexual and other types of exploitation' (target 5.2); 'to end abuse, exploitation, trafficking and all forms of violence against, and torture of, children' (target 16.2).[3]

2.2 We make this Call fully aware of safeguarding/Safe Church failures in religious institutions including churches of the Anglican Communion, as highlighted by government inquiries, reported cases and the media. There are people working within religious institutions, both clergy and lay persons, who have betrayed trust and abused children and adults for whom they had pastoral responsibility. There are religious leaders who have denied or minimised this abuse and its consequences. Religious institutions have compounded the impact of the initial abuse by failing to respond effectively. They have failed to take disclosures seriously, to report abuse immediately to the relevant authorities, to hold the perpe-trator accountable and/or to provide ongoing pastoral care to those who have been abused. As a result, the reputation of, and public trust in, many religious institutions has been damaged.

2.3 We declare:

- the witness of Scripture to God's love for all members of the human family and the priority given in Jesus' ministry to children, the vulner-able and the marginalised;
- the continuing relevance of the reflections of the Lambeth Conference 2008 upon the many forms of abuse of power within society and the church from which women and girls suffer disproportionately. Violence meted out to women and children within the body of Christ is violence done to the body of Christ. Violence takes many forms including phys-ical, financial, emotional, psychological, intellectual, cultural, sexual and spiritual abuse;
- that we will fulfil the Charter for the Safety of People within the churches of the Anglican Communion adopted by the Anglican Consul-tative Council in 2012 (at ACC-15). We will fulfil its five commitments of providing support where there is abuse; implementing effective responses to abuse; adopting and promoting standards for the practice of ministry; assessing suitability for ministry; and promoting a culture of safety;

- that we will implement the Protocol for disclosure of ministry suitability information between the churches of the Anglican Communion welcomed by the Anglican Consultative Council in 2016 (at ACC-16). We will implement the Protocol by having systems in place to share and assess information when church workers move between/within provinces;
- that we will follow the Guidelines to enhance the safety of all persons – especially children, young people and vulnerable adults – within the provinces of the Anglican Communion adopted by the Anglican Consultative Council in 2019 (at ACC-17). We will follow these Guidelines by having systems in place in our churches to prevent abuse and provide appropriate pastoral support to those who have been abused;
- that we will work with the Anglican Communion Safe Church Commission whose continuation was requested by the Anglican Consultative Council in 2019 (at ACC-17). We will work with the Commission as it provides assistance, and reports on progress, to enhance the safety of all people in the churches of the Anglican Communion.

## 3 Affirmation

3.1 We acknowledge with deep shame that some people working within the church, both clergy and lay persons, have engaged in sinful, and even criminal, behaviour by abusing those in their care. We apologise unreservedly to those who have been abused and harmed and who continue to live with the impacts of that harm. We are profoundly sorry for the failure of our churches to prevent harm, and to listen to and help those who have been abused. We acknowledge that our repentance must be demonstrated by intentional action towards enhancing the safety of our church communities and institutions.

3.2 We affirm that:

- a key part of the mission of the church and the discipleship of God's people is to create communities in which all people are safe and cared for. This conviction must be a core component of our theology and must therefore characterise our identity, thinking, words and actions in being God's Church for God's World;
- we will take action to make churches of the Anglican Communion places of enhanced safety for everyone, where church workers act with integrity; victims of abuse receive care and a just outcome; church

workers who commit abuse are held accountable; and church leaders do not conceal abuse.

## 4 Specific Requests (The Calls)

We, the bishops gathered at the Lambeth Conference, make the following Calls:

4.1 to ourselves as bishops, to fulfil our responsibility to protect all people in our care by:

- ensuring we ourselves are equipped with the necessary knowledge, understanding, compassion and discernment through training, listening to the experiences of those who have experienced abuse and ongoing sharing with fellow bishops;
- adopting the Charter for the Safety of People within the churches of the Anglican Communion;
- implementing the Protocol for disclosure of ministry suitability information;
- following the Guidelines to enhance the safety of all persons – especially children, young people and vulnerable adults – within the provinces of the Anglican Communion;
- ensuring that every diocese puts in place a Safe Church structure/system, appropriate to context and local resourcing, as a matter of urgency;
- fulfilling all legal requirements in our own countries to report abuse of children to the relevant authorities and services;
- advocating for changes in legislation and practice within government agencies to enhance the safeguarding of children, young people and vulnerable adults.

In so doing, we acknowledge that our progress is different in different parts of the Communion, and that some of our provinces and dioceses face situations such as war and natural disasters which pose unique challenges for this work;

4.2 to the Instruments of Communion, to make the safety of all persons in the provinces of the Anglican Communion a priority of their focus, resource allocation and actions;

4.3 to the people of our provinces and dioceses, to partner with us to protect everyone in our church communities and institutions by having systems, training and people in place to prevent abuse and provide appropriate pastoral support to those who have been abused;

4.4 to the leaders of the world, to take whatever steps are necessary to achieve SDG targets 5.2 and 16.2 (as per 2.1 above).

We undertake through our representatives to regularly report to the Instruments of Communion on progress in fulfilling our responsibility to protect all people in our care.

## Notes

1 World Health Organization, Fact sheet, Violence against children, 8 June 2020.

2 World Health Organization, Fact sheet, Violence against women, 9 March 2021.

3 The 2030 Agenda for Sustainable Development was launched by a United Nations Summit in September 2015 and is aimed at ending poverty in all its forms. It contains 17 Sustainable Development Goals and 169 targets.

# 32

# Lambeth Call 5
# Science and Faith

## 1 Introduction

1.1 The world faces multiple dangers in the coming decade from climate change and biodiversity loss, poverty, disease, war, famine and the careless use of new technologies. In the Call that follows, the bishops assembled at the Lambeth Conference invite every church of the Anglican Communion to recognise within science God-given resources for the life of faith and to offer the wisdom of faith to the work of science. We call on our churches to make this a priority and to support and equip church leaders and scientists in partnership for such courageous and confident leadership.

1.2 The bishops are issuing this Call because the biblical text they have been studying throughout the conference, 1 Peter, calls on God's people to be 'good stewards of the manifold grace of God' and to 'serve one another with whatever gift each of you have received' (1 Peter 4:10). There are many experienced scientists in our churches across the world, Anglicans who have the gifts of science to offer the church and the world; furthermore, many scientists look to the wisdom of faith and, in particular, the wisdom of Christianity for insight into the manifold grace of God. Also, 1 Peter is calling not only for the sharing of these gifts but to 'do so with the strength that God supplies' (1 Peter 4:11). In other words, Anglican scientists and church leaders should know that they are not on their own but can depend on the One in whom they live and move and have their being.

## 2 Declaration

2.1 Despite calls from successive Lambeth Conferences to the Communion for the church to engage with science and technology[1] and the more recent work of ECLAS,[2] the perception of a gap between science and faith has become more widespread and is expressed differently in different parts of the Communion. Often scientists have not been affirmed in their vocation as disciples and church leaders have not felt confident in bringing the wisdom of faith to scientific questions.

2.2 As the Archbishop of Canterbury has recently said, 'The relationship between science and faith presents us with a very real and a powerful route to lasting, major change. Our global reach [as the Anglican Communion], our commitment to local communities and our hope combined with the knowledge and expertise of science can forge a powerful alliance.'[3]

2.3 Furthermore, Pope Francis and an alliance of 40 global faith leaders issued the following powerful call in October 2021: 'Faith and science are essential pillars of human civilisation, with shared principles and complementarities ... We must address [the challenges we face] using the knowledge of science and the wisdom of religion: to know more and to care more.'[4]

## 3 Affirmation

3.1 As bishops we believe the perception of a rift between science and faith should be laid to rest in every part of our Anglican Communion over the coming critical decade, in order to fulfil our calling to be God's Church for God's World in this generation.[5]

3.2 This coming together of faith and science can only come about through partnership between scientists, theologians and church leaders and between the different churches of the Communion, recognising the complicated history that science has played in many countries and drawing on Anglican theological method (from Scripture, reason and tradition) to gain greater clarity over the relationship of Christian faith and science.
Therefore,

3.3 We the bishops assembled for the Lambeth Conference commit ourselves to welcome and enter into theological dialogue with science, establishing how it is understood in different regions of the Communion, recognising within it God-given resources for the life of faith and offering the wisdom of Christian faith to its work especially to the ethics of its use and unequal impacts across the world.

3.4 We call on our churches working with our ecumenical and interfaith partners and governments (where possible) to give this a high priority and to support and equip church leaders and scientists in partnership for such courageous and confident leadership, drawing on the collaboration that is already taking place through other Commissions, Networks and agencies in the Anglican Communion and in other churches.

## 4 Specific Requests (The Calls)

4.1 We call on all Anglicans as they participate in mission to enter into theological dialogue with science, establishing how it is understood in different regions of the Communion, recognising within it God-given resources for the life of faith and offering the wisdom of Anglican theological method (from Scripture, reason and tradition) to its work, especially to the ethics of its use and unequal impacts across the world. Using the Five Marks of Mission as a framework, this can happen in the following ways:

- *To proclaim the Good News of the Kingdom*: by recognising within science God-given resources for the life of faith, and thereby removing it as a barrier to proclamation and belief; by drawing on science as inspiration for our worship to the praise and glory of God;
- *To teach, baptise and nurture new believers*: by finding foundations within science for Christian faith and by affirming the dignity and value of new believers who have scientific backgrounds and vocations;
- *To respond to human need by loving service*: by using the resources of science in issues ranging from physical and mental health care to water and food security;
- *To transform unjust structures of society, to challenge violence of every kind and pursue peace and reconciliation*: by recognising how science may contribute to inequity and conflict, speaking to those issues from a position of confident scientific knowledge, offering the ethics and wisdom of faith to the deployment of new technologies such as AI, genetics and nuclear technologies;
- *To strive to safeguard the integrity of creation, and sustain and renew the life of the earth*: by contributing the Christian theological motivation for caring about the material world and responding to the ethical mandate to check greed and engage responsibly with God's creation.

4.2 We warmly welcome the establishing of the Anglican Communion Science Commission to lead and focus our work in this area, providing effective and easy communication of the work that stems from the Call.

4.3 We call on our schools, seminaries, theological colleges and training programmes to welcome and enter into theological dialogue with science as a God-given resource for the life of faith and to model how the wisdom of faith can be offered to the work of science, so that all God's people, lay and ordained, may be better equipped to do the same for those they serve as disciples and public ministers. We ask that the new Commission for Theological Education in the Anglican Communion take a lead on this.

4.4 We call on every church of the Communion to designate a lead Bishop for Science (if not already done so) and to explore the possibility of a Commission of scientists and church leaders in their provinces to take forward this agenda, to be connected with and supported by the Anglican Communion Science Project.[6] We especially ask that young scientists are invited onto these commissions.

4.5 We call on every Anglican disciple to grow in their understanding of science as integral to the wellbeing of all disciples and to the mission of every church, so that they can play a more active role as citizens of the world and be God's Church for God's World.

## 5 Implementation

The response to this Call will be led by the Anglican Communion Science Commission launched at Lambeth 2022 supported by a team of scientists and theologians from across the Communion. The work will be facilitated by the Anglican Communion Science Project, which will be based in two or three universities, such as Oxford, Cape Town and St Paul's University, Limuru, Kenya.

The Commission will report at regular intervals on its goals and progress.

The Commission will also report to the next Lambeth Conference on progress made across this critical decade.

## Notes

1 See, for example, Resolutions 1 and 2 of the 1978 Lambeth Conference and the accompanying commentary, pp. 65–67.

2 'Equipping Church Leaders in an Age of Science' (ECLAS) was established in 2013 and focused on the UK and latterly North America with similar aims, https://www.eclasproject.org.

3 The Archbishop of Canterbury, Address to Faith Leaders, February 2021, https://www.archbishopofcanterbury.org/speaking-writing/speeches/archbishop-canterbury-addressesinternational-faith-leaders-ahead-cop26.

4 Holy See: Faith and Science, An Appeal for COP 26 (a joint declaration from 40 faith leaders and leading scientists), https://www.gov.uk/government/news/holy-see-faith-and-science-an-appeal-for-cop26.

5 Science has not been innocent in colonial history and this is still felt in certain parts of the Communion. The rift is not simply between 'faith' and 'science' but is more complicated.

6 An application to fund this project has been made to a major global trust.

# 33

# Lambeth Call 6
# Human Dignity

*Blessed be the God and Father of our Lord Jesus Christ! By his great mercy he has given us a new birth into a living hope through the resurrection of Jesus Christ from the dead ...* (1 Peter 1:3)

## 1 Declaration

1.1 Within God's good gift of creation (Genesis 1:31), humanity is made in God's image and blessed by God's care and love (Genesis 1:26–28). This gives all human beings a dignity that cannot be taken away.[1] 'Whenever we face another, we see a reflection of God's infinite love and glory.'[2]

1.2 It is in Christ's mission that we know the grace of God and God's faithful love for every human being (John 3:16; Colossians 1:15–20; Romans 5:18–19; 1 Corinthians 15:22; 2 Corinthians 5:14–17; 1 Peter 2:9).[3] Humanity is offered new birth into a living hope through Christ's resurrection (1 Peter 1:3; 2 Peter 1:14). As God's image-bearers, human beings are called to love God and to love each other (1 John 4:11).[4]

1.3 The wonderful diversity of God's creation is echoed in the diversity of human beings. Every human being is 'a unique and deep mystery of inestimable value and dignity'.[5] This diversity among human beings and in all creation is good and beautiful. Pentecost – and the vision of Revelation 7:9 – show how diversity is a good gift from God when, in the unifying power of the Holy Spirit, it is used in God's service and for the good of one another.[6]

1.4 Only Christ is the perfect image of God (John 10:30; Colossians 1:15–16). All human beings turn away from God's love and mar God's image.[7] We acknowledge our sin and God's victory over sin at the cross (1 Peter 2:24, 3:18; Romans 5:8). Respecting, honouring, and preserving the dignity of each human being involves acknowledgment of sin, repentance and forgiveness. It is in Christ, through the power of the Holy

Spirit, that the full potential of the human person is seen.[8] It is in the gift of rebirth and renewed identity that the church, the body of Christ, is united. As a people redeemed by Christ, the church is called to bear God's image, to be the body of Christ on earth (1 Peter 3:9–10; Galatians 3:28).

1.5 Therefore, the church catholic declares that life is sacred and all persons are worthy of respect and worthy of conditions that make for life in all its fullness.[9] From such holy standards there can be no faithful dissent.

## 2 Affirmation

We are fellow-workers with God (1 Corinthians 3:9) called to protect the gift of human life and the dignity of all human beings.[10] As Jesus washed the feet of both his denier and betrayer, we are called to follow his example (John 13:12–17, 34–35). We are called to love one another.

Acts and attitudes against the dignity of God's children are sin. The legacies of colonialism, the trans-Atlantic slave trade, and other abuses of power continue to impact our communities.[11] Some have been enriched and some impoverished. International economic systems, built upon unjust structures of exploitation, have created dehumanising conditions. The deep inequalities in access to land, health and education, exploitation of the young, unjust labour practices, mistreatment of ethnic minorities, migrants and refugees, the inhumanity of human trafficking, religious persecution, pressures on those guided by their freedom of conscience, oppression of LGBTQ persons, gender-based violence, war and sexual violence in conflict, in part, reveal such sin. Hospitality to all and faithfulness to each are key marks of a godly community (1 Peter 4:8–10).

2.1 God intends life-giving inter-cultural community. Local missionary effort and contextual theology attest to a deep reception, contestation, adoption and adaptation of the Gospel of Jesus Christ within and across cultures.[12] However, international Anglicanism often emerged in the context of colonialism. We acknowledge the existence and ongoing impact of an imperialist Anglicanism involved in dehumanising practices predicated upon cultural and racial supremacy.[13] Christian commitment to human dignity must celebrate the rich diversities of contextual theologies and take account of Anglicanism's complicity in brutal and extractive colonialisms.

2.2 Unjust economic systems unfairly disadvantage the world's poorest communities.[14] Progress had been made in combating poverty.[15] However, a global pandemic, rising inflation and war has seen unprecedented reversals in the reduction of poverty. The ongoing climate emergency (seen in, for example, increased global temperature, rising sea levels, and ocean acidification) creates further instability and food insecurity, challenging efforts to eradicate poverty and create sustainable development now and in the future.[16] In 2020, an additional 120–124 million people were driven back into extreme poverty.[17] In 2022, it is estimated that between 657 million and 676 million people will live in extreme poverty.[18] We lament these figures and the ways such poverty disproportionately impacts women and girls.[19] A commitment to human dignity means the church stands in solidarity with the poor and the marginalised and stands in witness against injustice as the poor and the marginalised.

2.3 Prejudice on the basis of gender or sexuality threatens human dignity. Given Anglican polity, and especially the autonomy of provinces, there is disagreement and a plurality of views on the relationship between human dignity and human sexuality. Yet, we experience the safeguarding of dignity in deepening dialogue. It is the mind of the Anglican Communion as a whole that 'all baptised, believing and faithful persons, regardless of sexual orientation, are full members of the Body of Christ' and to be welcomed, cared for and treated with respect (1.10, 1998).[20] After careful theological reflection and a process of discernment, many Provinces continue to affirm that same gender marriage is not permissible. Lambeth Resolution 1.10 (1998) stated that the 'legitimising or blessing of same sex unions' is not advised.[21] Other provinces have blessed and welcomed same sex union/marriage after careful theological reflection and a process of discernment. As bishops we remain committed to listening and walking together despite our deep disagreement on these issues.

## 3 Specific Requests (The Calls)

The scriptures witness to the inherent dignity and equality of all human beings because all are made in the image of God. In the great ethnic and cultural diversities of the Anglican Communion all are made in the image of God. All are equal. Indeed, it is God's intent to curate the richness of the world's cultures in the final and full revelation of God's glorious redemption (Revelation 21:24). Therefore, the bishops gathered at the Lambeth Conference 2022 call on the church to protect the dignity of all creation, cultures and human beings. We call the Communion to:

### 3.1 *Support the Establishment of an Archbishop's Commission for Redemptive Action (ACRA)*

This work will have, at least, four foci. First, the Archbishop of Canterbury should convene the ACRA as a group of theologians in the Communion, under the chairmanship of a Majority World theologian (we have in view here a leader from a community that experienced colonialism and slavery). The ACRA will study the reports and forensic accounting being produced by the Church Commissioners for England into the church's historic links to transatlantic chattel slavery.[22]

Second, the ACRA will establish and publish holistic theologies of redemptive action and reparation, grounded in the great scriptural traditions of God's redemption in Christ, and the church's call to the ministry of reconciliation (2 Corinthians 5:17–19).[23] We call upon the Archbishop of Canterbury (as Chair of the Church Commissioners' Board of Governors) to ensure that this theology shapes the Church Commissioners' response to the church's links to colonialism and slavery.

Third, the ACRA, in consultation with the work of the Church Commissioners, will identify criteria, communities and programmes that would serve a Communion-wide witness to redemptive action.

The ACRA will provide quarterly progress reports to the Archbishop of Canterbury and the Standing Committee of the Anglican Consultative Council.

### 3.2 *Act for Funded Social Protection Measures across the Anglican Communion*

Such action will mean, where possible, lobbying governments for social protection measures. It will also mean the Anglican Communion acting for social protection.

First, in consultation with relevant sources and experts, at the next Primates' Meeting the Primates should explore together the meaning and implications of social protection in their contexts.[24] The Primates will take the lead in witnessing to the life-changing potential of social protection schemes while equipping their bishops and dioceses to do the same in local contexts.

Second, because poverty is 'a multifaceted problem that requires a multifaceted and integrated approach', resources that are economic, political, social, environmental, institutional, and spiritual need to be mobilised.[25] In a bid to deepen spiritual and imaginative approaches to the eradication of poverty, and especially youth poverty, we call the Anglican Consultative Council to establish an Anglican Innovation Fund

(AIF). This fund will disperse financial support for young people (18–30 years old) that establish projects or businesses that combat poverty through special attention to social protection. In reference to 3.1, this initiative may find ongoing funding as an outworking of the ACRA and the Church Commissioners' response to the historic injustice of slavery.

### 3.3 Extend the Work of the Anglican Communion Office to Promote Human Dignity with Attention to Sexuality as well as Gender

We call upon the ACC (informed by relevant networks and departments of the ACO and informed by Lambeth 1998 resolution 1.10) to examine whether its work on Gender Justice should be expanded to promote provincial and inter-provincial vision and practices towards human dignity with attention not only to gender but also sexuality. At ACC-19 provincial and inter-provincial reports on this matter should be received and further recommendations made.

### Notes

1 The Inter-Anglican Standing Commission on Unity, Faith & Order (IASCUFO), *Created in the Image of God: The Divine Gift and Call to Humanity: An Anglican Theological Anthropology*: Unity, Faith & Order Paper No. 3 (London: ACC, 2021), 9, 12, 14–25, 42, https://www.anglicancommunion.org/media/460188/UFO_IASCUFO_Papers-3-and-4-God-So-Loved-the-World_v2_en.pdf. See also Brian Brock and John Swinton, eds, *Disability in the Christian Tradition: A Reader* (Grand Rapids: Eerdmans, 2012); World Council of Churches, *The Gift of Being: Called to Be a Church of All and for All* (2016), https://tinyurl.com/7kyvdnrb.

2 IASCUFO, *Created in the Image of God*, 24.

3 International Commission for Anglican-Orthodox Theological Dialogue (ICAOTD), *In the Image and Likeness of God: A Hope-Filled Anthropology* ('The Buffalo Statement', 2015), 5–12. Lambeth 1998, 1.10c; IASCUFO, *Created in the Image of God*, 75–77.

4 IASCUFO, *Created in the Image of God*, 34–40.

5 IASCUFO, *Created in the Image of God*, 24.

6 IASCUFO, *Created in the Image of God*, 10–11.

7 IASCUFO, *Created in the Image of God*, 12, 50–57.

8 IASCUFO, *Created in the Image of God*, 9–11, 30–35.

9 ICAOTD, *In the Image and Likeness of God*; Lambeth 2008, Section C (Human and Social Justice); Lambeth 1998, 1.1, 2, 4, 5, 9, 14, 15; III.21, 22.

10 IASCUFO, *Created in the Image of God*, 26–30.

11 IASCUFO, *Created in the Image of God*, 53–54. See Jeremy M. Bergen, *Ecclesial Repentance: The Churches Confront their Sinful Pasts* (London: T&T Clark, 2011); International Labour Organization (ILO), Walk Free, and Interna-

tional Organization for Migration (IOM), *Global Estimates of Modern Slavery Forced Labour and Forced Marriage* (Geneva: ILO Publications, 2022).

12 See Lamin Sanneh, *Translating the Message: The Missionary Impact on Culture* revd edn (Maryknoll: Orbis, 2009); Jehu H. Hanciles, *Migration and the Making of Global Christianity* (Grand Rapids: Eerdmans, 2021); William L. Sachs and Robert S. Heaney, *The Promise of Anglicanism* (London: SCM Press, 2019).

13 See Rowan Strong, *Anglicanism and the British Empire* (Oxford: Oxford University Press, 2007); Ian T. Douglas and Kwok Pui-lan, eds, *Beyond Colonial Anglicanism: The Anglican Communion in the Twenty-First Century* (New York: Church Publishing, 2000).

14 See IASCUFO, *Created in the Image of God*, 52–54.

15 Andrea Peer and Sevil Omer, 'Global Poverty: Facts, FAQs, and how to help', https://www.worldvision.org/sponsorship-news-stories/global-poverty-facts, 23 August 2021, accessed 10 June 2022.

16 UN, General Assembly, 73rd Session (18 October 2018), Second Committee, Agenda item 24 (a), 'Eradication of poverty and other development issues: implementation of the Third United Nations Decade for the Eradication of Poverty' (2018–2027), 4. IASCUFO, *Created in the Image of God*, 12–13, 58–67.

17 https://sdgs.un.org/goals/goal1, accessed 10 June 2022.

18 'Extreme poverty' is measured as people living on less than $1.90 a day. See Daniel Gerszon Mahler, Nishant Yonzan, Ruth Hill, Christoph Lakner, Haoyu Wu and Nobuo Yoshida, 'Pandemic, prices, and poverty', https://blogs.worldbank.org/opendata/pandemic-prices-and-poverty, 13 April 2022, accessed 10 August 2022. See https://www.un.org/en/global-issues/ending-poverty accessed 11 June 2022. For information on climate change and migration patterns see Intergovernmental Panel on Climate Change, Working Group III contribution to the Sixth Assessment Report of the Intergovernmental Panel on Climate Change, 'Climate Change 2022: Mitigation of Climate Change' (April 2022), 2-54–2-55; 3-96–3-109, https://report.ipcc.ch/ar6wg3/pdf/IPCC_AR6_WGIII_FinalDraft_FullReport.pdf, accessed 27 June 2022.

19 UN, General Assembly, 73rd Session (18 October 2018), Second Committee, Agenda item 24 (a), 'Eradication of poverty and other development issues: implementation of the Third United Nations Decade for the Eradication of Poverty' (2018–2027), 3.

20 Lambeth 1998, 1.10 c, d.

21 Lambeth 1998 1.10 e.

22 https://www.churchofengland.org/sites/default/files/2022–06/Church%20 Commissioners%20research%20report%20final.pdf, accessed 28 June 2022.

23 IASCUFO, *Created in the Image of God*, 75–77. See IASCUFO, God's Sovereignty and Our Salvation: An Anglican Theological Statement: Unity, Faith & Order Paper No. 4 (London: ACC, 2021), 82–84.

24 Social protection is any scheme or system set in place to protect workers from dramatic or traumatic change in working conditions. Social protection means employers share risk with their employees. Such protection can be in the form of, for example, pension benefits, access to low-rate loans, and subsidized or free health care access. For more on the concept of 'risk sharing' see Truman Packard, Ugo Gentilini, Margaret Grosh, Philip O'Keefe, Robert Palacios, David Robalino and Indhira Santos, *Protecting All: Risk Sharing for a Diverse and Diversifying World*

*of Work* (Washington DC: International Bank for Reconstruction and Development/The World Bank, 2019), https://bitly.ws/zBmR, 21 June 2022.

25 UN, General Assembly, 73rd Session (18 October 2018), Second Committee, Agenda item 24 (a), 'Eradication of Poverty and Other Development Issues: Implementation of the Third United Nations Decade for the Eradication of Poverty' (2018–2027), 3.

# 34

# Lambeth Call 7
# Christian Unity

*Finally, all of you, have unity of spirit, sympathy, love for one another, a tender heart, and a humble mind.* (1 Peter 3:8)

## 1 Declaration

### Our Ecumenical Story

1.1 Just over one hundred years ago, the bishops of the Anglican Communion, assembled in the 1920 Lambeth Conference, issued An Appeal to all Christian People. In it, they spoke of their passionate desire to seek the unity of all Christians in a visibly united church, which would witness to the reconciling power of the Gospel and call all nations to repentance and faith. Meeting together as bishops in the 2022 Lambeth Conference we hear afresh their call, and now make our own commitment to strive for the unity of the church.

1.2 The Appeal to all Christian People represented a galvanising and stirring step forward in Anglican involvement in the worldwide ecumenical movement that had started in the late nineteenth century. Since then, this movement has made significant progress, and relations between the different Christian traditions have been transformed. No longer strangers, potentially hostile, to one another, there have been huge strides to deepen koinonia and mission. Anglicans have participated in the union of several churches in South Asia, and both global and regional commitments of full communion. We continue to celebrate the Bonn Agreement with the Union of Utrecht, and many warm and positive relationships of communion; for example, with some Lutheran churches. There are also other agreements of commitment and dialogue, including participation in multi-lateral instruments such as the World Council of Churches.

1.3 Ecumenism today takes many forms. Where churches have worked together on matters of peace and justice, our common life and witness has been immeasurably strengthened. Churches have increasingly spoken and worked together on the environment and care of creation. We welcome the growth of spiritual ecumenism, and the practice of Christians praying together, sometimes in the context of intentional ecumenical communities such as the Community of St Anselm, based at Lambeth Palace.

## Continuing Challenges

1.4 However, in recent years progress in bringing forward unity in matters of faith and order has slowed. Despite considerable convergence in doctrinal issues, agreement on patterns of governance has proved more difficult and different patterns of governance and ecclesiastical custom in the churches are not easily reconciled. At the local level the Lund Principle (that churches should seek to work together except where 'deep differences of conviction compel them to act separately') is generally acknowledged, but can be difficult to enact.

1.5 The disunity of the church is a continuing and damaging wound in the body of Christ. We regret that divisions between the baptised lead to estrangement: to a lack of mutual recognition of our sacraments and ministries and the abiding sadness of our inability to share Holy Communion together. Such division weakens the church's witness to the Gospel of reconciliation at a time when, in many parts of the world, government regulation, persecution and even terrorism make Christians vulnerable in their life and witness.

## 2 Affirmation

## Our Anglican Commitment

2.1 Beginning with the Chicago-Lambeth Quadrilateral (1886/1888), there have been many definitions of the goal of the unity we seek. The Anglican Consultative Council (ACC-14, 2009) adopted the following Four Principles of Ecumenism:

- The Goal: the full organic unity of the church;
- The Task: recognising and receiving the church in one another;
- The Process: unity by stages;
- The Content: common faith, sacraments and ministry.

2.2 We, the bishops of the Anglican Communion, now reaffirm our commitment to seeking the unity of Christ's body, the church. In our study of the First Epistle of Peter, we have been reminded that the church is God's creation, established on the one foundation stone, which is Jesus Christ. In God's vocation, the church is one 'chosen people, a royal priesthood, a holy nation, God's special possession', called to 'declare the praises of him who called [us] out of darkness into his wonderful light' (1 Peter 2:9).

2.3  We therefore affirm:

2.3.1  That the churches of the Anglican Communion are part of the one, holy, catholic and apostolic church;

2.3.2  That the vocation of the Anglican Communion includes a commitment to seek the visible unity of Christ's church;

2.3.3  That, despite our divisions, we recognise in other Christian churches the fruitfulness of the work of the Holy Spirit, commitment to the proclamation of the Gospel and loyalty to Jesus' institution of the Sacraments that we cherish in our own lives;

2.3.4  That at every level of church life Anglican churches can learn from other churches, communions and traditions and, in learning, receive gifts of grace;

2.3.5  That Anglicans should work together in mission and ministry with other churches wherever possible, on the way to the full organic unity which we believe is God's will and our calling.

## 3  Specific Requests (The Calls)

### 3.1  A Call to Action

We call upon the Instruments of Communion, the churches and the people of the Anglican Communion:

3.1.1  To renew their commitment to an urgent search for the full organic unity of the church;

3.1.2  To receive and carry forward the fruits of our ecumenical relationships;

3.1.3 To build strong, close relationships with the other churches in their provinces;

3.1.4 To seek reconciliation and unity even within the Anglican family of churches, recognising that disagreements within the Anglican Communion have led to the setting up of separated churches and groups from which, though standing within the same Anglican tradition, we are divided;

3.1.5 To work with our brothers and sisters in other churches in the mission of proclaiming the Good News of Christ and responding to the needs of the world;

3.1.6 To speak out with, for and on behalf of brothers and sisters who are persecuted: for when one part of the body suffers all suffer with it;

3.1.7 To see what is best in the other and to seek what we might receive from the riches of traditions that are not our own;

3.1.8 To seek opportunities for dialogue to overcome those theological and ecclesiological differences that remain as barriers to the full, visible communion of Christ's Church at local, regional and worldwide levels, establishing formal relationships of communion with other churches where possible and working towards the goal of full organic unity.

## 3.2 An Ecumenical Invitation

The World Council of Churches' Faith and Order document, The Church: Towards a Common Vision, describes ecumenical work as a call to the churches towards 'unity in faith, unity in sacramental life, and unity in service' (para. 67). In this spirit, we invite our ecumenical partners:

3.2.1 To assist us in understanding the depth and diversity of life in Christ, and what may be learned from one another;

3.2.2 To invite their neighbouring Anglican churches to share with them in local initiatives to proclaim the Gospel, to renew the life of the church and to serve society for the common good;

3.2.3 To work with us in sharing the riches of our common inheritance of faith, and those distinct gifts which God has bestowed on us in our separated histories and experiences (cf. 1 Peter 4:10);

3.2.4 To join with us in pursuing the steps leading to full organic unity;

3.2.5 In giving thanks for the achievements of the ecumenical movement, we urge one another to take ecumenical endeavour seriously in our lives and ministries, recalling at all times Our Lord's own prayer that all should be one (John 17:20).

# 4 Implementation

4.1 The task of encouraging and monitoring the implementation of this Call within the member churches and the Instruments of Communion lies principally with the Anglican Consultative Council, working through the Inter-Anglican Standing Commission on Unity, Faith and Order (IASCUFO) and the Anglican Communion Office;

4.2 We call upon the ACC and the Secretary General to ensure that adequate resources are available to enable this task;

4.3 We invite IASCUFO to monitor and oversee progress and to report regularly to the ACC;

4.4 We invite member churches to report regularly to IASCUFO, via the ACO's Department of Unity, Faith and Order, on developments and challenges in this area.

# 35

# Lambeth Call 8
# Mission and Evangelism

## 1 Introduction

1.1 As those called to serve Christ in episcopal ministry in Anglican churches we rejoice to announce this Call for Evangelism.

1.2 The people of God are chosen, set apart, equipped, and sent into God's world 'that you may declare the praises of him who called you out of darkness into his wonderful light' (1 Peter 2:9). For we who are recipients of God's great mercy in Christ, we who have been given 'new birth into a living hope through the resurrection of Jesus Christ from the dead', we who have an 'inheritance that can never spoil or perish', have been filled by the Holy Spirit 'sent from heaven' who turns us from serving ourselves to announce the beautiful Gospel – which angels have longed to look at – to all. Our unity of spirit, our lives lived in response to the grace that is ours, our suffering, our commitments, service, hospitality and hope are lived that all may glorify God who comes as judge of all people.

## 2 Declaration

2.1 Every church across the Anglican Communion joyfully and courageously shares this vocation to declare the Good News of God's salvation of the world in Christ Jesus. Our first Mark of Mission commits us: To proclaim the Good News of the Kingdom.

2.2 Evangelism is the proclamation of the Gospel of the one who was dead but is now alive – Christ Jesus and the Kingdom of God he inaugurates. Empowered by the Holy Spirit every Christian is a witness to Jesus Christ.

> *Do not fear what they fear, and do not be intimidated, but in your hearts sanctify Christ as Lord. Always be ready to make your defence to any-*

*one who demands from you an account of the hope that is in you; yet do it with gentleness and reverence.* (1 Peter 3:14–16)

2.3 All of our mission and evangelism begins with the mission of God; God chooses to be for us in creative and redeeming love. Christ Jesus is the great evangelist who, through the power of the Holy Spirit, is working constantly, faithfully and radically to draw all people to himself. Pope Francis states, 'It is first and foremost the Lord's work.' Empowered by his Holy Spirit, he calls his people to work with him, as his agents of the Good News.

2.4 Every church in our Communion has its origin in the mission of God. In 597 St Augustine arrived in Canterbury, sent by Pope Gregory the Great, to herald the Good News. Our Communion is testament to the vocation and power of the Good News of Christ in every country and culture. Each church was first established because God sent someone to proclaim the Good News of Christ and, through the enabling of the Holy Spirit, the church was formed in response.

2.5 As those called to oversight, we are those charged with serving the mission of the church; we are an apostolic sign of Christ's commission to preach the Gospel to the entire world and to make disciples of every nation.

## 3 Affirmation

Compelled by the love of Christ, that has been poured into our hearts by the Holy Spirit, we are convinced of the world's need to receive the salvation and redemption the Gospel proclaims – that all whom God has made hear the Good News, in such a way that they can respond in faith to all God has done in Christ. The good news of grace and mercy, of repentance and forgiveness, of reconciliation and stewardship, of hope and eternity is a message which the world is dying without hearing. But it is to this fallen world that the Gospel is addressed. 'God loves human beings. God loves the world. Not an ideal human, but human beings as they are; not an ideal world, but the real world' (Bonhoeffer). God calls every person through his great love, therefore it matters that those who have never heard this good news can hear it in a way they understand, so that they can respond to it. The Holy Spirit has been poured into our hearts so that we live as faithful witnesses to Jesus Christ.

## 4 Specific Requests (The Calls)

4.1 Each diocese and every church to seek fervently to be renewed by the wonder and power of the Good News of Christ.

4.2 Each diocese and every church to commit to prayer, listening and discernment, in the power of the Holy Spirit, so that we might live to bear faithful witness to Christ and authentically proclaim the Gospel. This to include praying for the Holy Spirit to work in hearts and minds so that the message of the Gospel would be received and bear fruit.

4.3 In obedience to Christ's own charge, every church to commit itself to actions which intentionally present the Good News of Christ so that all might hear the call of Christ and follow him.

4.4 Every Christian joyfully to embrace the calling to be a witness to Jesus Christ, praying that through this at least one other person each year might come to faith and grow as a disciple.

4.5 That we as the Anglican Communion pray for each other in this ministry and commit to listen to, learn from and find encouragement together in this Call.

4.6 For bishops to be equipped and enabled to lead in this evangelism. Following the apostolic example we bishops are to lead the people of God in God's world in bold proclamation.

4.7 For each diocese to cherish, train, send and receive evangelists.

4.8 For each diocese to make a fresh and creative commitment to revitalise churches and to plant new congregations in contextually appropriate ways, to reach those who have not yet heard the Gospel.

4.9 For the churches that are persecuted to be supported in their witness, that they may be protected and stand firm in their faith.

4.10 We call on the Secretary General to support and follow the progress in these areas with the help of the Commission on Evangelism and Discipleship, and to report back to the next ACC.

# 36

# Lambeth Call 9
# Inter Faith

## 1 Introduction

1.1 In a world of religious difference, like the context of those Christian disciples to whom the first letter of Peter was addressed, the church is a witness to the hope of the Good News of salvation in Jesus Christ (1 Peter 3:15–16), a sign of blessing and service to the wider community (1 Peter 2:12), and an anticipation of the glory of God in Christ that will be revealed to all by its faithfulness in the face of hostility and persecution (1 Peter 4:13–14).

## 2 Declaration

2.1 When Jesus Christ ascended into heaven, he promised the gift of the Holy Spirit to his disciples so that they may be empowered with his risen life to be his witnesses 'to the ends of the earth' (Acts 1:8).

2.2 A persistent challenge for Anglicans is how we are to be God's Church for God's World when living with people of diverse faiths. For some in the Anglican Communion there is the freedom to call people into baptism and discipleship, and our neighbours of other religious traditions can also become partners in work for the common good, tackling areas of shared concern such as the pandemic or climate change. In some contexts, however, Anglicans face hostility and even persecution. This is why the Network for Inter Faith Concerns for the Anglican Communion (NIFCON) was set up in 1993 on the authority of the Lambeth Conference of 1988 in order to share stories of encounter with other faiths across the different parts of the Communion.

2.3 At the Lambeth Conference of 2008, *Generous Love: the truth of the gospel and the call to dialogue,* was presented and received.[1] In the spirit of the important Roman Catholic Pastoral Constitution of Vatican II,

*Nostra Aetate*, the Lambeth Conference acknowledged that 'As members of the Church of the Triune God, we are to abide among our neighbours of different faiths as signs of God's presence with them, and we are sent to engage with our neighbours as agents of God's mission to them.' *Generous Love* recognised the diversity of contexts for both these patterns of presence and engagement across the Anglican Communion, 'whether as minority or majority communities, whether in places of vulnerability or security, whether in relations of dialogue or tension'.[2]

2.4 Whatever our context, our neighbours of other religious traditions are all made in the image of God, and as Christians we are called to love others as ourselves.

## 3 Affirmation

3.1 We the bishops of the Anglican Communion, assembled in the Lambeth Conference of 2022, therefore affirm our commitment to witnessing to Jesus Christ as Lord and Saviour by faithful, Christ-like service and in humble proclamation of this good news among people of different faiths and beliefs.

3.2 The church's rootedness in and indebtedness to the Jewish story means that there is a formative and primary encounter with other faiths in its encounter with Judaism, *most evident in those scriptures that are shared*. We acknowledge that the shameful history of Christian-Jewish relations gives the church a particular responsibility to reject and overcome anti-Judaism in its theology, liturgy and preaching.

3.3 We recognise that our commitment to the 'Five Marks of Mission' situates relations with people of other religious traditions within the mission of God in Christ, understood in a holistic sense, and each context and relationship will determine how these 'Marks of Mission' are held together.

3.4 In a world where there are increasing challenges which affect all our communities, how we work with other religious traditions for the common good testifies to our participation in the gracious work of God beyond the church. The Covid-19 pandemic has been one contemporary example of this, and the pressing challenge of climate change is another.

3.5 In a world of inter and intra religious violence, how we are agents of peace-making with neighbours from other faiths goes to the heart of the

Good News of the Gospel. Our calling to be agents of peace-making also means that we should be determined to reject and challenge all that exists within the church that might foster prejudice and hatred towards those of other religious traditions.

3.6 In a world of growing restrictions on religious freedom or belief, and heightened persecution of Christians, how the Anglican Communion (in the words of *Generous Love*) may 'offer our solidarity and support to Christians who have to witness to their faith in difficult circumstances'[3] honours our understanding of being part of the one Body of Christ, in sorrow and suffering, as well as in joy and resurrection.

3.7 In a world of growing restrictions on religious freedom or belief, there are increasing opportunities for Christians to work with members of other religious traditions in common cause of defence of these freedoms, including the freedom to *change one's religion or belief*, and in mutual advocacy.

## 4 Specific Requests (The Calls)

Based on our commitment to work for the common good with those of other religious traditions and beliefs, to neighbourly peace-making across religious communities, and to solidarity with our Christian sisters and brothers in struggling contexts for inter faith relations, we therefore make the following calls:

4.1 To all of us who are disciples of Christ, to witness to our neighbours of other religious traditions, in word and deed, and through humble service.

4.2 To bishops across the Anglican Communion, where possible in your local context, to forge a new friendship with a leader of another religious tradition, modelling our commitment to peace-making and the common good.

4.3 To invite leaders of other faith communities, to join with us in exploring how we can enable more effective collaborative work on tackling climate change and other challenges to our shared environment, alleviating poverty and care for the vulnerable.

4.4 To the Anglican Inter Faith Commission: to find funding for research by clergy or lay practitioners from across the Anglican Communion within a specialist track of inter faith relations with a view to resourcing a new generation of Anglican scholar-practitioners so that the good of theological learning about other religious traditions can be affirmed and fostered in the mission of the wider Communion.

4.5 To bishops and provinces of the Anglican Communion, where it is safe and possible, to set up links with those parts of our Communion facing hostility and persecution so that there can be exchange of information, prayerful support, and solidarity in friendship, including in the support of those who encounter hardship in the decision to convert to the Christian faith.

4.6 To all of us who are disciples of Christ, to commit to pray for the suffering persecuted church in its efforts in continuing to be a gentle and faithful witnessing presence even in the face of hostility and the struggle to form strong relationships with neighbours of other faiths.

## 5 Implementation

The Inter Faith Commission will promote and encourage:

- Practical ways to follow up outcomes of the call to a new friendship across faiths (4.2).
- Practical ways to follow up outcomes of the call to collaborative action with those of other religious traditions (4.3).
- Establishing research scholarships: delegated committee to oversee this, covering budgets for doctoral programmes, accommodation, etc. and feeding back into local, provincial and Communion-wide learning and practice (4.4).
- Practicalities of matching arrangements: how to identify the contexts looking for solidarity, how to make this informal: should it build on existing diocesan links or be separate or overlap? (4.5).

### Notes

1 *Generous Love: the truth of the gospel and the call to dialogue, an Anglican theology of inter faith relations*, Lambeth Conference 2008, page 10, available at https://www.acommonword.com/wp-content/uploads/2018/05/Generous_Love.pdf.

2 *Generous Love*, p. 8.

3 *Generous Love*, p. 10.

# 37

# Lambeth Call 10
# Reconciliation

*Come to him, a living stone, though rejected by mortals yet chosen and precious in God's sight, and like living stones, let yourselves be built into a spiritual house, to be a holy priesthood, to offer spiritual sacrifices acceptable to God through Jesus Christ. ... [Y]ou are a chosen race, a royal priesthood, a holy nation, God's own people, in order that you may proclaim the mighty acts of him who called you out of darkness into his marvellous light. Once you were not a people, but now you are God's people; once you had not received mercy, but now you have received mercy. (1 Peter 2:4–10)*


## 1 Introduction

God's reconciling mission is the ministry of the church today. We yearn for and commit to reconciliation through God's saving mercy and grace in Jesus, knowing fully that, without it, we are impoverished. We are redeemed as a holy nation and are called to work with God in living out this reconciliation.


## 2 Declaration

We believe in God who is three in one and one in three. In this Trinity, particularity and unity are held in the heart of God's being, as Father, Son and Holy Spirit. In the life, death, resurrection and ascension of Jesus Christ, God reaches out to an estranged and fractured humanity by becoming flesh – embodying and reconciling with humanity in an extraordinary, unique way. In the ultimate reconciliation on the cross, God in Christ bears witness to the cost and pain involved in reconciling. Each formed in God's image in unique ways and in different contexts, we are invited into covenantal partnership in God's mission of reconciliation. Our differences embodied in the Anglican Communion both challenge and deepen our experience of God in the other. As we join in God's mission of reconciliation through Jesus in the power of the Spirit, our diversity is celebrated and our divisions redeemed, as we are made whole in the body of Christ. In that diverse whole, we more fully reflect the image of God.

## 3 Affirmation

3.1 Relationships across difference can be holy and complex. We acknowledge that Scripture, in particular the 2022 Lambeth Conference's focal text of 1 Peter, has been interpreted over time by those wielding power, whether in nations, churches, cultures or households, to support the domination and oppression of other human beings. We are participants in systems that create division, disagreement and conflict both among us and within us. Reconciliation requires justice, accountability and change in society and in the church. Without these, oppression and division continue, diminishing the humanity of all caught up in those systems, regardless of their role. We call on the Holy Spirit to empower and inspire us as we seek right relations in Christ – among us, within each of us, with God, and with creation.

3.2 This Call reaffirms God's reconciling mission, the ongoing process of bringing us back to God in and through Christ, as the church's ministry. Recognising that those in power have sometimes used talk of reconciliation to maintain systems of power and impede efforts towards justice and wholeness, we seek a Communion-wide focus on this ministry as it is embodied in our different contexts.[1] As we witness together, we practise the reconciling habits highlighted at the Lambeth Conference: being curious and wondering about each other's unique experiences; being present with each other, listening attentively and without judgement; and reimagining our own contexts as our understanding is prayerfully expanded.[2] We seek to practise reconciliation in every aspect of our lives, both seen and unseen.

## 4 Special Requests (The Calls)

4.1 We call upon Anglicans worldwide to turn to God in prayer for refreshment in Christ's distinctive offering of mercy and grace amidst the fracture, division and polarisation around us and between us. We encourage engagement with the diverse liturgies used across the Anglican Communion which invite us to repentance and renewal and which give expression to God's gift of reconciliation.

4.2 We commit ourselves as bishops to urge our dioceses to join in this Communion-wide practice of reconciliation, utilising available reconciliation resources.[3] We affirm the Calls on the Environment and the Sustainable Development Goals and the Call on Ecumenism as examples of a Communion-wide commitment to reconciliation in relation to God's creation and other denominations.

4.3 We commit ourselves as bishops to encourage the next generation by celebrating their contribution to the ministry of reconciliation and nurturing their hopes. We will create space for listening and responding to their hurts and generational pain, and empowering their full participation in reconciliation initiatives.

4.4 We invite Anglican seminaries and training programmes around the Communion, supported by the new Commission on Theological Education and the Colleges and Universities of the Anglican Communion network, to create spaces for training and dialogue on reconciliation as a fundamental part of our identity as followers of Christ, hearing particularly from theologians in areas of the Communion that have historically had less power.

4.5 Acknowledging the pain of racial, cultural and caste discrimination and inspired by many Anglican churches' work in truth-telling and reckoning with these realities, we invite each province to an exercise of self-examination and reflection, listening respectfully to the experiences of those who have historically been, and continue to be, marginalised in their contexts and in their church.[4] And we call each Instrument of Communion to engage in a similar self-examining, listening exercise.

4.6 As we recognise the centrality of justice and accountability in God's reconciliation, we call upon the ACC to outline a plan for better understanding and interrogating the legacy of colonialism within the Anglican Communion. This might include, but is not limited to, mission practices grounded in imperialistic assumptions, and systems that remain complicit in colonialism. We hope it will build on work already done through the ACC.

4.7 We call upon the Archbishop of Canterbury, together with the ACC Standing Committee,[5] to renew and refresh the conversation with our sisters and brothers in provinces and dioceses unable to join us at Lambeth Conference 2022, seeking to build a fuller life together as an Anglican family of churches.

4.8 We call upon the Archbishop of Canterbury, the Primates and the ACC to raise the profile of existing funding streams and networks that will support peace-building responses and those standing for justice and wholeness in provinces experiencing acute conflict.

# 5 Implementation

5.1 We ask that each province engage with a reconciliation resource of their choice by the 2025 Primates' Meeting, in order to share stories from that experience and from listening to groups who have historically been marginalised.[6]

5.2 We invite the Commission on Theological Education to support seminaries creating spaces for dialogue and to report on resulting outcomes at ACC-19.

5.3 We ask the Instruments of Communion to receive questions and testimonies from each province in order to begin their exercises of self-examination. We hope they will respond with suggested actions by 2025.

5.4 We expect the ACC to report at the ACC-19 on its progress with, and plans for, studying the historic legacy of colonialism with fresh eyes and questioning mission practices that may still be grounded in imperialistic assumptions and practices, and systems that may continue to be complicit in colonialism, working with the Anglican Indigenous Network and others living with the continuing impact of colonialism.

5.5 We invite the peace-building function of the Archbishop of Canterbury's Reconciliation team, working with the Anglican Communion Fund and Anglican Peace and Justice Network, to report to Primates on ways to develop peace-building responses and support for individual peace-builders in provinces experiencing acute conflict.

5.6 We ask the Archbishop of Canterbury and the Standing Committee of ACC to report on the renewed conversation with those provinces and dioceses who were unable to join us at Lambeth 2022 at ACC-19.

5.7 We ask that the Anglican Communion Youth Network and the Archbishop of Canterbury's Reconciliation team present ideas for engaging young people in reconciliation initiatives as soon as practicable and celebrate what has been developed by young people at the following ACC.

## Notes

1 We acknowledge that the very term 'reconciliation' has become loaded in some contexts, either denoting one particular area of fractured relationships and/or becoming unhelpfully politicized. We also note that the concept of reconciliation is expressed differently among different contexts. For example, there is no word for reconciliation in Kiswahili but instead the notion of two sides meeting to move forward together. In Fiji, reconciliation is expressed by offering forgiveness as a gift. If it is received in humility, there is reconciliation and embrace. In Congo, the notion is expressed through a word meaning *shared inheritance*.

2 For more information about these habits, see the *Ministry in a Conflicted World* course offered to bishops in preparation for the Lambeth Conference: https://www.lambethconference.org/programme/ministry-in-a-conflicted-world/the-course/.

3 Resources may include those recommended by Anglican provinces or Anglican networks, e.g. the Anglican Indigenous Network or Anglican Peace and Justice Network, or the Difference course from the Archbishop of Canterbury's Reconciliation Ministry and his book *The Power of Reconciliation*.

4 See, for example, the Anglican Church in Canada, the Anglican Church in Aotearoa New Zealand and Polynesia, and the most recent work done on racism and white supremacy in The Episcopal Church.

5 The Standing Committee is responsible for the ongoing function of the ACC between meetings of the whole body.

6 Resources may include those recommended by Anglican Provinces or Anglican Networks, e.g. the Anglican Indigenous Network or Anglican Peace and Justice Network, or the Difference course from the Archbishop of Canterbury's Reconciliation Ministry and his book *The Power of Reconciliation*.

# 38

# The Statements of Support

Bishops at the Lambeth Conference were invited to draft statements of support for situations of need, suffering and opportunity in their own region. These were tabled towards the end of the conference and were collectively welcomed and supported by the bishops as a whole. They included Calls for an end to violence and peace in many different regions of the world. They are printed in full at http://www.lambethconference.org/wp-content/uploads/2022/08/Statements-of-Support-from-the-Lambeth-Conference-2022-1.pdf

Statement on the Anglican Church of Congo from Archbishop Titre Ande Georges, Congo

Statement of Support for Nigeria from Archbishop Justin Welby

Statement from The Episcopal Diocese of Jerusalem and the Middle East from Archbishop Hosam Naoum, Jerusalem

Statement of Support welcoming the Province of Alexandria in Egypt from Archbishop Sami Fawzi, Egypt

Statement of Support regarding the situation in Ukraine from Bishop Robert Innes, Diocese of Europe

Statement of Support for Sudan from Archbishop Ezekiel Kondo, Sudan

Statement of Support for Pakistan from Bishop Azad Marshall, Pakistan

Statement on the Anglican Church of South Sudan from Archbishop Justin Badi, South Sudan

Statement on the Anglican Church of Ceylon, from Bishop Keerthisiri Fernando, Sri Lanka

Statement of Support for the people of Myanmar/Burma from the Bishops of Myanmar

Statement of Support for Tanzania from Archbishop Maimbo Mndolwa, Tanzania

Statement on Indigenous People in Canada and the world from Archbishop Linda Nicholls, Canada

Statement of Support in response to the shootings in the USA from Bishop Michael Curry, USA

Statement on the Refugee and Migration Crisis from Archbishop Justin Welby

# 39

# Looking Ahead to Phase 3

For the first time the Lambeth Conference has a planned post-conference implementation process. This is now underway as this report is published. This phase is envisaged for three years, overseen by a group drawn from across the Anglican Communion and chaired by Archbishop Julio Murray of Panama. The resourcing of the phase comes from the funds raised for the conference. A post of Bishop for Episcopal Ministry in the Anglican Communion has been created to be the project lead, a post now filled by Bishop Jo Bailey Wells. The chair and project lead report to the Archbishop of Canterbury who, as host of the Lambeth Conference, retains ultimate oversight of this phase. The Anglican Consultative Council has taken over from the Lambeth Conference Company the responsibilities of facilitating this phase. What will it include?

As mentioned earlier in this report, the revised versions of the Calls printed above are now being promoted and disseminated across the churches of the Anglican Communion. These churches are invited to receive the Calls in synods and consultations, and reflect and respond to them in ways appropriate to their situations. They are a gift to be used in whatever ways may be right in their different contexts. The varied Responses to the Calls will be collected and collated by the Phase 3 group, wherever possible, not least to help resource others in shaping further Responses. Some elements of the Calls (Specific Requests) fall to particular Commissions, Networks and agencies. Part of the Phase 3 process will be to identify those elements of the Calls that can be taken forward cross-provincially and work together with those particular bodies as they, too, take up the Call.

Another element will be Bible study for bishops as well as for spouses. Many bishops commented on how foundational the small groups were and their study of the Bible for the conference as a whole. They were key to providing space for relationships to be built and for prayer and conversation in a safe space. These were the same groups that discussed the Calls during the conference. This means bishops spent a lot of time in them and many, during the conference, made plans to ensure they could go on meeting in some way, over Zoom or WhatsApp. A few Bible study groups have been reorganised, given that time zones have not been compatible and membership has changed as bishops have retired and stepped away from their group. Where possible their replacements are being invited to join the existing group, meaning that the new bishop would have immediate access to a number of other bishops around the world. The groups over time will change organically and help to build relationships as well as focus on the priority of being part of the Anglican Communion.

A third element will be coordination of cross-provincial training and support of new bishops, liaising with those who already provide these things, to assist co-ordination and extension of what is provided, particularly on what it means to be part of the Anglican Communion. Current providers of cross-provincial training and support include Canterbury Cathedral, the Council of Anglican Provinces in Africa (CAPA), The Episcopal Church's programme for new bishops supported by the Anglican Church of Canada, and USPG's mentoring programme of new bishops by experienced bishops. Phase 3 will support and extend this provision, using online webinars and courses, mentoring and coaching, involving formation as well as support, not least in the area of 'safe church'.

The setting up of a new Spouses' Network will also be part of Phase 3, a network that will become self-extending and self-supporting in the years ahead, with cross-provincial groups of spouses who can study the Bible, pray and support each other in ways that they fashion together. This will be a multilingual network.

The Phase 3 journey is bound to evolve as it moves forward, and as the bishops of the Anglican Communion continue to walk, listen and witness together serving God's Church for God's World.

# Afterword

*Phil George, Chief Executive of the
Lambeth Conference Company*

Following my appointment in the autumn of 2017 the three-year journey of planning and overseeing the (then) 2020 Lambeth Conference commenced. I soon realised this was going to be quite unlike any previous conference that I had been involved in. It was going to be seriously complex and yet, at the same time, exciting.

On Day One I had no team. I ordered a desk chair for myself and started to look at the archives from the 2008 Lambeth Conference. What followed was a series of conversations which included speaking with some of the previous conference team, a reconstruction of the finances and a realisation that as 12 years had passed, we really needed to start again.

Hearing Archbishop Justin's vision for the conference was a clear priority. It was a privilege to accompany him occasionally around the Anglican Communion's regions, meeting with Primates, archbishops and bishops to hear what was on their minds, their concerns and joys, and key topics they would like at the conference. Soon the theme of 'God's Church for God's World' emerged and, with the help of the Design Group chaired by Archbishop Thabo Makgoba of Southern Africa, the programme began to take shape. We were blessed with St Augustine Foundation of Canterbury helping to finance the preparations for Bible studies on 1 Peter.

One key directive was that all the costs must be covered. The budget was soon set and with 42% inflation since 2008 the cost per person was going to be high. Production expectations were high, the digital world had exploded into life over the past 12 years, interpretation across nine languages was essential, technology had advanced and live streaming needed to be factored in. With so many delegates requiring a bursary we had an immediate fundraising challenge ahead of us and so we approached a range of donors, who were all very generous.

My strategy was to recruit a small but highly effective staff team to lead in key areas and to outsource as many of the production tasks as possible. With many stakeholders involved it became clear that a dedicated Lambeth Conference head of communications would also be very useful, in addition to the existing three event project coordinators and one administrator. We were a team of only six, but all were recruited especially for this conference and were focused on what was required. I am so proud of our team – namely, Rachel Westall, Janet Miles, Caroline Thompson, Kari Loureiro and Brad Frey – for what together we eventually delivered.

Looking back, I also give thanks to the array of dedicated support teams plus volunteers who were involved in helping deliver the conference. We had a very good trustee team who supported and challenged me and a creative Design Group who helped put the programme together. In addition, we had New Testament biblical scholars from around the Communion helping prepare the expositions and Bible studies, a senior management team involving leaders from the Anglican Communion Office and Lambeth Palace staff. We were all pulling in the same direction, trying our best to make this as successful a conference as we could. We wanted to ensure all bishops and spouses could join in and attend the physical conference wherever finances were a challenge. In the end over half of those who attended drew on our bursary fund. Praise God for the generosity of our donors.

Then only four months before the 2020 conference Covid struck, affecting not only our plans but the whole world. What were we to do? Archbishop Justin encouraged us all to see the Lambeth Conference as a four-year journey across three phases, the first of which would take place online during the postponement period until the face-to-face conference, now rescheduled for 2022, which would be the second phase. A third phase would be the follow-up after the conference. A new Working Group chaired by Bishop Emma Ineson met frequently to think through the new plans surrounding this new journey. Before no time, over 500 bishops were meeting in conversation groups across provinces to discuss current themes and topics that were on the conference agenda. Several spouses' groups also met online either in provincial or cross-provincial groups. These conversations laid foundations for building strong relationships across the Communion and by 2022 when the face-to-face conference took place, bishops and spouses were very excited to meet in person.

Fortunately, when insurance for the conference was purchased in 2018 the risk of a 'communicable disease' to the conference finances was included in the policy. With the onset of Covid and all the disruption to the conference it has been necessary to draw down compensation based on this. At the time of writing the cost of two extra years of salaries have been covered and a similar amount is pending relating to additional costs incurred due to the two-year postponement. This is a significant and welcome boost financially.

With the in-person conference set for 2022, the whole programme was re-examined to ensure that the topics and themes were still relevant and a few new seminars were added. Almost all who booked for the 2020 conference were able to attend in person at Canterbury in 2022 and an online provision was made for what in the end was a small number of bishops and spouses who, for whatever reason, could not travel.

We are now in Phase Three, a three-year period of post-conference implementation. In this period the legacies of the conference will be strengthened and extended, not least the strengthening relationships between bishops and spouses across provinces and discussion of the Lambeth Calls across the Communion. A new Phase Three group is in place, as mentioned, chaired by Bishop Julio Murray of Panama.

The publication and distribution of this Lambeth Conference report is a good moment to reflect on the whole journey. Different people will have different views on how the journey has gone so far. From my perspective the pre-conference phase and the in-person conference were a huge success in bringing so many bishops and spouses together in a rich variety of ways. It was a real privilege to have been a part of this. The funds required were generously provided, all the teams worked extremely hard, and it has been great fun and something I will never forget. For other perspectives, why not ask those who attended? The Press wanted a story, and some have printed their own interpretations of what happened. The real story has yet to be told, I suspect. This conference was never intended to only be 12 days in Canterbury but rather to set the agenda for the decade ahead for the Anglican Communion and deepen the relationships and friendships that link us together. Yes, there are differences within the Communion that must be faced but we are 'God's Church for God's World, walking, listening, and witnessing together'. Archbishop Justin has asked that this be done to the maximum possible degree despite these differences.

My prayer is that we continue to make a significant difference wherever we are as Christians across the world with its pressing needs. This conference is calling us all to play our part in doing just that.